What Everyone Is Saying About WillMaker...

"By far the most comprehensive program we reviewed, offering guidance on everything...."

—USA Today

"The most complete of the five products we tried."

—The Wall Street Journal

"From a group of tough critics, Nolo's WillMaker got the most praise ... superior on every front."

—Kiplinger's Personal Finance Magazine

"The most ... comprehensive and widely praised of the will writing programs."

—Chicago Tribune

"You can complete the documents fairly quickly, or you can spend a great deal of time exploring all the clearly written definitions and explanations...."

—PC World

"Even if you know you should see a lawyer...[WillMaker]'s question-and-answer technique can help you sort through the options."

—BusinessWeek

"The most sophisticated legal software on the market."

—Worth

"The level of detail and complexity anticipated by the program makes WillMaker one of the leading legal-advice programs on the market."

—Inc.

Support, Updates, and Renewals for WillMaker & Trust

When you purchase Quicken WillMaker & Trust, you get customer support, legal updates, and technical improvements for one year from the date you activate your account. During that year, you can use WillMaker to make and revise estate planning documents for yourself and your immediate family. If you want to make or revise WillMaker documents after that year, you can renew your WillMaker account through your customer portal.

An Important Message to Our Readers

This product is not a substitute for legal advice from an attorney. We've done our best to give you useful, accurate legal information, but that's not the same as personalized legal advice. If you want help understanding how the law applies to your particular circumstances or deciding which estate planning documents are best for you and your family, you should consider seeing a qualified attorney. Estate planning documents are not valid in Louisiana, the U.S. Territories, or Canada.

2027 Edition

Quicken WillMaker & Trust

Book & Online Software Kit

NOLO
LAW for ALL

TWENTY-SEVENTH EDITION	OCTOBER 2026
Editor	BETSY SIMMONS HANNIBAL
Book Design	SUSAN PUTNEY
Proofreading	JENNIFER ARTER
Index	RICHARD GENOVA
Printing	SHERIDAN

ISSN: 2151-5808 (print)

ISBN: 978-1-4133-3377-0 (pbk)

This book covers only United States law, unless it specifically states otherwise.

MH Sub I, LLC dba Nolo, 909 N. Pacific Coast Hwy, 11th Fl, El Segundo, CA 90245

Table of Contents

Introduction to WillMaker

If you're like a lot of people, you have a nagging feeling that you need to make a will—but you haven't gotten around to it because it sounds hard or expensive or just unpleasant. (Or maybe this book interests you because you are the rare individual who loves to plan and get organized. We encourage those tendencies.) You're smart to pay attention to that nagging feeling: Almost everyone needs a will. It lets you leave your property, name a guardian for young children, and eliminate uncertainty about your wishes—all of which will spare your family headaches later.

With WillMaker, making a legal will doesn't have to be difficult. In fact, you can probably get it done in less than an hour.

And a will isn't the only thing to think about. In addition, you might want to make a living trust or transfer on death deed to help your family avoid probate court proceedings after your death. And everyone should consider preparing a living will and durable powers of attorney—important documents that can help you stay in control of your own health care and financial choices while saving your family lots of hassles and heartaches, too. You can use WillMaker to prepare these legal tools and more.

To get started, go to www.willmaker.com/redeem and use the single-use activation key (provided at the back of this book) to access your WillMaker portal. In the portal, you can start making your documents online or download WillMaker and make your documents using software that runs on your personal computer. Using either platform, you can make any or all of WillMaker's essential documents. However, these two versions of WillMaker do not share data, so you can't start a document on one platform and then finish it on the other.

Two Ways to Use WillMaker

With WillMaker & Trust you can choose whether to use WillMaker online or as downloadable software. Both versions provide the same time-tested estate planning documents. The difference is a matter of location. Would you rather make your documents online—from any device—using an internet browser? Or would you prefer to work directly on your personal computer, needing the internet only for the initial download and occasional updates? The choice is yours, and you can use both platforms. But keep in mind that data does not transfer from one to the other. For example, if you start your will using the software installed on your computer, you won't be able to access that document online.

To start making WillMaker documents, take the unique code from the back inside cover of this book and enter it at www.willmaker.com/redeem. Then you will be directed to your WillMaker portal, where you can learn more about WillMaker, start your estate plan, or choose to install the downloadable version of WillMaker. If you need help, you can look for answers at www.willmaker.com/support, or contact Nolo Customer Support at customersupport@nolo.com or 800-728-3555 (ext. 1). We are here to help you Monday through Friday, 9 a.m. to 6 p.m. Eastern Time.

RESOURCE

Get help online. Go to www.willmaker.com/support for answers to common questions and to learn more about WillMaker's documents.

When you're ready to start making your documents, our carefully designed question-and-answer format makes the process as easy as it can be. Our goal is to help you over any hurdles by providing clear guidance and encouragement at every step. After you select a document to begin, we'll ask you a series of straightforward questions. Then WillMaker uses your answers to make a legal document that's valid in your state.

If you're not sure how to answer a particular question, you'll find lots of practical and legal information within easy reach. Our onscreen help is there to guide you through questions large and small. (And we'll always alert you to situations in which you might benefit from help from a lawyer or another expert.) When you're done making a document, we'll tell you everything you need to know about how to finalize it and make it legal. Keep in mind that you can plan your estate a little bit at a time. Start by making just one document, such as your will. When you're ready, come back to WillMaker to make more. You can think of WillMaker as your estate planning companion, providing trustworthy legal and practical information along the path that's best for you.

Congratulations on starting your estate planning—it's a wonderful thing to do for your loved ones. We know from long experience that putting a sound estate plan into place can bring peace and satisfaction to those who take the time to do it.

Contributors

Authors & Editors

Nolo's lawyers and programmer friends created the first version of WillMaker more than 40 years ago. In the following decades, a handful of smart and dedicated lawyers continued to develop and nurture the program that has become America's best-selling estate planning software. Each of the following people—and many more—made meaningful contributions to the integrity and success of WillMaker.

Steve Elias received his law degree from the University of California College of the Law, San Francisco in 1969. He worked in California, New York, and Vermont as a legal aid lawyer and in Vermont as a public defender. Steve wrote and edited Nolo books on a wide range of topics, including wills, special needs trusts, criminal law, legal research, patents, trademarks, bankruptcy, and foreclosures. Steve lived in Lakeport, California, where he provided legal advice to people doing their own bankruptcies and cohosted several radio programs with his wife on community radio. Steve passed away in 2012, and he is much missed.

Betsy S. Hannibal specializes in estate planning content at Nolo and is the managing editor of WillMaker. She also edits several popular Nolo books, including *Make Your Living Trust* and *Estate Planning Basics*. She received her law degree from the Honors Lawyering Program at Golden Gate University School of Law.

Shae Irving was a Nolo editor and author for more than 20 years, specializing in health care directives and powers of attorney. She received her law degree from UC Berkeley Law in 1994. For many years, Shae was the managing editor of WillMaker. In addition, she wrote or cowrote many Nolo products, including *Prenuptial Agreements: How to Write a Fair & Lasting Contract* and *Get It Together: Organize Your Records So Your Family Won't Have To.*

Mary Randolph was Nolo's Editor in Chief for many years before leaving to work at a nonprofit environmental organization, Seacology. She earned her law degree from UC Berkeley Law. In addition to working on much of the material in WillMaker, she is the author of several Nolo estate planning and administration books, including *The Executor's Guide: Settling a Loved One's Estate or Trust* and *8 Ways to Avoid Probate.*

Ralph "Jake" Warner founded Nolo with Ed Sherman in 1972. When personal computers came along, he became a pioneer of self-help legal software, cocreating the first version of WillMaker in the early 1980s. In addition to running Nolo for several decades, Warner was an active editor and author of many books. Warner holds a law degree from UC Berkeley Law and an undergraduate degree from Princeton.

CHAPTER

1

Planning Your Estate With WillMaker

Estate planning is the process of arranging for what will happen to your property when you die. (Whatever you own at your death is called your estate.) It can also include:

- making arrangements for the care of your young children in the event of your death
- planning for your own care and the care of your property in case someday you can't make decisions on your own
- taking steps so that your inheritors can avoid probate court proceedings after your death, and
- if you own a very large amount of property, planning to avoid federal or state estate tax.

WillMaker can help you with all of these issues and a few others as well. What follows is a discussion of the legal documents you can create with WillMaker, so you can see what they accomplish and decide whether or not they fit your situation.

Wills

Perhaps the most essential reason to make an estate plan is to have a say about who gets your property when you die. A will is the easiest way to do this.

If you don't use a will or some other legal method to transfer your property when you die, state law determines what happens to your possessions. (See "Dying Without a Will" in Chapter 2.)

In addition to specifying who will inherit your property, you can also use your will to:

- name alternates, in case your first choices die before you do
- choose an executor—someone you trust to oversee the distribution of your property after your death
- name a guardian to raise your young children if you can't, and
- name a trusted adult to manage the property that a child or young adult inherits from you. (WillMaker gives you several ways to handle this; they're explained in Chapter 7.)

Property That Doesn't Pass Through a Will

Usually, you cannot use a will to leave certain kinds of assets, including:

- property you leave through a living trust
- bank accounts for which you have named a pay-on-death beneficiary
- stocks and bonds or vehicles for which you have named a transfer on death beneficiary
- real estate left through a transfer on death deed
- property owned as "community property with right of survivorship," which automatically goes to the survivor when one co-owner dies
- property owned in joint tenancy or tenancy by the entirety, which automatically goes to the surviving owners at your death, and
- retirement accounts (IRAs and 401(k) plans) and some pension funds that go to the beneficiary you named in forms provided by the account custodian.

Other Ways to Leave Property

A will is not the only way—and, in some cases, not the best way—to transfer ownership of your property when you die. Especially if you own a fair amount of property, you should consider whether it makes sense to plan now to help your inheritors avoid time-consuming and expensive probate court proceedings after your death. To learn more about using a will as part of a larger estate plan, see Chapter 13.

Living Trusts

Consider using a living trust if you want your property to avoid probate after you die. Any property that passes through a living trust can be transferred directly to beneficiaries without going through probate court, often saving time and money.

Living trusts are a popular and useful estate planning tool, but not everyone needs a living trust. Those with simple or small estates might find that the benefits of keeping property out of probate do not justify the hassle of creating a living trust, transferring property, and maintaining the trust. And a large amount of your property could pass directly to your beneficiaries even without a living trust. For example, these kinds of property do not go through probate: retirement accounts, financial accounts with a named beneficiary, any real estate for which you've made a transfer on death deed, and life insurance proceeds.

Your decision about whether to make a living trust depends on:

- what kinds of property will be in your estate
- your estate planning goals, and
- your financial and family circumstances.

Reading Chapter 13 might help you make this decision. Also, the last section of Chapter 6 will help you weigh the pros and cons of using your will to "pour" property from your will into your living trust.

To learn more about living trusts or about how to use WillMaker's living trust, go to www.willmaker.com/legal-manual/living-trusts.

Quitclaim Deeds

WillMaker's quitclaim deed is a limited-use deed designed to help you (or you and your spouse) transfer your home or other real estate into your living trust. To learn more or to start your deed in WillMaker, go to the screen that lists all of WillMaker's documents and look for Quitclaim Deed in the Estate Planning section. WillMaker's quitclaim deed is available in most states.

Transfer on Death Deeds

In the majority of the U.S. states, you can use a transfer on death (TOD) deed to name a beneficiary for real estate, like your home. The property transfers to your beneficiary when you die, without probate. Before your death, you still own the property, and you can revoke the deed (or make a new one) at any time.

Transfer on death deeds provide some of the best features of both wills and living trusts. Like living trusts, TOD deeds keep the property out of probate. Like wills, they are simple to make, revise, and revoke. So for many people, particularly those whose largest asset is their house, TOD deeds can replace the need for a living trust. (You'll still almost certainly need a will.)

To learn more about WillMaker's transfer on death deeds, go to www.willmaker.com/legal-manual/transfer-on-death-deeds.

Durable Power of Attorney for Finances

It's a good idea for almost everyone with property or an income to make a durable power of attorney for finances. It's particularly important, however, if you fear that health problems might make it impossible for you to handle your financial matters.

Making a durable financial power of attorney ensures that someone you trust will be on hand to manage the many practical financial tasks that will arise if you become incapacitated. For example, bills must be paid, bank deposits must be made, and someone must handle insurance and benefits paperwork. Many other matters might need attention as well, from property repairs to managing investments or a small business. In most cases, a durable power of attorney for finances is the best way to take care of tasks like these. If you ever need to revoke your power of attorney, use the revocation form that prints with your document. Or, if you want to revoke a previously made power of attorney, you can use WillMaker's Revocation of Power of Attorney. See Chapter 14 for more information.

Health Care Directives (Living Will and Power of Attorney)

It's vitally important that those close to you understand the kind of medical treatment you would—or would not—want if you were unable to speak for yourself. You can use a WillMaker health care directive to describe your health care wishes and name a trusted person to oversee them. The person you name can also make other necessary health care decisions for you if you are too ill or injured to direct your own care.

WillMaker helps you prepare documents that are legal in your state. Depending on where you live, you might get a single document (often called an advance health care directive) or two separate documents (typically called a living will and a durable power of attorney for health care). If you ever need to revoke your health care directive, use the revocation form that prints with your document. Or, if you want to revoke a previously made health care directive, you can use WillMaker's Revocation of Health Care Directive.

You'll find much more information about health care directives in Chapter 15.

Final Arrangements Document

As you create your estate planning documents, your thoughts might turn to how you want your body to be handled after your death.

With our final arrangements document, you can let your loved ones know whether you wish to be buried or cremated, what kind of memorial ceremonies you have in mind, and other details related to the final disposition of your body. During a difficult time, this document can provide much-needed guidance for your survivors.

To learn more about the final arrangements document, see Chapter 16.

Information for Caregivers and Survivors

With the download version of WillMaker, you can make a document called Information for Caregivers and Survivors, which is a comprehensive guide to the details of your life, from information about your bank accounts to people you'd like contacted in the event of your illness or death.

When you prepare this form, WillMaker walks you through the particulars of your life, asking you to provide details on many topics, including things your loved ones might not know—such as the names of your doctors, whether you have life insurance, or how to access your online accounts. This interview creates a comprehensive document that will greatly aid those who need to care for you or manage your estate.

Letter to Survivors

When working on your estate plan, you might find that you want to explain certain things to your loved ones. For example, you might want to let them know why you left a large gift to charity, why you named your sister (and not your brother) to look after your child's finances, or where you keep important papers or passwords. Or maybe you simply want to leave some thoughts about your life.

One way to convey these things is to write a letter that will be passed on to your loved ones when you die. The letter can be in any format you like, from a handwritten note to a more formal typed letter. If you'd like some help, try WillMaker's Letter to Survivors. It prompts you about many types of information—you pick and choose the topics that you want to write about. Type in your thoughts and ideas, and WillMaker will compile them into a letter for you. Learn more in Chapter 12.

Forms for Home and Family

WillMaker also provides a range of forms you can use to take care of your loved ones, pets, and property. For example, there are authorizations granting others permission to care for your child, and for pet care. Here's some information about each of the forms for your home and family.

Child Care Agreement

If you want to hire someone to care for your children in your home, you should prepare a child care agreement.

WillMaker's Child Care Agreement allows you to spell out the exact responsibilities of the position and to specify the child care provider's hours, amount and schedule of payment, benefits, and other important aspects of the job.

Child Care Instructions

Use this form to provide important information for babysitters and child care providers, such as names and phone numbers of doctors and emergency contacts and instructions about meals, naps, and other details of your child's care.

Authorization for Minor's Medical Treatment

Creating a medical care authorization allows another adult to authorize necessary medical or dental treatment if your child is injured or becomes ill while not with you—for example, while playing on a sports team or staying with a babysitter.

Authorization for International Travel With Minor

If your young child will be traveling outside the United States with another adult, you should prepare an authorization for international travel. The form provides necessary proof that you have consented to the travel.

Temporary Guardianship Authorization

If you leave your child in the care of another adult for a few days, weeks, or months, you should authorize the caretaker to make any necessary decisions about your child's medical, educational, and other care. You can do this by preparing a temporary guardianship authorization.

Elder Care Agreement

WillMaker's elder care agreement is for people who wish to sign an agreement with an elder care provider who will take care of an older parent or other elderly relative at home. The agreement allows you to spell out the exact responsibilities of the position and to specify the worker's hours, amount and schedule of payment, benefits, and other important aspects of the job.

Pet Care Agreement

If you're going on a trip or will otherwise be unable to care for your pet for a period of time, you might leave your animal in the care of a friend, relative, neighbor, or professional pet sitter. If you do, it's a good idea to prepare this written agreement that sets out clear instructions for your pet's care and clarifies each party's responsibilities and expectations.

Housekeeping Services Agreement

If you hire someone to clean or take care of your house on a regular basis, you can use our housekeeping services agreement. It allows you to spell out the exact responsibilities of the position and to specify the housekeeper's hours, benefits, and other details.

Housesitting Instructions

Use this form to provide detailed housesitting instructions for a person who will care for your home while you are away. You can specify your wishes about your plants and garden, newspapers and mail, telephone calls, appliances, computers, lights and security, tools and supplies, vehicles, and other matters. You can also include important information, such as how you can be reached while you are away and whom the housesitter can contact for help in your absence.

Authorization to Drive a Motor Vehicle

Lending your vehicle to someone isn't always as simple as handing over the keys. If the person who borrows your car is pulled over by the police or is involved in an accident, the borrower will want to quickly prove that you agreed to the use. Otherwise, the driver might be detained while police investigate whether the car is stolen.

This simple authorization takes just a few minutes to complete, and it provides important legal proof that you've given someone else permission to drive your vehicle. The form is designed for a car, but it will work fine for a motorcycle, truck, or other motor vehicle, such as a motorboat.

Personal Finance Forms

Finally, WillMaker offers some forms to help you with basic financial matters. There are forms to use if you need to borrow or lend money and a few other useful documents—such as a power of attorney you can use to have someone take care of a specific financial transaction if you're unavailable. Here's a little more information about each form.

General Bill of Sale

Use this form to record the terms of the sale of an item of personal property, such as a car, computer, or guitar. When you sell an item with a written bill of sale, you reduce the chance of a dispute arising after the sale.

Limited Power of Attorney for Finances

A limited power of attorney for finances lets you appoint someone (called your "agent" or "attorney-in-fact") to help you with one or more clearly defined tasks involving your finances or property. For example, you might want to name someone to monitor certain investments for you while you are on vacation—and sell them if necessary. Or you might need someone to sign business or legal papers for you while you are unavailable. This form lets you temporarily delegate authority to someone you trust.

Revocation of Power of Attorney

If you've made a power of attorney, you can change your mind and cancel it at any time. Use this notice of revocation to put an end to any power of attorney, including a durable power of attorney (one that is designed to remain in effect even after you become incapacitated).

Promissory Notes

If you are borrowing or lending money, you should create a promissory note. Like an IOU, a promissory note records the terms of the loan, including the period of repayment and the interest rate (if interest will be charged), as well as the borrower's promise to pay back the loan. The promissory note you make with WillMaker offers a choice of three payment plans.

Installment payments. This type of promissory note requires the borrower to make the same monthly payment for a specified number of months. You can choose whether or not the borrower will pay interest on the loan.

One lump-sum payment. As the name indicates, this note requires the borrower to make just one payment on a specified date. You can choose whether the borrower will pay interest on the loan.

Payments of interest only. With this type of note, the borrower pays only the interest on the loan each month for a specified number of months, with a balloon payment of the principal and any remaining interest at the end of the loan term.

Organizing Your Records

Working on your estate plan is a good time to consider how you will organize and store all of your important documents—such as your living trust documents, list of passwords, or life insurance policy—so that others can easily find them. To do this, you'll need to come up with a system that works for you. Here are a few ideas that might help.

- **Using a document.** With the download version of WillMaker, you can make an Information for Caregivers and Survivors form to help with this task. With this document, you can provide a comprehensive guide to the details of your life—ranging from information about your property and your financial accounts to the names and addresses of people you want contacted in the event of your death. To begin this document, click the "Your Documents" button at the top of the screen and select "Information for Caregivers and Survivors" from the list.
- **Using a binder or file box.** If you like the idea of using a printed book to help you get organized, consider using *Get It Together: Organize Your Records So Your Family Won't Have To,* by Melanie Cullen (Nolo), which gives you step-by-step instructions for finding, organizing, and storing the important details of your life.

  Or if you'd prefer a filing system that's already set up for you, look into Nokbox, which gives you a ready-made file box with prelabeled files and checklists to help you find and store your records.
- **Using an online vault.** If you like the idea of keeping things online, you'll find several reliable programs that provide a digital storage space for documents and information. Most also offer a system to grant your executor (or whoever you designate) access to your account in the event of your death or incapacity. Some popular online options include Quicken LifeHub, Everplans, and Trustworthy.

Most people will need to use a combination of online and physical systems because some information is better stored online (like lists of accounts and passwords), while other information can only be stored in a hardcopy or tangible form (like your will or house keys).

No matter how you approach it, it will take some time and effort to collect the important details of your life. But it will be worth the work because your loved ones won't have to spend weeks or months poking around your belongings for the information they need to manage your property or wrap up your estate.

CHAPTER

2

About Wills

Making a will is an excellent way to ensure that your plans for leaving property to family, friends, and organizations of your choice are carried out after you die. You can efficiently and safely write your own legal will using WillMaker. But before you start, it is a good idea to read this chapter and Chapter 3, which explain generally how wills work and how you can use WillMaker to meet your needs.

Legal Requirements

For a will to be legally valid, both you—the person making the will—and the will itself must meet some technical requirements.

Who Can Make a Will

Before you start your will, make sure you qualify to make one in the eyes of the law.

Age

To make a will, you must be either:

- at least 18 years old, or
- living in a state that permits people under 18 to make a will if they are married, in the military, or otherwise considered legally emancipated.

Mental Competence

You must be of sound mind to prepare a valid will. The laws generally require that you must:

- know what a will is, what it does, and that you are making one
- understand the relationship between you and the people who would normally be provided for in your will, such as a spouse or children
- understand the kind and quantity of property you own, and
- be able to decide how to distribute your belongings.

This threshold of mental competence is not hard to meet. Very few wills are successfully challenged based on the charge that the testator (the person making the will) was mentally incompetent. It is not enough to show that the person was forgetful or absentminded.

To have a probate court declare a will invalid usually requires proving that the testator was totally overtaken by the fraud or undue influence of another person—and that person then benefited from the wrongdoing by becoming entitled to a large amount of money or property under the will.

Interestingly, the great majority of undue influence contests are filed against attorneys who draw up wills in which they are named to take clients' property. If a person was very old, ill, or suffering from dementia when making the will, it is obviously easier to convince a judge that undue influence occurred.

SEE AN EXPERT

If a contest seems possible. If you have any serious doubts about your ability to meet the legal requirements for making a will, or if you believe your will is likely to be contested by another person for any reason, consult an experienced lawyer. (See Chapter 17.)

Will Requirements

State law determines whether a will made by a resident of the state is valid. And a will that is valid in the state where it is made is valid in all other states.

Contrary to what many people believe, a will need not be notarized to be legally valid. But adding a notarized document to the will verifying that the will was signed and witnessed can be helpful when it comes time to file the will in probate court. This option is available in all but a handful of states. (See "The Self-Proving Option" in Chapter 10.)

There are surprisingly few legal restrictions and requirements in the will-making process. In most states, a will must:

- include at least one substantive provision—either giving away some property or naming a guardian to care for minor children who are left without parents
- be signed and dated by the person making it
- be witnessed by at least two other people who are not named to take property under the will, and
- be clear enough that others can understand what the testator intended. Nonsensical, legalistic language such as "I hereby give, bequeath, and devise" is both unwise and unnecessary.

Handwritten and Oral Wills

In about half the states, unwitnessed, handwritten wills—called holographic wills—are legally valid. And a few states accept oral wills under very limited circumstances, such as when a mortally wounded soldier utters last wishes.

But handwritten wills are fraught with possible legal problems. Most obviously, after your death, it might be difficult to prove that your unwitnessed, handwritten document was actually written by you and that you intended it to be your will. And it might be almost impossible to prove the authenticity of an oral will.

A typewritten, properly signed, witnessed will is much less vulnerable to challenge by anyone claiming it was forged or fabricated. If need be, witnesses can later testify in court that the person whose name is on the will is the same person who signed it and that making the will was a voluntary and knowing act.

Electronic Wills

Electronic wills are signed and witnessed electronically. Currently, about a dozen states have adopted laws to allow electronic wills, and more are sure to follow. However, until these new laws settle and a majority of states have figured out how electronic wills will work (both practically and legally), stick to making your will on paper. Read more about electronic witnessing in Chapter 10.

Dying Without a Will

If you die without a valid will, property you own at death (that does not have named beneficiaries) will be divided and distributed to others according to your state's intestate succession laws. These laws divide that property among the relatives who are considered closest to you according to a set formula—and completely exclude friends and charities.

These legal formulas often do not mirror people's wishes. For example, many married people would want their spouse to get their entire estate. However, in some states, if there are no children, the intestate succession laws split the estate between the spouse and the parents. The situation is even worse for unmarried couples. Except in a few states, unmarried partners receive nothing. And even in the states that offer exceptions, benefits aren't automatic—eligible couples must register their partnerships with the state or prove that they have a "common law" marriage (see Chapter 4).

RESOURCE

Learn more about intestate succession. You can read more about intestate succession—including detailed information about the laws in your state—at www.nolo.com/legal-encyclopedia/intestate-succession.

If you have minor children, another important reason to make a will is to name a personal guardian to care for them. This is an important concern of most parents, who worry that their children will be left without a caretaker if both parents die. Intestate succession laws do not deal with the issue of who will take care of your children. If you don't name a guardian in your will, it is left up to the courts and social service agencies to find and appoint a personal guardian.

Making Basic Decisions About Your Will

Making a will is not difficult, but it is undeniably a serious and sobering process. Before you begin, get organized and focus on these important questions:

- What do you own? (See Chapter 5.)
- Who should get your property? (See Chapter 6.)
- If you have minor children, who is the best person to care for them, and who is best suited to manage property you leave them? (See Chapter 4 and Chapter 7.)
- Who will see that your property is distributed according to your wishes after your death? (See Chapter 8.)

This manual offers guidance on how to use WillMaker to give legal effect to your decisions in all of these areas. The ultimate choices, however, are up to you.

But you might have a question about your particular situation that WillMaker does not answer. Or perhaps you have a very large estate and want to engage in some sophisticated tax planning. Or you might simply be comforted by having a lawyer give your WillMaker will a once-over. Whenever you have concerns such as these or simply feel that you are in over your head, it might be wise to consult an attorney with knowledge and experience in wills and estate planning. A good lawyer can give you personalized legal advice that WillMaker cannot provide. (See Chapter 17.)

Helping Someone Else Make a Will

You can use WillMaker to help a loved one or friend make a will. But you must be sure that your role is only to type in the will maker's wishes. In other words, the will maker, not you, must decide on the terms of the will. If your role exceeds these limits, a court could declare the will invalid—and you might even face legal charges.

If you decide to help someone else prepare a will, you might want to take an extra step to document your role: Make an audio or video recording of the process or ask someone else to be present as a witness while you follow the will maker's directions.

> EXAMPLE: Betty asks her neighbor, James, to help her make her will because her hands shake too badly to type her responses into WillMaker. She dictates her answers to James and he types them in at her direction. She also tells James to print out the document for her to sign. For extra security, Betty's friend Wendy watches as a witness so she can later testify to James's role, if necessary.

If the person you want to help cannot clearly direct the will-making process, or if you have any concern that the person might not fully understand what it means to make a will, see an experienced estate planning attorney for help.

Helping Someone Else Make a Will

CHAPTER

3

About WillMaker Wills

Because wills reflect how people want to leave their property, they can be as complex and intricate as life. While state laws broadly regulate the procedures for valid will making, you are generally free to write a will to meet your needs. If you aren't familiar with legal paperwork, this level of flexibility can feel daunting.

WillMaker offers considerable help. WillMaker works by asking you to systematically answer questions. As you will soon see, either you already have enough information to answer them easily, or you can quickly get it.

What You Can Do With a WillMaker Will

This section gives you a quick survey of what you can do with the WillMaker will. Each topic is discussed in greater detail in the onscreen help and in other chapters in this manual.

Tailor Your Will to Your Needs

WillMaker provides you with unique guidance and options based on the state in which you live, your marital status, whether you have children, whether your children are minors, and how you want to leave your property. Recognizing that some people have very simple wishes for leaving their property while those of others are more complex, WillMaker lets you choose from among several approaches designed to meet your needs. For instance, if you are married, you can choose to:

- leave all property to your spouse
- leave most property to your spouse, with several specific property items going to people you name, or
- divide property among many different people and organizations. (See Chapter 6.)

Name Beneficiaries to Get Specific Property

WillMaker lets you make an unlimited number of separate gifts—called specific bequests—of cash, personal property, or real estate. You can choose to leave these bequests to your spouse, children, grandchildren, or anyone else—including friends, business associates, charities, or other organizations. You can also use your will to leave property to a living trust, if you've established one. (See Chapter 6.)

EXAMPLE 1: Using the WillMaker will, Marcia leaves her interest in the family home to her spouse, Duane, her valuable vinyl record collection to one of her children, her boat to another child, her computer to a charity, and $5,000 to her two aunts, in equal shares.

EXAMPLE 2: Raymond, a lifelong bachelor, follows the WillMaker directions and leaves his house to his favorite charity. He divides his personal possessions among 15 different relatives and friends.

EXAMPLE 3: Darryl and Floyd have lived together for several years. Darryl uses the WillMaker will to leave Floyd all of his property, which includes his car, timeshare ownership in a condominium, art collection, and miscellaneous personal belongings.

Name Someone to Take All Remaining Property

WillMaker also allows you to name people or organizations to take whatever property is left over after you have made the specific bequests. This property is called your residuary estate. (See "Naming Residuary Beneficiaries" in Chapter 6.)

EXAMPLE: Annie wants to make a number of small bequests to friends and charities but to leave the bulk of her property to her friend Maureen. She accomplishes this by using specific bequests to make the small gifts, and then names Maureen as residuary beneficiary. There is no need for her to list the property that goes to Maureen. The very nature of the residuary estate is that the residuary beneficiary—in this case, Maureen—gets everything that is left over after the specific bequests are distributed.

If you leave your entire estate to one person or to a group of people without making any specific bequests, then your estate will have no residuary beneficiary.

Name Alternate Beneficiaries

Using WillMaker, all beneficiaries you name take the property you leave them under your will only if they survive you by 45 days. WillMaker imposes this 45-day rule because you do not want to leave your property to a beneficiary who dies very shortly after you do. When that happens, the property you left to that beneficiary would then be passed along to that person's inheritors, who are not likely to be the ones you would have chosen to receive your property.

To account for the possibility that your first choices of beneficiaries will not meet the survivorship requirement, WillMaker allows you to name alternate beneficiaries for each of your bequests. (See Chapter 6.)

Avoiding Legalese: Per Stirpes and Per Capita

"Per stirpes" and "per capita" are legal jargon for the way children inherit property in place of a deceased parent—for example, one of these terms might govern how a granddaughter would inherit property left to her mother under a will, if her mother died before the will maker. It's not necessary for your will to include these terms. In fact, it's better to avoid them, because they can be interpreted in different ways. Instead, your WillMaker will lets you set out exactly whom you want to inherit your property, who will take the property if your first-choice beneficiary doesn't survive you, and the shares that they will inherit.

If you prefer to use "per capita" or "per stirpes" instead of naming each of your beneficiaries, get help from an attorney who can address how those words will apply to your specific circumstances.

Name a Guardian to Care for Your Children

You can use WillMaker to name a personal guardian—either an individual or a couple—to care for your minor children until they reach age 18, in case there is no other legal parent to handle these duties. You can name the same guardian for all your children or different guardians for different children. (It is important, however, that both parents name the same person or couple as guardian for any particular child; see the example below.) You will also have the opportunity to explain your choices in your will.

If your children need a guardian after your death, a court will formally review your choice. Your choice will normally be approved unless the person or couple you name refuses to assume the responsibility or the court becomes convinced that your children would be better off in the care of someone else. (See "Your Children" in Chapter 4.)

> **EXAMPLE:** Millicent names her friend Vera to serve as personal guardian in the event that her husband, Frank, dies at the same time she does or is otherwise unavailable to care for their three children. Millicent and Frank die together in an accident. No one questions Vera's ability to care for them, so the court appoints her to be the personal guardian for all three children.
>
> If Frank had written a will naming another person to serve as guardian, however, the court would have to choose between those nominated. For this reason, parents should choose the same people as personal guardians, if possible.

Name a Manager for Children's Property

Property left to minors—especially cash or other liquid assets—will usually have to be managed by an adult until the minors turn 18. In many cases, it might be most prudent to have an adult manage property left to minors until they are even older.

Property management involves safeguarding and spending the property for the young person's education, health care, and basic living needs; keeping good records of these expenditures; and seeing that income taxes are paid.

RESOURCE

Providing for beneficiaries with special needs. It is common to set up management for property that will pass to a beneficiary who has a disability. One common way to provide this management is through a "special needs trust." You can use your WillMaker will to leave money or property to a preexisting special needs trust. However, you cannot use your WillMaker will to set up a special needs trust or any other kind of property management for a person with special needs. If you need this type of management, you can turn to Nolo's book *Special Needs Trusts: Protect Your Child's Financial Future*, by Kevin Urbatsch and Jessica Farinas Jones, or consult an attorney who specializes in dealing with the needs of people with disabilities. (See Chapter 17.)

WillMaker allows you to name a trusted person to manage property you leave to young beneficiaries through your will. Separately, the program can also help you name a property guardian to manage property that your children might acquire outside of your will (through income or inheritance, for example).

Setting up property management for children is discussed in detail in Chapter 7.

Name a Caretaker for Your Pet

While many of us consider our pets to be members of the family, in the eyes of the law, pets are property. That means you can't leave money or other items directly to your pet—but you can use your will to leave your pet to a trusted caretaker. Doing so is a good way to ensure that your pet has a loving home when you die.

With the WillMaker will, you can name a caretaker for your pet and leave money to that person for your pet's care. If you choose to leave money to the caretaker, your document will state that you leave it "with the hope that the money will be used for the costs of owning" your pet. It will be up to the honor of the caretaker to use the gift as you intend. This shouldn't be a problem if you choose someone you trust to care for your pet.

You can also name an alternate in case your first-choice caretaker is not available when you die. (See "Your Pets" in Chapter 4.)

Cancel Debts Others Owe You

You can use WillMaker to relieve any debtors who owe you money at your death from the responsibility of paying your survivors. All you need to do is specify the debts and the people who owe them. WillMaker will then include a statement in your will canceling the debts. If a debt is canceled in this way, WillMaker also automatically wipes out any interest that has accrued on the debt as of your death. (See "Debts Others Owe to You" in Chapter 9.)

EXAMPLE: Cynthia lent $25,000 at 10% annual interest to her son George as a down payment on a house. She uses WillMaker to cancel this debt. At Cynthia's death, George need not pay her estate the remaining balance of the loan or the interest accrued on it.

Name an Executor

With WillMaker, you can name an executor for your estate. This person or institution, officially called a personal representative in many states, will be responsible for making sure the provisions in your will are carried out and your property distributed as your will directs. WillMaker also produces a letter to your executor that generally explains what the job requires.

The executor can be any competent adult. Commonly, people name a spouse or another close relative or friend or—for large estates or where no trusted person is able to serve—a financial institution, such as a bank or savings and loan. You are free to name two people or institutions to share the job, but doing so is often unwise. (See Chapter 8.)

It is also a good idea to use WillMaker to name an alternate executor in case your first choice becomes unable or unwilling to serve.

> EXAMPLE 1: Rick and Phyllis both use WillMaker to complete wills naming each other as executor in case the other dies first. They both name Rick's father as an alternate executor to distribute their property in the event they die at the same time.

> EXAMPLE 2: Pat and Babs do not wish to burden their relatives with having to take care of their fairly considerable estate. Each names the Third National Bank as executor after checking that their estate is large enough that this bank will be willing to take the job.

What You Cannot Do With a WillMaker Will

WillMaker allows you to produce a valid and effective will designed to meet most needs. But there are some restrictions built in. Some are designed to prevent you from writing in conditions that might not be legally valid. Others are intended to keep WillMaker simple and easy to use.

Make Bequests With Conditions

You cannot make a bequest that will take effect only if a certain condition occurs—an "if, and, or but," such as "$5,000 to John if he stops smoking." Such conditional bequests are confusing and usually require someone to supervise the beneficiaries to be sure they satisfy the conditions in the will. Consider that someone would have to constantly check up on John to make sure he never took a puff—and someone would have to wrench away his property if he ever got caught in the act.

So, to use WillMaker, you must be willing to leave property to people outright; you cannot make them jump through hoops or change their behavior to get it.

Write Joint Wills

In the past, it was common for a couple who had an agreed-upon scheme for how to distribute all their property to write one document together: a joint will. But time has shown that setup to be crawling with problems. WillMaker requires that each spouse make a separate will, even if both agree about how to distribute their property. This limitation is not imposed to annoy people or defeat their intentions; there is solid legal reasoning behind it.

Creating Identical Wills

While you can't create a joint will using WillMaker, you can create identical wills—that is, two separate wills in which all the provisions (such as beneficiaries, children's guardians, and executors) are the same. If you want to do this, WillMaker provides an easy shortcut.

Here's how:

1. Complete a will for one spouse, naming the second spouse on the marital status screen.
2. On the document preview screen for that will, click the "Duplicate for Spouse" button.
3. On the next screen under Helpful Information, read about "Creating Identical Wills for Couples." Then click the "Duplicate for Spouse" button. This will prompt WillMaker to create a second will, duplicating key information from the first will.
4. Find this new will on the "Your Documents" menu under the name of the second spouse.
5. Step through each screen of the new will, reviewing and revising the duplicated information as needed.

Joint wills are intended to prevent the surviving spouse from changing the couple's plan after the first spouse dies. The practical effect is to tie up the property for years in title and probate determinations—often until long after the second spouse dies. Also, many court battles are fought over whether the surviving spouse is legally entitled to revoke any part of the joint will.

There are still some lawyers who will agree to write joint wills, but they take the risk that such wills might become cumbersome or might even be found invalid in later court challenges. For these reasons, it is best for both spouses to write separate wills—a bit more time-consuming, perhaps, but a lot safer from a legal standpoint.

CAUTION

Review wills to avoid conflicts. People who jointly own property or have children together should review their wills together to be sure they do not provide conflicting information—such as each naming two different guardians for any one child.

Explain the Reasons for Leaving Your Property

Most of the time, the act of leaving property to people—or choosing not to leave them anything—speaks for itself. Occasionally, however, people making wills want to explain to survivors the reasons they left property as they did. This might be the case, for example, if you opt to leave one of your two children more property than the other to compensate for the loan you made during your lifetime to help one of them buy a house. Although the desire to make such explanations is understandable, WillMaker does not allow you to do it in your will because doing so could add legally confusing language to the document.

However, WillMaker does provide an easy and legally safe way to provide your heirs with explanations for your bequests. You can draft a Letter to Survivors to keep with your will, explaining your reasons for leaving property to some people—or not leaving it to others. (See Chapter 12.)

Name Coguardians for Children's Property

You can name only one guardian to care for the property left to your young children. While you can choose different property guardians for different children, you cannot name two people to share the responsibility. (See Chapter 7.)

At first glance, it might seem to be a good idea to divide up the job—after all, sometimes two heads are better than one. But naming more than one property guardian often presents more problems than it solves because those two people will have to make every decision together. A difference of opinion could require court intervention, which will cost both time and money. It is better to name just one trustworthy person to make decisions about your children's property, and then name a second equally trustworthy person to take over the job if the first one becomes unavailable.

In contrast, WillMaker does allow you to name a couple to serve as your children's *personal* guardians. Personal guardians step in when a child's other legal guardian is not available. They make decisions about the well-being of the children, rather than the children's property. When those types of decisions will be made in a family setting with two adults, the ability to name a couple is important—so that either adult can take the child to the doctor or to school, for example.

Control Property After Death

Property given to others in a WillMaker will must go to them as soon as you die. You cannot make a bequest by will that gives property to one person for life and then gives the same property to a second person when the first person dies. Such an arrangement involves too many unique variables to address in a DIY will. You will need a lawyer to carry out this type of plan. (See Chapter 17.)

EXAMPLE: Emory wants his grandchildren to get his house when he dies but wants his wife to have the right to live in the house until her death. Emory cannot use WillMaker to accomplish this. Instead, Emory hires an attorney to write a trust that leaves his house to his spouse for her life and then to his grandchildren upon his spouse's death.

Require a Bond for Executors or Property Managers

A bond is like an insurance policy that protects the beneficiaries in the unlikely event that the executor wrongfully spends or distributes estate property. Because the premium or fee that must be paid for a bond comes out of the estate—leaving less money for the beneficiaries—most wills for small or moderate estates do not require one.

Following this general practice, the will produced by WillMaker does not require a bond. Instead, take care to appoint someone you know to be trustworthy.

Although the WillMaker will does not require a bond, a court might still require one—especially if the executor or property manager lives out of state. You can read more about this in Chapter 8.

Leave Property to Your Pet

Animals aren't legally permitted to own property, so you can't use your will to make gifts to your pet. If you name your pet to receive property through your will, that gift will be void and the intended gift and the pet will become part of your residuary estate.

That said, using WillMaker's will, you can name a new owner for your pet and leave money to that person requesting that they use it to care for your pet. In most states you can also create a "pet trust" to set up a legal obligation to care for your pet after you die. (See "Your Pets" in Chapter 4.)

Make a Plan for Foreign Property

You cannot use the WillMaker will to make a plan for property that is located in a country other than the United States. The laws of that country will affect how the property passes to beneficiaries, and owning foreign property can affect your taxes. If you own property in another country, get help from a lawyer who has experience dealing with that country's property, probate, and tax laws.

Include a No-Contest Clause

The WillMaker will does not include a no-contest clause. A no-contest clause states that a beneficiary who challenges your will after your death forfeits any gifts you have made to that beneficiary under your will. Many people believe that including a no-contest clause will dissuade any would-be beneficiaries from challenging the will.

However, most states will not uphold a no-contest clause if the challenger has a good reason to object to the will—for example, if the challenger shows that the will is not valid because the signer's name was forged. Other states go further and do not uphold no-contest clauses for any reason. WillMaker's will does not include a no-contest clause because no-contest clauses give the will maker a false sense of security about possible will challenges, when in reality, such clauses are often not enforced.

If you want to include a no-contest clause anyway, or if you think that there is a good chance that someone will challenge your will, see an experienced estate planning lawyer for help. If you need it, a good lawyer should be able to craft a no-contest clause that creates maximum protection for your specific situation. And in some states, a lawyer might be able to help you "prevalidate" your will, which would greatly reduce the possibility of a challenge.

A Look at a WillMaker Will

You might find it helpful to take a look at a WillMaker will, but do not be alarmed if the sample will does not match the one you produce. Your WillMaker will is tailored to your property, circumstances, and state laws. Nearly every paragraph or clause of the sample will is followed by an explanation.

Will of Willy WillMaker

Part 1. Personal Information

I, Willy WillMaker, a resident of the State of California, Alameda County, declare that this is my will.

Part 2. Revocation of Previous Wills

I revoke all wills and codicils that I have previously made.

> *This provision makes clear that this is the will to be used—not any other wills or amendments to those wills, called codicils, that were made earlier. To prevent possible confusion, all earlier wills and codicils should also be physically destroyed.*

Part 3. Marital Status

I am married to Wilma WillMaker.

> *Here you identify your spouse if you are married—or your partner, if you are in a registered partnership, civil union, or other marriage-like relationship recognized by your state. If you are not married or in a registered partnership, this provision will not appear in your will.*

Part 4. Children

I have the following children now living: Sammie WillMaker and Chester WillMaker.

> *This part of your will should list all of your biological and adopted children; your stepchildren should not be included here. By naming all your children, you will prevent a child from claiming to have been accidentally overlooked in your will. It will also ward off later claims that any child is entitled to take a share of your property against your wishes.*

/////

/////

Page 1 Initials: _____ _____ _____ _____ Date: ______________

Part 5. Pets

I leave my Boston terrier, Clementine, and $1,500 to Marjani Mohamed, with the hope that the money will be used for the costs of owning Clementine. If Marjani Mohamed does not survive me, I leave Clementine and $2,000 to Julian Rosen, with the hope that the money will be used for the costs of owning Clementine.

Here you can leave your pet to a trusted caretaker. You can also leave money to the caretaker with a request that the caretaker use the money for your pet's care.

Part 6. Disposition of Property

A beneficiary must survive me for 45 days to receive property under this will. As used in this will, the phrase "survive me" means to be alive or in existence as an organization on the 45th day after my death.

This language means that to receive property under your will, a person must be alive for at least 45 days after your death. Otherwise, the property will go to whomever you named as an alternate. This language permits you to choose another way to leave your property if your first choice dies within a short time after you do.

This will clause also prevents the confusion associated with the simultaneous death of two spouses, when it is hard to tell who gets the property they have left to each other. Property left to a spouse who dies within 45 days of the first spouse, including a spouse who dies simultaneously, will go to the person or organization named as alternate.

If I leave property to be shared by two or more beneficiaries, and any of them does not survive me, I leave that beneficiary's share to the others equally unless this will provides otherwise.

This clause states that if you leave a gift to two or more beneficiaries without stating the percentage each should receive, the beneficiaries will share the gift equally. This clause is included as a catchall; you can determine the shares for almost every shared gift.

Page 2 Initials: ______ ______ ______ ______ Date: ____________

My residuary estate is all property I own at my death that is subject to this will that does not pass under a general or specific bequest, including all failed or lapsed bequests.

> *This definition is included so that you and your survivors are clear on the meaning of "residuary estate." If you leave no specific bequests (including pets), this clause will not appear in your will.*

I leave $10,000 to Jasmine Hernandez. If Jasmine Hernandez does not survive me, I leave this property to Fumiko Tanaka.

> *This language leaves a specific item of property—$10,000—to a named beneficiary, Jasmine Hernandez. If Jasmine Hernandez does not survive the testator, then Fumiko Tanaka will get the money.*

I leave my rare stamp collection to Marjani Mohamed, Sven Olsson, and Nadia Dimitrov in the following shares: Marjani Mohamed shall receive a 1/4 share. Sven Olsson shall receive a 1/4 share. Nadia Dimitrov shall receive a 1/2 share.

> *This language leaves a specific item of property—a stamp collection—to three people in unequal shares.*

I leave my collection of Nash cars to The Big Sky Auto Museum and Richard Jenkins in equal shares. If Richard Jenkins does not survive me, I leave his share of this property to Patricia Jenkins.

> *This will leaves specific property to an organization and a person equally. Since the testator here was concerned about providing for the possibility that the person would not survive to take the property, the testator named an alternate.*

I leave my residuary estate to my spouse, Wilma WillMaker.

> *This clause gives the residuary estate—all property that does not pass under this will in specific bequests—to the testator's spouse. Your residuary estate may be defined differently depending on your plans for leaving your property.*

Page 3 Initials: _____ _____ _____ _____ Date: _______________

If Wilma WillMaker does not survive me, I leave my residuary estate to Sammie WillMaker and Chester WillMaker in a children's pot trust to be administered under the children's pot trust provisions.

> *If the person named here to take the residuary estate does not survive the testator, the residuary estate will pass to the two people named: the testator's children. The property will be put in one pot for both of the children to use as they mature. Specifics of how this pot trust operates are explained later in the will. Keep in mind that, in this example, the pot trust will come into being only if the testator's spouse does not survive the testator by at least 45 days.*

If both of these children are age 18 or older at my death, my residuary estate shall be distributed to them directly in equal shares.

> *This clause makes clear what should happen if the children are older than the age at which the testator specified the pot trust should end. In this case, no pot trust will be created; the children will get the property directly and divide it evenly.*

If either of these children does not survive me, I leave that child's share to the other child.

> *This clause explains that if either child here does not survive, the other will get the property directly.*

If Wilma WillMaker, Sammie WillMaker, and Chester WillMaker all do not survive me, I leave my residuary estate to Peter Chen.

All personal and real property that I leave in this will shall pass subject to any encumbrances or liens placed on the property as security for the repayment of a loan or debt.

> *This language explains that whoever gets any property under this will also gets the mortgage and other legal claims against the property, such as liens. And anyone who takes property that is subject to a loan, such as a car loan, gets the debt as well as the property.*

Page 4 Initials: ____ ____ ____ ____ Date: __________

Part 7. Custodianship Under the Uniform Transfers to Minors Act

All property left in this will to Peter Chen shall be given to Amaya Adebayo as custodian under the California Uniform Transfers to Minors Act, to be held until Peter Chen reaches age 21. If Amaya Adebayo is unwilling or unable to serve as custodian of property left to Peter Chen under this will, Michelle Lee shall serve instead.

> *This clause provides that all property left to the child named in the clause will be managed by the person named as the custodian until the child turns the age indicated. An alternate custodian is also named in case the first-choice custodian is unable or unwilling to serve when the time comes.*

Part 8. Children's Pot Trust

A. Beneficiaries of Children's Pot Trust

Sammie WillMaker and Chester WillMaker shall be the beneficiaries of the children's pot trust provided for in this will. If a beneficiary survives me but dies before the children's pot trust terminates, that beneficiary's interest in the trust shall pass to the surviving beneficiaries of the children's pot trust.

B. Trustee of Children's Pot Trust

Mele Tupou shall serve as the trustee of the children's pot trust. If Mele Tupou is unable or unwilling to serve, Alisi Tupou shall serve instead.

C. Administration of the Children's Pot Trust

The trustee shall manage and distribute the assets in the children's pot trust in the following manner.

The trustee may distribute trust assets as trustee deems necessary for a beneficiary's health, support, maintenance, and education. Education includes, but is not limited to, college, graduate, postgraduate, and vocational studies and reasonably related living expenses.

In deciding whether or not to make distributions, the trustee shall consider the value of the trust assets, the relative current and future needs of each beneficiary, and each beneficiary's other income, resources, and sources of support. In doing so, the trustee has the discretion to make distributions that benefit some beneficiaries more than others or that completely exclude others.

Page 5 Initials: ______ ______ ______ ______ Date: ____________

Any trust income that is not distributed by the trustee shall be accumulated and added to the principal.

D. Termination of the Children's Pot Trust

When the youngest surviving beneficiary of this children's pot trust reaches age 18, the trustee shall distribute the remaining trust assets to the surviving beneficiaries in equal shares.

If none of the trust beneficiaries survives to the age of 18, the trustee shall, at the death of the last surviving beneficiary, distribute the remaining trust assets to that beneficiary's estate.

Part 9. Individual Child's Trust

A. Beneficiaries and Trustees

All property left in this will to Fumiko Tanaka shall be held in a separate trust for Fumiko Tanaka until Fumiko Tankaka reaches age 25. The trustee of the Fumiko Tanaka trust shall be Filipe Santos.

This clause provides that all property given to the child named in the clause shall be held in trust—that is, managed strictly for the benefit of the child—by the person named as the trustee until the child turns the age indicated. An alternate trustee can also be named in case the first-choice trustee is unable or unwilling to serve when the time comes.

B. Administration of an Individual Child's Trust

The trustee of an individual child's trust shall manage and distribute the assets in the trust in the following manner.

Until the trust beneficiary reaches the age specified for final distribution of the principal, the trustee may distribute some or all of the principal or net income of the trust as the trustee deems necessary for the child's health, support, maintenance, and education. Education includes, but is not limited to, college, graduate, postgraduate, and vocational studies and reasonable living expenses.

This clause lets the trustee spend the trust principal and income for the child's general living, health, and educational needs. The clause gives the trustee great latitude in how this is done and what amount is spent.

In deciding whether or not to make a distribution to a beneficiary, the trustee may take into account the beneficiary's other income, resources, and sources of support.

This clause lets the trustee withhold the trust principal or income from the trust beneficiary if, in the trustee's opinion, the beneficiary has sufficient income from other sources.

Any trust income that is not distributed by the trustee shall be accumulated and added to the principal.

Every trust involves two types of property: the property in the trust—called the trust principal—and the income that is earned by investing the principal. This clause ensures that the trustee must add to the trust principal any income that is earned on the principal, unless the income is distributed to the trust beneficiary.

C. Termination of an Individual Child's Trust

An individual child's trust shall terminate as soon as one of the following events occurs:

- the beneficiary reaches the age stated above, in which case the trustee shall distribute the remaining principal and accumulated net income of the trust to the beneficiary
- the beneficiary dies, in which case the principal and accumulated net income of the trust shall pass under the beneficiary's will or, if there is no will, to the beneficiary's heirs, or
- the trust principal is exhausted through distributions allowed under these provisions.

/////

/////

Page 7 Initials: ______ ______ ______ ______ Date: ________________

This clause sets out three events that may cause the trust to end. The first is when the minor or young adult reaches the age specified for the trust to end. If the trust ends for this reason, the minor or young adult gets whatever trust principal and accumulated income are left. The trust will also end if the minor or young adult dies before the age set for the trust to end. If the trust ends for this reason, the principal and income accumulated in the trust go to whomever the young adult named in their will to get them or, if there is no will, to the minor or young adult's legal heirs—such as parents, brothers, and sisters. A third occurrence that will cause the trust to end is when there is no trust principal left—or so little left that it's no longer financially feasible to maintain it.

Part 10. General Trust Administration Provisions

All trusts established in this will shall be managed subject to the following provisions.

A. Transferability of Interests

The interests of any beneficiary of all trusts established by this will shall not be transferable by voluntary or involuntary assignment or by operation of law and shall be free from the claims of creditors and from attachment, execution, bankruptcy, or other legal process to the fullest extent permitted by law.

This important clause removes the trust principal and accumulated income from the reach of the minor or young adult's creditors—while they are being held in the trust. Also, this clause prevents the minor or young adult from transferring ownership of the principal or accumulated interest to others—again, while it is in the trust. After property is distributed to the minor or young adult, however, there are no restrictions on how it can be used.

B. Powers of the Trustee

In addition to other powers granted a trustee in this will, a trustee shall have the powers to:

Page 8 Initials: ______ ______ ______ ______ Date: ______________

1. Invest and reinvest trust funds in every kind of property and every kind of investment, provided that the trustee acts with the care, skill, prudence, and diligence under the prevailing circumstances that a prudent person, acting in a similar capacity and familiar with such matters, would use.
2. Receive additional property from any source and acquire or hold properties jointly or in undivided interests or in partnership or joint venture with other people or entities.
3. Enter, continue, or participate in the operation of any business, and incorporate, liquidate, reorganize, or otherwise change the form or terminate the operation of the business and contribute capital or loan money to the business.
4. Exercise all the rights, powers, and privileges of an owner of any securities held in the trust.
5. Borrow funds, guarantee or indemnify in the name of the trust and secure any obligation, mortgage, pledge, or other security interest, and renew, extend, or modify any such obligations.
6. Lease trust property for terms within or beyond the term of the trust.
7. Prosecute, defend, contest, or otherwise litigate legal actions or other proceedings for the protection or benefit of the trust; pay, compromise, release, adjust, or submit to arbitration any debt, claim or controversy; and insure the trust against any risk and the trustee against liability with respect to other people.
8. Pay themselves reasonable compensation out of trust assets for ordinary and extraordinary services, and for all services in connection with the complete or partial termination of this trust.
9. Employ and discharge professionals to aid or assist in managing the trust and compensate them from the trust assets.
10. Make distributions to the beneficiaries directly or to other people or organizations on behalf of the beneficiaries.

This list of powers should cover the gamut of activities that trustees might be called upon to exercise in administering any trust set up in this will.

Page 9 Initials: ______ ______ ______ ______ Date: ____________

C. Severability

The invalidity of any trust provision of this will shall not affect the validity of the remaining trust provisions.

> *This language ensures that in the unlikely event that a court finds any individual part of this trust to be invalid, the rest of the document will remain in effect.*

Part 11. Personal Guardian

If at my death a guardian is needed to care for my children, I name Marjani Mohamed as personal guardian. If this person is unable or unwilling to serve as personal guardian, I name Michelle Lee to serve instead.

Reasons for my choice for guardian for all my children: Marjani Mohamed has established a close relationship with all of the children. She frequently takes care of them when my wife and I must work on weekends—and her training as a doctor makes her especially knowledgeable about handling their health care needs. Best of all, she is a loving and trustworthy friend who has unerring judgment and common sense—an excellent choice to raise the children if Wilma and I cannot.

No personal guardian shall be required to post bond.

> *This clause names someone to provide parental-type care for a minor child if there is no legal (biological or adoptive) parent able to provide it. The clause also provides for an alternate to step in if the first choice is not able or willing to act when the moment comes. When making your own will, be aware that if there is another legal parent on the scene, that parent will usually be awarded custody of the children, unless a court concludes that the children would be at risk of harm. The explanation provided for the choice helps ensure that a court will follow your reasoning and approve your choice of guardian. The clause also provides that the personal guardian need not provide a bond—a kind of insurance of good performance—to guarantee faithful performance of the guardian's duties.*

Page 10 Initials: ______ ______ ______ ______ Date: ______________

Part 12. Property Guardian

If at my death a guardian is needed to care for any property belonging to Sammie WillMaker or Chester WillMaker, I name Sven Olsson as property guardian. If Sven Olsson is unwilling or unable to serve as property guardian, I name Jasmine Hernandez to serve instead.

No property guardian shall be required to post bond.

This clause appoints someone to manage property that passes to your children outside of your will. For example, if your children receive an inheritance from another relative, proceeds from a life insurance policy, or income from a trust, and those instruments do not provide a property guardian, you can name an adult to manage those funds until the children become adults. You can also appoint an alternate property guardian in case your first choice is not able or willing to serve when the time comes. Finally, this clause provides that the property guardian need not provide a bond to guarantee that the guardian will act faithfully.

Part 13. Forgiveness of Debts

I wish to forgive all debts specified below, plus accrued interest as of the date of my death:

Debtor:	Glenda Cyprus
Date debt was incurred:	May 5, 2019
Amount to be forgiven:	$10,000

Forgiving a debt is equivalent to making a bequest of money. It is a common way to equalize what you leave to all your children when you have loaned one of them some money—that is, the amount that you would otherwise leave that child can be reduced by the amount of the debt being forgiven.

Part 14. Executor

I name Wilma WillMaker to serve as my executor. If Wilma WillMaker is unwilling or unable to serve as executor, I name Marjani Mohamed to serve as my executor.

No executor shall be required to post bond.

Page 11 Initials: ______ ______ ______ ______ Date: ______________

> *This clause identifies the choices for executor and an alternate executor who will take over if the first choice is unable or unwilling to serve when the time comes.*

Part 15. Executor's Powers

I direct my executor to take all actions legally permissible to have the probate of my will done as simply and as free of court supervision as possible under the laws of the state having jurisdiction over this will, including filing a petition in the appropriate court for the independent administration of my estate.

> *This clause sets out the specific authority that the executor will need to competently manage the estate until it has been distributed under the terms of the will. The will language expresses your desire that your executor work as free from court supervision as possible. This will cut down on delays and expense.*
>
> *When you print out your will, a second paragraph will list a number of specific powers that your executor will have, if necessary. It also makes clear that the listing of these specific powers does not deprive your executor of any other powers provided by the law of your state. The general idea is to give your executor as much power as possible, so that your executor will not have to go to court and get permission to take a particular action.*

Part 16. Payment of Debts

Except for liens and encumbrances placed on property as security for the repayment of a loan or debt, I direct all debts and expenses owed by my estate to be paid in the manner provided for by the laws of California.

Part 17. Payment of Taxes

I direct that all estate and inheritance taxes assessed against property in my estate or against my beneficiaries to be paid in the manner provided for by the laws of California.

/////

/////

/////

Page 12 Initials: _____ _____ _____ _____ Date: ____________

These hashmarks will automatically appear to fill up the rest of the page so that your signature appears with some text of the will—one way to help guard against an unethical survivor tampering with the document.

Part 18. Severability

If any provision of this will is held invalid, that shall not affect other provisions that can be given effect without the invalid provision.

This is standard language that ensures that in the unlikely event that a court finds any individual part of your will to be invalid, the rest of the document will remain in effect.

SIGNATURE

I, Willy WillMaker, the testator, sign my name to this instrument, this ________________ day of ____________________________, ____________, at ____. I declare that I sign and execute this instrument as my last will, that I sign it willingly, and that I execute it as my free and voluntary act. I declare that I am of the age of majority or otherwise legally empowered to make a will, and under no constraint or undue influence.

Signature: ______________________________

WITNESSES

We, the witnesses, sign our names to this document, and declare that the testator willingly signed and executed this document as the testator's last will.

In the presence of the testator, and in the presence of each other, we sign this will as witnesses to the testator's signing.

To the best of our knowledge, the testator is of the age of majority or otherwise legally empowered to make a will, is mentally competent, and is under no constraint or undue influence. We declare under penalty of perjury that the foregoing is true and correct, this ________________ day of ________________________, ________, at ______________________ ____.

/////

Page 13 Initials: _____ _____ _____ _____ Date: ________________

First Witness

Sign your name: ______________________________

Print your name: ______________________________

Address: ______________________________

City, State: ______________________________

Second Witness

Sign your name: ______________________________

Print your name: ______________________________

Address: ______________________________

City, State: ______________________________

Page 14 Initials: _____ _____ _____ _____ Date: ______________

CHAPTER

4

About You and Yours

The interview for WillMaker's will first asks you to answer a number of questions about yourself and your family. This chapter discusses those questions in the order in which they appear.

Your Name

Enter your name—first, middle if you choose, then last—in the same form that you use on other formal documents, such as your driver's license or bank accounts. This might or might not be the name that appears on your birth certificate.

If you have used more than one name for business purposes, enter all of them, separated by a.k.a., which stands for "also known as."

Your name is needed here to identify you and all the property you own. Be sure to include all names in which you have held bank accounts, stocks, bonds, real estate, or other property. There is room for you to list several names. But use your common sense—you need not list every nickname, or names you use for nonbusiness purposes.

Your Social Security Number

At the end of the will interview, WillMaker will give you the option to enter your nine-digit Social Security number. If you choose to enter it, the number will *not* be included in your will, where it could become part of the public record. Instead, WillMaker will print your Social Security number in a letter for your executor that prints with your will.

CAUTION

Wills valid in the United States only. WillMaker produces valid wills for all of the United States except for Louisiana—and it guides you by showing you screens geared specifically to the state of residence you indicate when using it.

Because the property and probate laws in Puerto Rico and Guam, for example, might differ from those of the state you have selected to use in making your will, WillMaker cannot guarantee that its will is valid there. However, some users who reside outside the United States do use WillMaker to help draft their wills and then have them looked over by an experienced local professional.

Your State

You are asked to specify the state of your legal residence, sometimes called a domicile. This is the state where you make your home now and for the indefinite future.

Your state's laws affect:

- marital property ownership
- property management options for young beneficiaries
- how your will can be admitted into probate, and
- whether your property will be subject to state inheritance or estate taxes.

If you live in two or more states during the year and have business relationships in both, you might not be sure which state is your legal residence. Choose the state where you are the most rooted—that is, the state in which you:

- are registered to vote
- register your motor vehicles
- own valuable property—especially property with a title document, such as a house or car
- have checking, savings, and other investment accounts, and
- maintain a business.

To avoid confusion, it is best to keep all or at least most of your roots in one state, if possible. For people with large estates (in the millions), ideally this should be in a state that does not levy estate or inheritance taxes. (See "Estate and Inheritance Taxes" in Chapter 9.)

SEE AN EXPERT

If your choice is not clear. If you do not maintain continuous ties with a particular state, or if you have homes in both the United States and another country, consult a lawyer to find out which state to list as your legal domicile when using WillMaker.

Living Overseas

If you live overseas temporarily because you are in the armed services, your residence will be the home of record you declared to the military authorities.

Normally, your home of record is the state you lived in before you received your assignment, where your parents or spouse live, or where you now have a permanent home. If there is a close call between two states, consider the factors listed above for determining a legal residence or get advice from the military legal authorities.

If you live overseas for business or education, you probably still have ties with a particular state that would make it your legal residence. For example, if you were born in Wisconsin, lived there for many years, registered to vote there, and receive mail there in care of your parents who still live in Milwaukee, then Wisconsin is your legal residence for purposes of making a will.

Your County

Including your county in your will is optional but recommended. Including it will help others identify you and track down your property after your death.

Also, a county name can provide those handling your estate with important direction, because wills go through probate in the court system of the county where you last resided, no matter where you died.

The one exception is real estate: That property is probated in the court of the county in which it is located.

When you enter your county name, use the entire name, including the word "county," for example: Kings County or County of Alameda. If you live in an area that does not use the term "county," use the term most commonly used to describe the area of your state where your city is located. For example, if you live in Healy, Alaska, you would enter "Denali Borough." If there is no county-like descriptor for the area where you live, leave this box blank.

The Importance of Your Marital Status

You should make a new will whenever you marry or divorce. (See Chapter 11.)

If your marital status changes but your will does not, your new spouse or ex-spouse might get more or less of your property than you intend. For example, if you remarry after making a will and do not provide for the new spouse—either in a will or through transfers outside the will—in many states, your new spouse might be entitled to claim a big share of your property at your death.

Also, if you name a spouse in a will, then divorce or have the marriage annulled and die before making a new will, state laws will produce different, often unexpected, results. In most states, the former spouse will automatically get nothing. In other states, the former spouse is entitled to take the property as set out in the will.

A few states continue to offer registered partnerships that come with similar rights and responsibilities as marriage. In those states, changes in your partnership status might affect the distribution of your property. Therefore, like married folks, you should make a new will whenever your registered partnership status changes.

Marital or Registered Partnership Status

WillMaker asks you to indicate your marital or registered partnership status. The law treats married people and registered partners differently than other will makers, so your answer to this question is important. Rest assured, however, that you will be able to leave your property in almost any way you please, regardless of your relationship status.

It will probably be easy to select your relationship status. However, if you are separated, have filed for divorce, or think you might have a common law marriage, the answer might not be clear. Read the following sections to help you make the best choice.

If you are married or in a registered partnership, you should also review the property ownership laws affecting married and partnered people. (See "Property Ownership Rules for Married People" in Chapter 5.)

TIP

Legally registered relationships that aren't marriage. In this book, "registered partnership" means any marriage-like partnership registered with a state government, including civil unions and reciprocal beneficiary relationships.

Divorce

If you're not sure whether you are legally divorced, make sure you see a copy of the final order signed by a judge. To track down a divorce order, contact the court clerk in the county where you believe the divorce occurred. You will need to give your first and last name and that of your former spouse and make a good guess at what year the divorce became final. If the divorce was supposed to have taken place outside the United States, it might be difficult to verify. If you cannot locate a final decree of divorce, it is safest to assume you are still legally married.

If you have any reason to think that someone you consider to be a former spouse might claim to be married to you, consult a lawyer. (See Chapter 17.)

Separation

Many married couples, contemplating divorce or reconciliation, live apart from one another, sometimes for several years. Although this might feel like a murky limbo while you are living it, for will-making purposes, your status is straightforward: You are legally married until a court issues a formal decree of divorce, signed by a judge. This is true even if you and your spouse are legally separated as declared in a legal document. Note that many separation agreements, however, set out rights and restrictions that might affect your ownership of property.

TIP

Widows and widowers. If you were married but your spouse died (and you haven't remarried), then you may consider yourself a widow or widower. However, because you don't have a living spouse, for the purposes of will making, you are legally "not married." While you won't be able to mention your deceased spouse in your will, if you wish, you can leave a tribute to your spouse in a separate letter or note to your loved ones. (See Chapter 12 for more about leaving a Letter to Survivors.)

Common Law Marriage

It is uncommon to have a common law marriage. In fact, in most states, it is impossible to create a common law marriage.

But in the states listed in the chart below, couples can become legally married if they live together and either present themselves to others as a married couple or actually intend to be married to one another. When these conditions are met, the couple is legally married. And the marriage will still be valid even if they later move to a state that does not allow couples to form common law marriages there.

No matter what state you live in, if either you or the person you live with is still legally married to some other person, you cannot have a common law marriage.

As you can see, some states recognize common law marriages only if they were created long ago. If you live in one of these states and you entered into what you believe to be a common law marriage, consult a lawyer to determine the legal status of your relationship.

There is no such thing as a common law divorce; no matter how your marriage begins, you must go through formal divorce proceedings to end it.

SEE AN EXPERT

If you're not sure of your marital status. If you're confused about the legal status of your relationship, you're not alone. Find a good estate planning or family law attorney to help you figure it out based on the details of your specific situation.

States That Recognize Common Law Marriage

The following states recognize some form of common law marriage.

Alabama (if created before 1/1/2017)	Nebraska (if created before 1923)
Colorado	Nevada (if created before 3/29/1943)
District of Columbia	New Hampshire (for inheritance purposes only)
Florida (if created before 1/1/1968)	New Jersey (if created before 12/1/1939)
Georgia (if created before 1/1/1997)	New York (if created before 4/28/1933)
Idaho (if created before 1/1/1996)	Ohio (if created before 10/10/1991)
Illinois (if created before 6/30/1905)	Oklahoma*
Indiana (if created before 1/1/1958)	Pennsylvania (if created before 1/1/2005)
Iowa	Rhode Island
Kansas	South Carolina (if created before 7/24/2019)
Michigan (if created before 1/1/1957)	South Dakota (if created before 7/1/1959)
Minnesota (if created before 4/26/1941)	Texas
Mississippi (if created before 4/5/1956)	Utah (if petition is filed before 5/5/2027)
Montana	

* Available through case law, not statute.

Registered Partnerships

Registered partnerships are not as common as they were before same-sex couples could legally marry. But some states still allow partnership registration or at least recognize registered partnerships that were made previously.

RESOURCE

Learn more. Get lots of free information about LGBTQ law—including information about registered partnerships and same-sex marriage—at www.nolo.com/legal-encyclopedia/lgbt-law.

WillMaker needs to know if you are in a registered partnership because it can affect how the law sees your partner in terms of inheritance.

If you and your partner have a registered partnership in a state that offers marriage-like benefits to registered partners, you still live in that state, and your state has not converted your relationship to marriage (see below), choose "I have a registered partner" when WillMaker asks for your relationship status. Although states use different terms (such as "domestic partners," "civil union partners," or "reciprocal beneficiaries"), WillMaker generally uses "registered partners" to refer to a couple that has registered their relationship with their state. Your finished document will contain the correct term for your state. (If you live in New Jersey or Hawaii, you will be asked to select the appropriate term for your relationship.)

Keep in mind that several states that once offered registered partnerships have automatically converted those legal relationships to marriage. So it is possible that you are married, even though you entered a domestic partnership or civil union. If you're unsure about the legal status of your relationship, get help from an expert in your state.

If you registered your relationship with your city or county—but not your state—do not indicate that you have a registered partner. Probate courts follow state law, so unless you are registered with the state, the probate court is unlikely to recognize your partnership. If you want to acknowledge your partnership outside of your will, consider doing so in a Letter to Survivors. (See Chapter 12.) If you have concerns about your partnership status or are uncertain about your status, get help from a local attorney who is familiar with the registered partnership laws in your area.

Neither Married Nor Registered

If you and your partner are not married and have not registered with your state, or if you no longer live in the state where you registered, you should make your will as a single person by choosing "I'm not married, nor do I have a registered partner."

Indicating that you are single does not limit your ability to leave property to your partner or to name your partner as executor of your will or guardian of your young children. You can do all of those things in your will.

Your Spouse or Registered Partner

WillMaker prompts you to provide the full name of your spouse or registered partner. As with your own name, list all names used for business purposes, following the tips suggested for entering your own name, above.

Your Children

Becoming a parent might be what motivated you to buckle down to the task of writing your will in the first place.

If you are the parent of young children, your will is the perfect place to address some driving concerns you are likely to have if you die before they are grown. These concerns include:

- who will care for your children, and
- who will manage their property.

WillMaker lets you make these decisions separately. This gives you the option of placing the responsibilities in the hands of the same person or, if need be, naming different people. Here, you'll be asked to identify your living children and name someone to care for them if you (and their other parent) cannot. Later you'll be able to name someone to take care of their property. (See Chapter 7.)

Inheritance for Children Conceived After a Parent Dies

If a child is conceived before your death but is born after you die, that child will most likely be entitled to part of your estate even if your will doesn't mention the child. But what about children conceived *after* the death of a parent using that parent's preserved sperm, eggs, or embryos? These children are called posthumously conceived children, and their inheritance rights depend on the state.

States generally fall into three categories on this issue:

- **States with inheritance rights under strict circumstances.** Most states that have laws about this issue allow inheritance by a posthumously conceived child only if the deceased parent gave explicit consent for their genetic material to be used to create a child and the child is conceived within a specific time frame (usually two or three years, depending on the state).
- **States that deny inheritance rights.** A few states have laws that expressly deny inheritance to children conceived after a parent's death.
- **Silent states.** The remaining states (about half of all states) do not have laws on this issue. A posthumously conceived child will inherit based on the terms of the deceased parent's estate plan, if the deceased parent had one. If the deceased parent did not have an estate plan, the child's inheritance rights will be determined by a court's application of intestacy and parentage laws on the facts of the case. Outcomes from such cases vary dramatically.

If you are curious about this issue or planning to have a posthumously conceived child, get help from a knowledgeable estate planning lawyer.

Identifying Your Children

WillMaker asks you whether or not you have any living children and, if you do, asks you to name each of them. You are not required to leave property to your children, but it is important that you at least state each child's name. If you don't, it might not be clear whether you intentionally left a child out of your will or whether the child was accidentally overlooked (called "pretermitted," under the law). Children unintentionally omitted from your will—usually because you made your will before they were born—have a right to take a share of your estate.

To list your children, enter their full names in the sequence and format you want the names to appear in your will.

Deceased Children

When naming your children, you should include all living children born to you or legally adopted by you. Do not name children who have died, as they cannot receive property from you. However, do name any children of those children in the Grandchildren section of the interview. If you don't, those grandchildren could also be entitled to a portion of your property under the "omitted child" laws, discussed above. To name or honor a child who has predeceased you, use WillMaker's Letter to Survivors. (See Chapter 12.)

TIP

If your parental rights have ended. If you are the parent of a child who has been legally adopted by a person other than your spouse or partner—or you have otherwise given up your legal parental rights—then you need not name that child in your will.

Stepchildren

You should not name stepchildren you have not adopted, since they are not entitled by law to a share of your property when you die. The pretermitted heir rule does not apply to them. Also, WillMaker offers a number of options that include your children as a group, and if you include stepchildren in the list and use one of these options, your will might contain provisions you did not intend.

However, you are free to leave your stepchildren as much property in your will as you wish. If you want to treat your children and stepchildren equally and not differentiate between them, when WillMaker asks how you wish to leave your property, choose the option labeled "Leave it some other way." (See Chapter 6.)

CAUTION

Name your children individually. Some people are tempted to skip naming their children individually and want to fill in "all my children," "my surviving children," "my lawful heirs," or "my issue." However, such shorthand language is less clear than listing each child by name.

Similarly, naming your "unborn" children creates more uncertainty than simply naming your existing children and then updating your will when others are born.

WillMaker requires you to list each of your existing children by name. If you feel strongly about grouping them together or including children who haven't yet been born, see a lawyer for help.

Your Children's Birthdates

WillMaker also asks you to enter your children's dates of birth—month, day, and year. It will automatically compute their ages in years—an important consideration when you are asked to name a personal guardian and provide management for property you or others leave them.

Personal Guardians for Your Minor Children

Among the most pressing concerns of parents with minor children is who will care for the children if one or both parents die before the children reach adulthood. Although contemplating the possibility of your early death can be wrenching, making this decision is important and should be a key aspect of your estate plan.

This section discusses using WillMaker to choose a *personal* guardian to care for the children's basic health, education, and other daily needs. Choosing a person to manage your children's *property* is discussed in Chapter 7.

Reasons for Naming a Personal Guardian

The general legal rule is that if there are two parents willing and able to care for a child and one parent dies, the other parent will take over physical custody and responsibility for caring for the child. In many states, the surviving parent might also be given authority by a court to manage any property the deceased parent left to the child—unless the deceased parent has specified a different property management arrangement in a will.

But there is no ready fallback plan if both parents of a minor child die or, in the case of a single parent, there is not another parent able or willing to do the job. Using WillMaker, you can deal with these concerns by naming a personal guardian as well as an alternate. The person you name will normally be appointed by the court to act as a surrogate parent for your minor child if both of the following are true:

- There is no surviving biological or adoptive parent able to properly care for the child.
- The court agrees that your choice is in the best interests of the child.

If both parents are making wills, each should name the same person as guardian for each child. This will help avoid the possibility of a dispute and perhaps even a court battle should the parents die simultaneously. But remember, if one parent dies, the other will usually assume custody and will then be free to make a new will naming a different personal guardian. In short, if both parents are active caretakers, the personal guardian named in a will cares for the child only if both parents die close together in time.

However, if you feel strongly that the other parent is not the best person to care for your child, be sure to explain your reasoning when WillMaker prompts you to do so. (See "Explaining Your Choice," below.)

Naming Different Guardians for Different Children

One obvious concern when choosing a personal guardian for your children is to keep them together if they get along well with one another. This suggests that it is best to name the same personal guardian for all the children.

There are families, however, where the children are not particularly close to one another but have strong attachments with one or more adults outside the immediate family. For instance, one child might spend a lot of time with a grandparent while another child might be close to an aunt and uncle. Also, in a second or third marriage, a child from an earlier marriage might be closer to a different adult than a child from the current marriage is.

In these situations and others, logic dictates other advice: Choose the personal guardian you believe would best be able to care for the child. This might mean that you will choose different personal guardians for different children.

Choosing a Personal Guardian

To qualify as a personal guardian, your choice must be an adult—18 in most states—and competent to do the job. For obvious reasons, you should first consider an adult with whom the child already has a close relationship—a stepparent, grandparent, aunt or uncle, older sibling, babysitter, close friend of the family, or even neighbor. Whoever you choose, be sure that person is mature, good-hearted, and willing and able to assume the responsibility.

Naming More Than One Person as Guardian

In many cases, it's a poor idea to name more than one person to serve as guardian for your children. Naming coguardians raises the possibility that they might disagree about the best way to raise a child, resulting in conflict and perhaps even requiring court intervention. However, there is one situation in which naming two guardians makes good sense: when you want to name a couple to care for your children.

If you know a couple—for example, your sister and her husband—who are willing and able to take good care of your children, it's fine to name them both as coguardians. The couple will act as your children's surrogate parents. Both of them will be allowed to do things for your children that require legal authority, such as picking up your children from school, authorizing field trips, or taking them to the doctor.

Keep in mind, however, that if you name a couple as coguardians, they must be able to agree on what's best for your children. Any severe difference of opinion between them could require court intervention—and this would be upsetting to your kids and difficult for the couple. Also, if you name a couple that parts ways while you are still alive, you should revise your will to name one or the other to care for your children or choose a different couple to act as coguardians.

Choose carefully when naming a couple as personal coguardians for your children. Select a couple that can make joint decisions without conflict, has a unified parenting style, and is likely to stay together a long time. If you have any reservations about the longevity of the couple's relationship or any concerns about either person's parenting style, you might be better off just naming one of them—for example, name just your sister without naming her husband. If you like, you can explain the reasons for your choice in your will. See "Explaining Your Choice," below.

Choosing an Alternate Personal Guardian

WillMaker lets you name a backup or alternate personal guardian to serve in case your first choice for each child is unable to (or does not want to) do the job at your death. The considerations involved in naming an alternate personal guardian are the same as those you pondered when making your first choice: maturity, a good heart, familiarity with the children, and willingness to serve.

If you name a couple as coguardians, the alternate will become the personal guardian only if both coguardians are unable or unwilling to serve.

Explaining Your Choice

WillMaker gives you the option to include a brief statement in your will that explains your choice for personal guardian. Leaving a written explanation of why you made a particular choice for a personal guardian might be a good idea if you think a judge might have reason to question your decision or if you want to give a judge more information about your situation. Explanations might be especially important when the other parent might not make a good guardian or when the best choice for guardian might not be obvious. Consider these situations:

- "I have custody of my three children. I don't want my ex-husband, who I believe is emotionally destructive, to get custody of our children if I die. Can I choose a guardian to serve instead of him?"
- "I have legal custody of my daughter and I've remarried. My present wife is a much better mother to my daughter than my ex-wife, who never cared for her properly. What can I do to make sure my present wife gets custody if I die?"
- "I live with a man who's been a good parent to my children for six years. My father doesn't like the fact that we aren't married and might try to get custody of the kids if I die. What can I do to see that my partner gets custody?"

None of these situations has a clear-cut solution. If you die while your children are young, a judge will assess your family situation and make a determination about what is best for your kids. What you can do is name the person you believe is the best choice and also leave a note in your WillMaker will that explains your decision and provides the judge with information that can help confirm your choice.

If you don't want the other parent to have custody. You might have strong ideas about why your child's other parent should not have custody of your minor children. In this case, you can and should name someone else as guardian and include an explanation of your decision in your will. However, even if you do, the judge will likely grant custody to the other parent, unless that parent:

- has legally abandoned the child by not providing for or visiting the child for an extended period
- is clearly unfit as a parent, or
- declines custody and a better choice is available.

EXAMPLE: Susan and Fred, an unmarried couple, have two minor children. Although Susan loves Fred, she does not think he is capable of raising the children on his own. She uses WillMaker to name her mother, Elinor, as guardian. If Susan dies, Fred, as the children's other parent, will be given first priority as personal guardian over Elinor despite Susan's will, assuming the court finds he is willing and able to care for the children. However, if the court finds that Fred should not be personal guardian, Elinor would get the nod, assuming she is fit.

It is usually difficult to prove that a parent is unfit, absent serious and obvious problems, such as chronic drug or alcohol abuse, mental illness, or a history of child abuse. The fact that you do not like or respect the other parent is never enough, by itself, for a court to deny custody to that person.

If you honestly believe the other parent is incapable of caring for your children properly—or simply will not assume the responsibility—you should reinforce that belief by providing information that supports your opinion and by explaining why the person you named would be a better choice.

When your partner is not a legal parent to your children. If you coparent your children with a partner who is not legally your children's other parent, you will likely want to nominate that person to be your children's personal guardian. If so, also consider leaving an explanation about your choice so that a judge would have all of the information needed to fully grasp the importance of the relationship between your children and your partner.

> EXAMPLE: Justine and Paula live together with Justine's minor children from an earlier marriage. The children's biological father has not spent time with the kids for many years, and Justine believes he has no interest in parenting them. Justine wants Paula to have custody because she knows the children well and loves them. Justine can use WillMaker to name Paula as personal guardian and add a statement making the reasons for this choice clear. If Justine dies and the biological father does not want custody of the kids (or the court decides that he is not fit to parent), Justine's explanation will give the court good reason to name Paula the children's personal guardian.

In sum, if there is any reason for a judge to question your choice for personal guardian or if there is information you want a judge to have when deciding who will take care of your children, take the opportunity to leave an explanation about your choice in your will document. In contrast, explanations about other choices in your will—like who will get your property or who you named as executor—do not belong in your will document. You can leave explanations about those things and anything else in a Letter to Survivors. (See Chapter 12.)

Tips on What to Include

When deciding who should become a child's personal guardian, the courts of all states are required to act in the child's best interests. In making this determination, the courts commonly consider a number of factors, which you might want to mention when explaining your choice for personal guardian. They include:

- whom the parents nominated to become the personal guardian
- whether the proposed personal guardian will provide the greatest stability and continuity of care for the child
- which person will best be able to meet the child's needs
- the quality of the relationship between the child and the adults being considered for guardian
- the child's preferences to the extent these can be gleaned, and
- the moral fitness and conduct of the proposed guardians.

RESOURCE

Learn more about nontraditional families and the law. For free information about how the law deals with all types of families, go to www.nolo.com/legal-encyclopedia/children.

Your Grandchildren

WillMaker asks you to name your grandchildren. Name all of them—including those to whom you leave no property. Include children adopted by your child and those born while your child was not married.

It is important that you name all grandchildren, because the rule that allows unintentionally omitted children to take a share of your estate also applies to grandchildren you might have overlooked in your will if their parent—that is, your child—dies before you do. (See "Your Children," above.)

As it does for your own children, WillMaker automatically provides the statement that if you have not left any property to a grandchild, that is intentional—and therefore eliminates the problem. Again, you are free to leave the grandchild property if you choose. If you have additional grandchildren after making your will, it is wise to make a new will that includes them.

SEE AN EXPERT

If you don't know your children or grandchildren. If family estrangement or other circumstances leave you thinking that you might not know the names of all of your grandchildren—or even your children—seek the advice of a good estate planning lawyer. You'll want to be certain that your will is not subject to unexpected claims.

Keep Your Will Current

Here are two situations in which you should make a new will.

If a child is born to or legally adopted by you after you make your will. You should draft a new will to list the new child. If you do not, that child might challenge your will and receive a share of what you leave.

If one of your children dies before you do and leaves children of their own. The laws of many states require that you name and provide for the children of deceased children. If you do not, they might be considered accidentally overlooked and entitled to part of your property. To protect against this, make a new will naming these grandchildren so that you can signal that you are aware that these grandchildren exist. You are still free to leave them as little or as much property as you wish in your will.

(See Chapter 11 for information on updating your will.)

Finding a Loving Home for Your Pet

If you're not able to find someone both willing and able to take care of your pet after you die, you're not without options. Programs exist across the country that help assure people that their pets will have a loving home when they can no longer care for them.

If you find an organization that interests you, carefully check its references (and perhaps its history with the Better Business Bureau) to make sure that the organization is likely to still be around when your pet needs it.

SPCA programs. The San Francisco SPCA was the first to offer a special service to find good homes for the pets of its deceased members. Other SPCAs have created similar programs. Contact local SPCAs and similar organizations in your area for more information.

Veterinary school programs. A number of veterinary schools take in pets whose owners leave substantial endowments to the school. These programs typically provide a homelike atmosphere and lifetime veterinary care for the animals. Here are a few:

- Purdue University, College of Veterinary Medicine Peace of Mind Program
- Kansas State University, KSU Foundation Perpetual Pet Care Program
- Oklahoma State University, Cohn Pet Care Facility, OSU College of Veterinary Medicine
- Texas A&M University, Stevenson Companion Animal Life-Care Center, School of Veterinary Medicine

Private organizations. There are also many private organizations that look after pets whose owners have passed away. Some keep the pets in their facilities for the pets' lifetime; others find new homes for those pets. Typically, they require a flat fee of a few thousand dollars. To find an organization near you, search online for "pet lifetime care" and the name of your city, county, or state.

Your Pets

You can use the WillMaker will to leave your pet to someone you trust. You can also leave money to that person to help with the costs of owning your pet, although your will cannot force the new owner to use the money that way. If you want the new owner to be legally bound to use the money for the care of your pet, you will need a pet trust. (See "Setting up a trust for your pet," below.)

Using a will to provide for your pet is a simple and inexpensive way to make sure your pet has a caring home after your death. It is not the only way to provide for your pet, but most folks find that it makes the most sense.

However, if you plan to leave your entire estate—including your pet—to one person, there is no need to make a separate pet bequest. When you use WillMaker to leave everything to one person, that person will get your pet and can use money from your estate to care for your pet. Separately, you can leave instructions about how to care for your pet; see below.

Leaving Details About Your Pet's Care

In addition to naming a new owner for your pet, you might want to leave information and suggestions about your pet's habits and needs. You can use WillMaker's Information for Survivors and Caregivers form (in the download version of WillMaker) for this purpose. It allows you to leave specifics about each animal, including health needs, food and exercise requirements, and sleeping habits. You can also use the document to organize many important details of your life. See "Organizing Your Records" in Chapter 1.

SEE AN EXPERT

Setting up a trust for your pet. You can leave your pet money in a trust, managed by a trustee you name. The main advantage of creating a pet trust is that under a pet trust, the person who cares for your pet is legally obligated to follow the instructions you lay out in your trust document. However, for most people, this legal obligation is not necessary because they're confident that the person they name will follow their wishes without a court getting involved. An additional benefit of creating a pet trust is that it can go into effect quickly after death, or even before death if the trust is set up to cover the pet owner's incapacity. If you do want to create a pet trust, you'll need to hire an attorney to be sure the document is properly drafted and valid in your state.

CHAPTER

5

About Your Property

This chapter discusses the grist of will making: what you own, how you own it, and what legal rules affect how you can leave it. Once you have considered the information about property in this chapter, you will be ready to use WillMaker to leave it to others—a task discussed in detail in Chapter 6. If you have children, see Chapter 7 for a discussion of their right to inherit property and your right to disinherit them.

Many readers will not need the information in this chapter. If you plan to leave your property in a lump—that is, without giving specific items of property to specific people—it makes little difference what you own and how you own it. That will be sorted out when you die, and the people you have named to take all your property will get whatever you own.

This chapter is important for you to read if either of the following is true:

- You are married or in a registered partnership and you plan to name someone other than your spouse or partner to receive all or most of your property. This includes everyone who has not received a final decree of divorce or dissolution.
- You plan to leave specific items of property to specific people or organizations.

TIP

Keeping track of your property. There are many things your survivors will need to know about your property—and it will help them to have some relevant information about it, including:

- the location of some items
- the location of ownership, warranty, and appraisal papers
- the value of some items—especially if they have special significance
- how to access your online accounts
- directions for maintaining the property, and
- details about caring for your pets.

You can use the Information for Caregivers and Survivors form for this task (in the download version of WillMaker).

Inventory Your Valuable Property

The first step is to take inventory—write down the valuable items of property you own. The categories listed below should jog your memory. Even if you plan to leave everything to your spouse or children, it's wise to make a list to keep you from overlooking things.

To help you with this task, WillMaker provides a property worksheet that you can fill out and keep with you as a reference while you make your estate planning documents. You can access the property worksheet from the screen called Leaving Your Property, which introduces you to the topic of leaving your property to others. Click the Property Worksheet link to start making your list.

Foreign Property

If you own property in another country, have an attorney help you with your estate plan. The laws of that country might affect how the property passes to beneficiaries, and owning property in another country might affect your estate's taxes. Choose a lawyer who has experience dealing with foreign property because the lawyer will need to understand or learn the other country's laws, as well as any international laws that might apply. If necessary, your lawyer can work with an attorney in that country to ensure that local rules are understood.

To be clear, you can use WillMaker to deal with property you own in any U.S. state, but if you own property in another country (or in any of the U.S. territories), you need help from an attorney.

Property You Should Not Include in Your Will

In almost all cases, your will does not affect property that you have arranged to leave by another method. (There's an exception in the State of Washington; see below.)

Types of Property You Can Include in Your Will

- Animals
- Antiques
- Appliances
- Art
- Books
- Business interests
  - Corporation
  - Limited partnership
  - LLC
  - Partnership
  - Sole proprietorship
- Business property*
- Cameras and photo equipment
- Cash accounts
  - Certificates of deposit
  - Checking
  - Money market funds
  - Savings
- Cell phones
- China, crystal, and silver
- Coins and stamps
- Collectibles
- Computers, tablets, and e-readers
- Copyrights, patents, and trademarks
- Documents (digital or printed)
- Electronic equipment
- Furniture
- Furs
- Jewelry
- Music collections (digital, vinyl, CD, or other)
- Photos (digital or printed)
- Precious metals
- Real estate
  - Agricultural land
  - Boat/marina dock space
  - Co-ops
  - Condos
  - Duplexes
  - Houses
  - Mobile homes
  - Rental property
  - Timeshares
  - Undeveloped land
  - Vacation houses
- Retirement accounts
- Royalties
- Securities
  - Bonds
  - Commodities
  - Mutual funds
  - Stocks
  - U.S. bills, notes, and bonds
- Tools
- Vehicles
  - Bicycles
  - Boats
  - Cars
  - Motorcycles
  - Motor homes/RVs
  - Planes

* If you own a sole proprietorship

SEE AN EXPERT

Frozen embryos and other genetic material. If you have frozen embryos, eggs, or sperm in storage, what will happen to them if you die? You might have already made a decision about this (knowingly or not) because fertility clinic and storage facility contracts often include provisions for what will happen to embryos and other genetic material in case of death of the parents or donors. However, if no plan is in place and you want to make one, see an attorney for help. The law about who has a right to own, transfer, use, or destroy embryos and genetic materials is complex and state-specific. You'll need to find an experienced attorney who knows the laws in your state.

Property with a right of survivorship. If you hold property in joint tenancy, tenancy by the entirety, or community property with right of survivorship, your share of that property automatically belongs to the surviving co-owner after you die. A will provision leaving your share would have no effect unless all co-owners die simultaneously.

Property you place in a trust. Property you place in a trust passes automatically to the beneficiary named in the trust document; you cannot pass this property in your will. This includes property placed in a revocable living trust. (To learn more about living trusts, see Chapter 13.)

Property for which you've already named a beneficiary. There are many ways to pass property without a will or trust. You shouldn't include in your will any type of property on this list:

- real estate for which you've made a transfer on death deed
- vehicles for which you've named a transfer on death beneficiary
- funds in bank accounts for which you've named a pay-on-death beneficiary
- securities, like stocks, bonds, or mutual funds, for which you've named a transfer on death beneficiary
- proceeds of a life insurance or annuity policy for which you've named a beneficiary, or
- money in a pension plan, individual retirement account (IRA), 401(k) plan, or other retirement plan for which you've named a beneficiary.

These types of property will pass to the named beneficiaries outside of your will and without probate. So the only effect of including them in your will would be to create confusion. To learn more about how these types of property fit into your estate plan, see Chapter 13.

Note for Washington Readers

The State of Washington has changed some of the rules discussed above. If you like, you can leave the following types of property in your will:

- your share of joint tenancy bank accounts
- pay-on-death bank accounts
- transfer on death securities or security accounts, and
- property in a living trust.

If you set up one of these devices for leaving your property and then later use your will to change the beneficiary, the property goes to the person you name in your will. However, if you designate a new beneficiary after you make your will—for example, by updating the paperwork for a pay-on-death account or changing your living trust—the gift in the will has no effect. (Wash. Rev. Code § 11.11.020.)

Property You Own With Others

If you are not married or in a registered partnership, and you own property with someone else, you probably own it in tenancy in common. This is the most common way for unmarried people to own property together. All co-owners are free to sell or give away their own interest during life or leave it to another at death in a will. To tell whether you own property as tenancy in common, check the deed or other title document; it should specifically note that the property is held as a tenancy in common.

CAUTION

More rules for married or registered partnered people making wills. If you are married or in a registered partnership, a whole host of legal rules can affect what property you own jointly and separately. (See "Property Ownership Rules for Married People," below.)

Property Ownership Rules for Married People

Most people who are married or are in registered partnerships leave all or the greatest share of their property to their surviving spouses or partners. For them, the nuances of marital property law are not important, since the survivor gets the property anyway.

But if you plan to leave your property to several people instead of, or in addition to, your spouse or partner, the picture becomes more complicated. Under your state's laws, your spouse or partner might own some property you believe is yours. And if you do not own it, you cannot give it away—either now or at your death. Questions of which spouse or partner owns what property are important if your spouse or partner does not agree to your plan for property disposition.

There are two issues to consider:

- What do you own?
- Will your spouse or partner have the right to claim a share of your property after your death? (See "Your Spouse's Right to Inherit From You," below.)

This section will help you determine what you own and so can leave to others in your will. To figure it out, you need to know a little about the laws in your state. When it comes to property ownership, states are broadly divided into two types: community property states and common law property states.

Community Property States		
Arizona	Louisiana	Texas
California*	Nevada*	Washington*
Idaho	New Mexico	Wisconsin

* Registered domestic partners are also covered by community property laws.

Alaska, Florida, Kentucky, South Dakota, and Tennessee allow a married couple to make a written agreement stating that they wish certain property to be treated as community property. (See a lawyer if you want to make this kind of agreement.)

Common Law States
All other states

Community Property States

If you live in a community property state, there are a few key rules to keep in mind while making your will:

- You can leave your separate property to anyone you wish.
- You can leavc half of the community property (property you and your spouse or partner own together) to anyone you wish.
- After your death, your spouse or partner automatically keeps their half of the community property.
- The community property rules that apply to married couples might also apply to registered partners.
- If you want to leave everything to your partner, you might be able to avoid probate by owning your property "with right of survivorship" or by making a "community property agreement." (See Chapter 13.)

Your Separate Property

The following property qualifies as separate property in all community property states:

- property that you own before marriage
- property that you receive after marriage by gift or inheritance
- property that you purchase entirely with your separate property, and
- property that you earn or accumulate after permanent separation.

In some states, additional types of property—such as personal injury awards received by one spouse during marriage—might also qualify as separate property. (See "Property That Is Difficult to Categorize," below.)

Community property states differ in how they treat income earned from separate property. Most hold that such income is separate. But a number of states take the opposite approach, treating income from separate property as community property.

Normally, separate property stays separate as long as it is not:

- so mixed with marital property that it is impossible to tell what is separate and what is not, or
- transferred in writing by the separate property owner into a form of shared ownership.

Just as separate property can be transformed into shared property, community property can be turned into separate property by a gift from one spouse to the other. The rules differ somewhat from state to state, but, generally speaking, gifts made to transform one type of property into another must be made with a signed document.

Community Property

The basic rule of community property is simple: During a marriage, all property earned or acquired by either spouse or registered partner is owned 50-50 by each spouse or partner, except for property received by only one of them through gift or inheritance.

More specifically, community property usually includes:

- All income received by either spouse or partner from employment or any other source (except gifts to or inheritance by just one spouse or partner)—for example, wages, stock options, pensions and other employment compensation, and business profits. This rule generally applies only to the period when the couple lives together as spouses or registered partners. Most community property states consider income and property acquired after the spouses or partners permanently separate to be the separate property of the spouse or partner who receives it.
- All property acquired with community property income during the marriage.
- All separate property that is transformed into community property under state law. This transformation can occur in several ways, including when one spouse or registered partner makes a gift of separate property to both of them or when property is so mixed together that it's no longer possible to tell what property is separate (lawyers call this "commingling").
- As mentioned above, in a few community property states, income earned during marriage from separate property—for example, rent, interest, or dividends—is community property. Most community property states consider such income to be separate property, however.

EXAMPLE: Beth and Daniel live in Idaho, one of the few community property states where income earned from separate property belongs to the community. Beth inherits 22 head of Angus cattle from her father. Those cattle go on to breed a herd of more than 100 cattle. All the descendants of the original 22 animals are considered income from Beth's separate property and are included in the couple's community property estate.

Classifying Property in Community Property States: Some Examples

Property	Community or Separate	Why
A painting you inherited while married	Separate; you can leave it in your will.	Inherited property belongs only to the person who inherited it.
A car you bought before you got married	Separate; you can leave it in your will.	Property owned before marriage is not community property.
A boat you bought with your income while married and registered in your name	Community; you can leave only your half-interest in your will.	It was purchased with community property income (income earned during the marriage).
The family home you and your spouse own together	Community; you can leave only your half-interest in your will.	It was purchased with community property income (income earned during the marriage).
A loan made to your brother during your marriage or partnership	Community; you can leave only your half-interest in your will.	The loan was made from community property funds and belongs half to you and half to your spouse.
A fishing cabin you inherited from your father	Separate; you can leave it in your will.	Inherited property belongs only to the person who inherited it.
Stock you and your spouse bought with savings from your spouse's earnings	Community; you can leave only your half-interest in your will.	It was purchased with one spouse's earnings, which are community property during marriage.

Agreements About Community Property

In all community property states, married couples can choose to turn separate property into community property—this normally must be done in writing. Further, although Alaska, Florida, Kentucky, South Dakota, and Tennessee are not community property states, married couples who live in those states can choose to hold property as community property.

Most community property states also allow married couples to make an agreement that leaves all community property to the surviving spouse without probate. These agreements are often called "community property agreements" or CPAs.

In some states you can use a CPA to accomplish both tasks—that is, to agree that certain property (1) is community property, and (2) should pass to the surviving spouse without probate. You can learn a little more about this in Chapter 13.

TIP

WillMaker can help Washington residents make a CPA. When making a will with WillMaker, if Washington residents indicate that they want all of their property to go to their spouse, WillMaker includes an optional CPA with the printed will documents.

Property That Is Difficult to Categorize

Normally, classifying property as community or separate property is easy. But in some situations, it can be a close call. There are several potential problem areas.

Businesses. Family businesses can create complications, especially if they were owned before marriage by one spouse or registered partner and expanded during the marriage or partnership. The key is to figure out whether the increased value of the business is community or separate property. If you and your spouse or partner do not have the same view of how to pass on the business, it might be worthwhile to get help from a lawyer or an accountant.

Money from a personal injury lawsuit. Usually, but not always, awards won in a personal injury lawsuit are the separate property of the spouse or partner receiving them. There is no easy way to characterize this type of property. If a significant amount of your property came from a personal injury settlement, research the specifics of your state's law or ask an estate planning expert.

Pensions. Generally, for married people, the part of a pension gained from earnings made during the marriage is considered to be community property. This is also true of military pensions. However, some federal pensions—such as Railroad Retirement benefits and Social Security retirement benefits—are not considered community property, because federal law deems them to be the separate property of the employee earning them. Also, because the federal government does not recognize registered partnerships, community property rules will not apply to federal benefits acquired by registered partners.

Common Law Property States

Common law property states are all states other than the community property states listed above.

In these states, you own:

- all property you purchased using your property or income, and
- property you own solely in your name if it has a title slip, deed, or other legal ownership document.

In common law states, the key to ownership for many types of valuable property is whose name is on the title. If you and your spouse or registered partner take title to a house together—that is, both of your names are on the deed—you both own it. That is true even if only you earned or inherited the money you used to buy it. If your spouse or registered partner earns the money, but you take title in your name alone, you own it.

If the property is valuable but has no title document, such as a computer, then the person whose income or property is used to pay for it owns it. If joint income is used, then you own it together. You can each leave your half in your will, unless you signed an agreement providing for a joint tenancy or a tenancy by the entirety.

EXAMPLE 1: Will and Jane are married and live in Kentucky, a common law property state. They have five children. Shortly after their marriage, Jane created a very successful app that helps doctors diagnose illness. Over the next 10 years she earned about $200,000 per year from licensing the app. Jane has used that money to buy a car, boat, and mountain cabin—all registered in her name alone. The couple also owns a house as joint tenants. In addition, Jane owns a number of family heirlooms that she inherited from her parents. Throughout their marriage, Jane and Will have maintained separate savings accounts. Will works as a computer engineer and has deposited all of his income into his account. Jane put her unspent licensing income in her account, which now contains $75,000.

Jane owns:

- the savings account listed in her name alone
- one-half interest in the house (which, because it is held in joint tenancy, will go to Will at Jane's death)
- the car, boat, and cabin, since there are title documents listing them in her name (if there were no such documents, she would still own them because they were bought with her income), and
- her family heirlooms.

Will owns:

- the savings account listed in his name alone, and
- one-half interest in the house (which, because it is held in joint tenancy, will go to Jane at Will's death).

EXAMPLE 2: Martha and Scott, who are married, have both worked for 30 years as schoolteachers in Michigan, a common law state. Generally, Scott and Martha pooled their income and jointly purchased a house worth $400,000 (in both their names as joint tenants), cars (one in Martha's name and one in Scott's), a share in a vacation condominium (in both names as joint tenants), and household furniture. Each maintains a separate savings account, and they also have a joint tenancy checking account containing $2,000. In addition, Scott and his sister own a piece of land as tenants in common.

Martha owns:

- her savings account
- one-half interest in the house, the joint checking account, and the condo (which, because they are held in joint tenancy, will go to Scott at her death)
- her car, and
- half the furniture.

Scott owns:

- his savings account
- one-half interest in the house, the joint checking account, and the condo (which, because they are held in joint tenancy, will go to Martha at his death)
- his car
- half the furniture, and
- a half-interest in the land he owns with his sister.

Moving From State to State

Complications might set in when a husband and wife acquire property in a common law property state and then move to a community property state. California, Idaho, Washington, and Wisconsin treat the earlier-acquired property as if it had been acquired in the community property state. The legal term for this type of property is "quasi-community property." Wisconsin calls it "deferred marital property."

The other community property states do not recognize the quasi-community property concept for will-making purposes. Instead, they go by the rules of the state where the property was acquired. If you and your spouse move from a non–community property state into one of the states that recognizes quasi-community property, all of your property is treated according to community property rules. However, if you move to any of the other community property states from a common law state, you must assess your property according to the rules of the state where the property was acquired.

Couples who move from a community property state to a common law state face the opposite problem. Generally, each spouse retains one-half interest in the community property the couple accumulated while living in the community property state. However, if there is a conflict after your death, it can get messy; courts dealing with the issue have not been consistent.

SEE AN EXPERT

If you move. If you move from a community property state to a common law one, and you and your spouse have any disagreement or uncertainty as to who owns what, it might be wise to check with a lawyer. (See Chapter 17.)

SEE AN EXPERT

Registered partnerships. If you are moving from the state in which you registered your relationship as a civil union or domestic partnership, there is a good chance that the state you are moving to will not recognize the property rights you received through your partnership status. Consider consulting a knowledgeable attorney in your new state to be sure you both fully understand your property rights and have an appropriate plan in place.

Your Spouse's Right to Inherit From You

If you intend to leave your spouse or registered partner very little or no property, you might run into some legal roadblocks. All common law property states (see above) protect a surviving spouse or partner from being completely disinherited—and most ensure that a spouse has the right to receive a substantial share of a deceased spouse's property. Community property states offer a different kind of protection.

Spousal Protection in Common Law States

In a common law state, a shortchanged surviving spouse or registered partner usually has the option of either taking what the will provides, called "taking under the will," or rejecting the gift and instead taking the minimum share allowed by state law, called "taking against the will." In some states, your spouse or partner might have the right to inherit the family residence or at least use it for the duration of their life. The Florida constitution, for example, gives a surviving spouse the deceased spouse's residence.

Laws protecting spouses and registered partners vary among the states. In many common law property states, a spouse is entitled to one-third of the property left in the will. In a few, it is one-half. The exact amount of the spouse's minimum share can also depend on whether there are also minor children and whether the spouse has been provided for outside the will by trusts or other means.

> **EXAMPLE:** Leonard's will leaves $50,000 to his second wife, June, and the rest of his property, totaling $400,000, to May and April, his daughters from his first marriage. June can choose instead to receive her statutory share of Leonard's estate, which will be far more than $50,000. To the probable dismay of May and April, their shares will be substantially reduced; they will share what is left of Leonard's property after June gets her statutory share.

Of course, these are just options. A spouse who is not unhappy with the share the will provides is free to let it stand. And in almost all states, one spouse or partner can give up all rights to inherit any property by completing and signing a waiver. If you want to make that type of arrangement, consult a lawyer. (See Chapter 17.)

Family Allowances

Some states provide additional, relatively minor protections for immediate family members. These vary from state to state in too much detail to discuss here. Generally, however, these devices attempt to ensure that your spouse and children are not left without support after your death, by allowing them temporary protection (such as the right to remain in the family home for a short period) or funds (typically, living expenses while an estate is being probated).

In many common law states, how much the surviving spouse is entitled to receive depends on what that spouse receives both under the will and outside of the will—for example, through joint tenancy or a living trust—as well as what the surviving spouse owns. The total of all of these is called the augmented estate.

While the augmented estate concept is rather complicated, its purpose is easy to grasp. Basically, almost all property of both spouses is taken into account, and the surviving spouse gets a piece of the whole pie.

SEE AN EXPERT

Leaving little to a spouse. If you do not plan to leave at least half of your property to your spouse or registered partner in your will and have not provided for them generously outside your will, consult a lawyer.

Spousal Protection in Community Property States

Most community property states do not give surviving spouses or registered partners the right to take a share of the deceased spouse's or partner's estate. Instead, they try to protect spouses and registered partners while both are still alive by granting each spouse or partner half ownership of property and earnings either spouse or partner acquires during the marriage. (See "Community Property States," above.)

However, in a few states—under very limited circumstances—a surviving spouse or registered partner can elect to take a portion of the deceased spouse's community or separate property. These laws are designed to prevent spouses and registered partners from being either accidentally overlooked—for example, if one spouse or partner makes a will before marriage or partnership and forgets to change it afterward to include the new spouse or partner—or deliberately deprived of their fair share of property. These protections are available in Alaska (Alaska Stat. §§ 13.12.201 and following), Arizona (Ariz. Rev. Stat. § 14-2301), California (Cal. Prob. Code §§ 21610 and following), Idaho (Idaho Code §§ 15-2-202 and following), New Mexico (N.M. Stat. § 45-2-301), Washington (Wash. Rev. Code §§ 26.16.240 and following), and Wisconsin (Wis. Stat. §§ 861.02 and following). If you want to learn more about them, consult a lawyer. (See Chapter 17.)

Property on Which You Owe Money

Using WillMaker, if you leave property on which you owe money, the beneficiary who takes it at your death will also take over the debt owed on that property. This means the beneficiary of the property is responsible for paying off the debt. (But your survivors will not inherit debt not attached to property. For example, if you die with nothing to your name except credit card debt, your survivors will not be responsible for paying those bills.) If you don't want your beneficiaries to take over debt you owe on property, see a lawyer for help.

Your Digital Assets

When you're thinking about a plan for your property, don't forget to consider the fate of your digital assets—the online accounts and digital files that will be left behind when you die.

Here are some things to think about:

- Do you want someone to have access to your email accounts?
- What should be done with your social media—for example, Facebook, LinkedIn, or Instagram?
- Do you want someone to make final posts on your blog or YouTube channel?
- Should your online communities be notified of your death?
- What should happen to photos, music, books, or documents that you store on your computer, phone, or tablet or in the cloud?

Having access to your digital assets can make your executor's job easier, as they will be better able to find your contacts, close accounts, pay bills, distribute property, and more. If you want to give your executor access to your digital assets, you'll need to take two steps: (1) make sure your executor knows about your wishes for your digital assets, and give your executor the login information needed to access the accounts, and (2) give your executor the legal authority to manage your digital assets.

Leaving Instructions and Login Information for Your Executor

The easiest way to give your executor practical access to your digital assets is to leave a letter for your executor that provides instructions about what to do. For example, if you want your executor to archive your blog posts, leave your executor details about how to get into the admin area of the blog, how to archive the data, and what to do with it afterward. Leave this information in a letter separate from your will.

You'll also need to provide the login information for your accounts, either in this same letter or by giving your executor access to any password managers you use.

Giving Your Executor the Legal Authority to Manage Your Digital Assets

Your WillMaker will grants your executor the power to access and control your digital assets. This means that when you make a will through WillMaker, you are giving your executor the authority to access your emails, social media, online file storage, and other digital assets. However, your executor's legal authority might also be affected by:

- the law in your state
- whether you used a particular company's online tool to name a legacy contact or someone to manage your account after death, and
- each company's terms of service agreement.

Even with the legal authority provided in your will, without your login information, your executor's ability to access your digital assets might depend on each company's willingness to be helpful. If a company refuses to provide the access to which your executor is entitled, your executor might have to get a court order, which will take time and money. All of that said, in practice if you leave clear and detailed access information, your executor will be able to follow your wishes by managing or deleting your accounts as you would.

For more about an executor's rights to access digital assets in your state, go to www.nolo.com/legal-encyclopedia/digital-assets. (For more about leaving instructions for your digital assets, see Chapter 12.)

CHAPTER

6

How to Leave Your Property

The heart of will making is deciding who gets your property when you die. For many, this is an easy task: You want it all to go to your spouse or partner, your kids, or your favorite charity. For others, it's a little more complicated—for example, you want most of your property to go to your spouse, partner, child, or charity, but you also want certain items to go to other people. You might even have a fairly complicated scheme in mind that involves dividing your property among a number of people and organizations.

Chapter 5 introduced some basic concepts about your property and whether you can leave it to others in your will. This chapter explains how to put your plan into effect using WillMaker. If you want to leave all or most of your property to a loved one or favorite charity, WillMaker offers you some shortcuts. It also accommodates more complex wishes.

After you name those who will get your property, WillMaker lets you name alternates—that is, who should get property if your first choices do not survive you.

You do not need to read all of this chapter to figure out how to write the will you want. Start with the discussion that is tailored to your situation:

- married or in a registered partnership, with children
- married or in a registered partnership, with no children
- not married or in a registered partnership, with children, or
- not married or in a registered partnership, with no children.

In this chapter, when we refer to "registered partners," we're talking about domestic partnerships *registered with a state government* (including civil unions and reciprocal beneficiaries). Registration is important because, legally, it gives the partnership marriage-like qualities that don't apply to unmarried or unregistered partners. Read more about these rules in Chapter 4.

Married or in a Registered Partnership, With Children

Many married or partnered people have simple will-making needs. They want to leave all or most of their property to their spouses or partners. As alternates, they might want to choose their children or name another person or organization. WillMaker lets you choose any of those paths easily. And if you do not want to make your spouse or partner the main beneficiary of your will, that option is available, too.

Choosing Beneficiaries

WillMaker prompts you to choose one of three approaches to leaving your property. You can:

- Leave it all to your spouse or registered partner.
- Leave most of it to your spouse or registered partner, with some specific exceptions.
- Leave it some other way, making a plan that might or might not include your spouse or registered partner.

The third option offers flexibility. You should choose it if you want to divide up your property more evenly among a number of beneficiaries or if you want to give all or most of your property to someone other than your spouse or registered partner. But if you do choose this approach to making your will, be sure that you understand the rules governing what you own and the rights of your spouse or partner. (See "Property Ownership Rules for Married People" and "Your Spouse's Right to Inherit From You" in Chapter 5.)

EXAMPLE 1: Anne and Robert are a married couple with one young child. Anne wants a simple will in which she leaves all of her property to Robert. She chooses the first option—everything to your spouse—to get a will that reflects her wishes.

EXAMPLE 2: Arnie wants his wife to receive most of his property when he dies, but he has a valuable violin that he wants to go to his best friend, Eddie, and a coin collection that he wants his nephew to receive. Arnie chooses the second option—most to your spouse. Then he can name Eddie to receive his violin and his nephew to receive his coin collection.

EXAMPLE 3: Sylvia is married to Fred. She wants to leave him her share of their investment portfolio and family business but also wants to leave a number of specific property items to different friends, relatives, and charities. So she chooses the third option. WillMaker then prompts her to list specific property items and the person or organization she wants to receive each one. Before she does, Sylvia reviews Chapter 5 to make sure she understands what property is appropriate to leave in her will.

SKIP AHEAD

When you can skip ahead. If you do not want to name your spouse or registered partner to receive all or most of your property, skip the rest of this section and go to "Making Specific Bequests," below, for a discussion of what comes next.

Choosing Alternates for Your Spouse or Partner

If you want your spouse or registered partner to receive all or most of your property, your next task will be to choose an alternate for your spouse or partner.

The will you create with WillMaker provides that all beneficiaries—including your spouse—must survive you by 45 days to receive the property you leave them. This is a standard will provision, called a survivorship requirement. It is based on the assumption that if a beneficiary survives you by only a few days or weeks, you would prefer the property to go to another beneficiary that you choose and name in your will.

The alternate or alternates you choose will receive the property only if your spouse or registered partner dies less than 45 days after you do.

Depending on your previous choices, WillMaker offers two or three options for alternates. You can name:

- your child or children, or
- other alternate beneficiaries.

These two approaches to naming alternates are shortcuts. You won't specify which items go to which beneficiaries because these alternates will receive all of the property that would have gone to your spouse or partner.

You also have a third option: You can make a completely new plan for leaving your property that will take effect only if your spouse does not survive you by at least 45 days. If you make this choice, you can divide your property among a number of alternate beneficiaries.

Each of these approaches to naming alternates is discussed below.

Naming Your Children as Alternates

It is common for married or partnered people who have children to simply leave all or most of their property to the surviving spouse or partner and name the children to take the property as alternates. This means if your spouse or partner does not survive you by 45 days, the property your spouse or partner would have received will pass to your child or children.

If you have more than one child, you must decide how the children should share the property.

> **EXAMPLE:** Meg and Charlie have three grown children. When Charlie makes his will, he leaves everything to Meg and names the children as alternates for her. He directs that all three children should receive equal shares of his property if Meg doesn't survive him and they take it instead.

If any of your children are minors or young adults, you can:

- specify the share each child will receive; later, you can designate how each child's share will be managed and doled out if a child is younger than 35 when you die, or

- direct that the property be held in one undivided fund, called a pot trust; under this option, the person you select to serve as trustee will use the assets in the trust for all your children as needed, until your youngest child turns an age you choose—up to age 25.

(See Chapter 7 for a discussion of these methods for managing property left to children.)

> EXAMPLE 1: Julia and Emanuel have three young children. When Julia makes her will, she names Emanuel to inherit most of her property and leaves a few small items to her sister. As alternates for her husband, she picks her children. But because they are too young to manage money or property, she names her sister to manage any property the children may take under her will while they are still young.

> EXAMPLE 2: Barry and his wife, Marta, have two young daughters close in age. In his will, Barry leaves Marta all his property and chooses the children as alternate beneficiaries. He also picks the pot trust option and names his mother as trustee. If Marta does not survive him by at least 45 days, all of Barry's property will go into a trust for the two girls, administered by Barry's mother.

WillMaker also lets you name a second level of alternates—that is, alternates who will take the property a child would have received, if that child does not survive you. You can name an alternate for each child or, if you have two or more children, you can designate that the surviving children receive any property that would have gone to the deceased child.

Naming Alternates Who Are Not Your Children

If you decide to specify alternates to receive the property left to your spouse or registered partner, you can name whomever you want. You are not constrained, as with the first option, to naming only your children as alternates. For instance, you can name a charity, a friend, or just one of your children. If your spouse or partner does not survive you by 45 days, the alternates you name will receive the property your spouse or partner would have received. If you name more than one person or organization, you can specify what share each is to receive.

> **EXAMPLE:** Celeste is married with two grown children. The children have both been provided for nicely with money from trusts and are financially secure. In her will, Celeste leaves her husband most of her property, with a few exceptions of some heirlooms for her children. As an alternate for her husband, she names the university where she taught for many years.

You can also name a second level of alternates—that is, alternates to take the property should both your spouse or partner and a first level of alternates you name all die before you do. You can name a backup alternate for each alternate. If you named more than one first-level alternate, you can also designate that the survivors receive any property that would have gone to a deceased alternate.

Making a Different Plan

This option—Plan B—is available only if you choose to leave all your property to your spouse or registered partner.

It lets you create a whole new plan to take effect if, and only if, your spouse or partner doesn't survive you by 45 days. This option is for people who think like this: I want to leave all my property to my spouse, period. But in case my spouse does not survive me, instead of leaving all of my property to one person—or to several people to share—I want to make a "Plan B" that divvies up my belongings, giving certain items to specific people.

Your Plan B can include as many specific bequests as you wish. (See "Making Specific Bequests," below.) After you have made all your specific bequests, you can also name someone to take the rest of your property. This is called your residuary beneficiary. (See "Naming Residuary Beneficiaries," below.) Again, all of these Plan B bequests will take effect only if your spouse or registered partner does not survive you by 45 days.

EXAMPLE: Sean wants to leave all his property to Eva, his wife, if she's alive when he dies. But thinking about what he would want to happen if Eva were not around to take everything, he decides that he would want to divide his property among several friends, relatives, and charities.

When he sits down with WillMaker to make his will, Sean names Eva to get all his property. Then, when it's time to name alternates, he chooses the Plan B option and leaves $10,000 to a local food bank, his piano to his niece, and the rest of his property to his brother.

If You Do Not Name Alternates

If you leave your entire estate to one person or a group of people, you do not name alternate beneficiaries, and your primary beneficiaries do not survive you, then your estate will be distributed according to the laws of your state. (See "Dying Without a Will" in Chapter 2.)

An Important Option for Washington Residents

You and your spouse or partner have another option if you live in the State of Washington. In Washington, WillMaker can help you make a "community property agreement" (CPA)—a document that leaves all of your property to each other, without probate. A CPA overrides your will if there is a conflict between those two documents. So a CPA can replace your will as your primary estate planning document. However, even if you make a CPA, you still need a will to name an executor, guardians for children, and beneficiaries for the unlikely possibility that you and your spouse die at the same time.

When you make a will with WillMaker, and you indicate that you live in Washington and that you want all of your property to go to your spouse, a Washington CPA (and detailed instructions for completing it) will print out with your will document. You don't have to use it, but it's there for you in case you want it. (See Chapter 13 for more about probate and CPAs.) (Wash. Rev. Code § 26.16.120.)

Married or in a Registered Partnership, No Children

Many married or partnered people have simple will-making needs. They want to leave all or most of their property to their spouses or registered partners. Then, as alternates, they might name one or more other people or organizations. WillMaker lets you choose this path easily. And if you do not want to make your spouse or partner the main beneficiary of your will, that option is available, too.

Choosing Beneficiaries

WillMaker prompts you to choose one of three approaches to leaving your property. You can:

- Leave it all to your spouse or registered partner.
- Leave most of it to your spouse or registered partner, with some specific exceptions.
- Leave it some other way, making a plan that might or might not include your spouse or registered partner.

The third option offers flexibility. You should choose it if you want to divide up your property more evenly among a number of beneficiaries or if you want to give all or most of your property to someone other than your spouse or partner. If you choose it, be sure that you understand the rules governing what you own and the rights of your spouse or registered partner. (See "Property Ownership Rules for Married People" and "Your Spouse's Right to Inherit From You" in Chapter 5.)

EXAMPLE 1: Mark and Abby are a young married couple with no children. Mark wants simply to leave everything to Abby in his will. He chooses the first option—everything to your spouse—so that his will reflects his intentions.

EXAMPLE 2: Paul wants his wife to receive most of his property when he dies, but he wants his golf clubs to go to his best friend, Eric, and wants his niece to take his photography equipment. Paul chooses the second option—most to your spouse. Then he can name Eric to receive his golf clubs and his niece to receive the photography equipment.

EXAMPLE 3: Eleanor is married to William. She wants to leave William her share of their investment portfolio and family business, but also wants to leave a number of specific items to different friends, relatives, and charities. She chooses the third option when using WillMaker—make a different plan. WillMaker then prompts her to list specific property items and the person or organization she wants to receive each of them. Before she does, Eleanor reviews Chapter 5 to make sure she understands what property is appropriate to leave in her will.

SKIP AHEAD

When you can skip ahead. If you do not want to name your spouse or registered partner to receive all or most of your property, skip the rest of this section and go to "Making Specific Bequests," below, for a discussion of what comes next.

Choosing Alternates for Your Spouse or Partner

If you want your spouse or registered partner to receive all or most of your property, your next task will be to choose an alternate or alternates for your spouse or partner.

The will you create with WillMaker provides that all beneficiaries—including your spouse or registered partner—must survive you by 45 days to receive the property you leave them. This is a standard will provision, called a survivorship requirement. It is based on the assumption that if a beneficiary survives you by only a few days or weeks, you would prefer the property to go to another beneficiary that you name in your will.

The alternate or alternates you choose will receive the property only if your spouse or partner does not live at least 45 days longer than you do.

The simplest ways to provide for alternates are to name:

- one person or organization to receive everything your spouse or partner would have received, or
- more than one person or organization to share the property.

If you choose either of these options, the alternate or alternates you name will receive all the property that would have gone to your spouse or partner, so you won't specify which items go to which beneficiaries.

Or you can make a different plan for leaving your property—Plan B—which will take effect only if your spouse or partner does not survive you by 45 days. If you choose to make a different plan, you can leave specific items of property among several alternate beneficiaries.

These approaches to naming alternates are discussed below.

Naming Alternates for Your Spouse or Partner

You can name whomever you want as the alternate for your spouse or registered partner. For instance, you can name a charity, friend, or relative. If your spouse or partner does not survive you by 45 days, the alternate you name will receive the property your spouse or partner would have received. If you name more than one person or organization, you can specify what share each is to receive.

> EXAMPLE: In her will, Sharon leaves most of her property to her husband, Alex, with a few exceptions of some small items for friends. As an alternate for Alex, she names the charity at which she volunteered for many years.

You can also name a second level of alternates—that is, alternates to take the property should both your spouse and alternate not survive you. You can name a backup alternate for each alternate. Or if you named more than one first-level alternate, you can designate that the surviving alternates receive any property that would have gone to a deceased alternate.

Making a Different Plan

If you choose to leave all of your property to your spouse or registered partner, you can create a whole new plan to take effect if, and only if, your spouse or partner doesn't survive you by 45 days. This option is for people who think like this: I want to leave all my property to my spouse, period. But in case my spouse does not survive me, instead of leaving all of my property to one person—or to several people to share—I want to make a "Plan B" that divvies up my belongings, giving certain items to specific people.

Your alternate plan can include as many specific bequests as you wish. (See "Making Specific Bequests," below.) After you have made all your specific bequests, you can also name someone to take the rest of your property. This is called your residuary beneficiary. (See "Naming Residuary Beneficiaries," below.) Again, all of these Plan B bequests will take effect only if your spouse or registered partner does not survive you by 45 days.

EXAMPLE: Sean wants to leave all his property to Eva, his wife, if she's alive when he dies. But thinking about what he would want to happen if Eva were not around to take everything, he decides that he would want to divide his property among several friends, relatives, and charities.

When he sits down with WillMaker to make his will, Sean names Eva to take everything. Then, when it's time to name alternates, he chooses to create a different plan and leaves $10,000 to a local food bank, his piano to his niece, and everything else to his brother.

If You Do Not Name Alternates

If you leave your entire estate to one person or a group of people, you do not name alternate beneficiaries, and your primary beneficiaries do not survive you, then your estate will be distributed according to the laws of your state. (See "Dying Without a Will" in Chapter 2.)

Not Married or in a Registered Partnership, With Children

If you have children, they probably figure prominently in your plans for distributing your property after your death. With that in mind, WillMaker offers some shortcuts when making your will.

Choosing Beneficiaries

WillMaker prompts you to choose one of three approaches to leaving your property. You can:

- Leave it all to your child or children.
- Leave most of it to your child or children, with some specific exceptions.
- Leave it some other way, making a plan that might or might not include your children.

The third option offers flexibility. You should choose it if you want to divide your property more evenly among a number of beneficiaries or if you want to give all or most of your property to someone other than your children. If you choose it, be sure that you understand the rules governing what you own. (See Chapter 5.)

EXAMPLE 1: Raquel is a divorced mother of two young children. She wants to leave all her property to the children, in equal shares. She chooses the first option.

EXAMPLE 2: Carlo, a widower, has one son, who is now 40 years old. Carlo wants to leave most of his property to his son but also make a few small bequests to charities. He chooses the second option. Then he can name the charities and the amounts he wants to leave to each.

EXAMPLE 3: Brenda has three children, all of whom are grown and financially healthy. She wants to leave a number of specific property items to her children but also to many different friends, relatives, and charities. She chooses the third option. WillMaker then asks her to list specific property items and the person or organization she wants to receive each one. Before doing this, Brenda reviews Chapter 5 to make sure she understands what property she can leave in her will.

SKIP AHEAD

When you can skip ahead. If you do not want to name your child or children to receive all or most of your property, skip the rest of this section and go to "Making Specific Bequests," below, for a discussion of what comes next.

Designating Children's Shares

If you have more than one child, you must decide how you want them to share the property they receive through your will.

> EXAMPLE: Charlie has three grown children. When Charlie makes his will, he names the children to receive everything. He directs that all three children should receive equal shares of his property.

If any of your children are minors or young adults, you can:

- specify the share each child will receive; later, you can designate how each child's share will be managed and doled out if a child is younger than 35 when you die, or
- direct that the property be held in one undivided fund, called a pot trust; under this option, the person you select to serve as trustee will use the assets in the trust for all your children as needed, until your youngest child turns an age you choose, up to age 25.

(See Chapter 7 for an explanation of all of these methods for managing property left to children.)

> EXAMPLE 1: Tess has three children, two teenagers and one 26-year-old son. When she makes her will, she leaves the children most of her property and leaves a few small items to her sister. Because her oldest child is self-supporting, she leaves him just a 1/5 share and leaves the two younger younger children come to own while they are still young.

> EXAMPLE 2: Frank has two young sons close in age. In his will, he leaves them all his property. He then picks the pot trust option and names his sister as trustee. That means that if the boys inherit Frank's property while they are still young, all of it will go into a trust for them, administered by Frank's sister.

Explaining Your Bequests to Your Children

Using WillMaker, you are free to divide your property among your children as you see fit. If your children are already responsible adults, your prime concern will likely be fairness—given the circumstances and the children's needs. Often, this will mean dividing your property equally among your children. Sometimes, however, the special health or educational needs of one child, the relative affluence and stability of another, or the fact that you are estranged from a child will be the impetus for you to divide the property unevenly.

Doing this can sometimes raise serious angst; a child who receives less property might conclude that you cared for that child less. To clear up confusion, you might wish to explain your choices. Because of the risk of adding illegal or confusing language, WillMaker does not allow you to make this explanation in your will. Fortunately, there is a sound and sensible way to express your reasons and feelings. Simply prepare a separate letter to accompany your will. (See Chapter 12.)

Choosing Alternates for Your Children

If you choose your child or children to receive all or most of your property, your next task will be to decide who should get that property if a child were to predecease you.

The will you create with WillMaker provides that a beneficiary must survive you by 45 days to receive property through the will. This is a standard will provision, called a survivorship requirement. It is based on the assumption that if a beneficiary survives you by only a few weeks, you would prefer the property to go to another beneficiary that you name in your will.

The alternate you choose for a child will receive the property only if the child does not survive you by at least 45 days.

If you have one child, you can either:

- name one or more alternates for that child, or
- make a different plan that allows you to divide up specific items of property among several other people or organizations.

If you have more than one child and have designated a share for each child, you can either:

- name one or more alternates for each child, or
- specify that if one child doesn't survive you, the surviving children should take the deceased child's share.

If you chose a pot trust, you need not name alternates. If any child does not survive you, the others will share the property.

Naming Alternates for Your Children

You can name whomever you want—for instance, a charity, friend, or relative—as the alternate for a child. If the child does not survive you by 45 days, the alternate will receive the property the child would have received. If you name more than one alternate, you can specify the share each is to receive.

> EXAMPLE: In her will, Sharon leaves her daughter most of her property and gives the rest to friends. As an alternate for her daughter, she names her daughter's two young children.

Surviving Children

If you have more than one child, rather than name alternates for each of your children, you might want to provide that whatever property you leave them will go to all the children who survive you.

> EXAMPLE: In his will, Patrick leaves his daughter and two sons all of his property. He specifies that each should receive an equal share. When WillMaker asks him to name alternates for the children, he specifies that the survivors should take the share of any deceased child.

If you have only one child and you choose to leave all of your property to that child, you can create a whole new plan to take effect if, and only if, your child doesn't survive you by 45 days. This option is for people who think like this: I want to leave all my property to my child, period. But in case my child does not survive me, instead of leaving all of my property to one person—or to several people to share—I want to make a "Plan B" that divvies up my belongings, giving certain items to specific people.

Your alternate plan can include as many specific bequests as you wish. (See "Making Specific Bequests," below.) After you have made all your specific bequests, you can also name someone to take the rest of your property. This is called your residuary beneficiary. (See "Naming Residuary Beneficiaries," below.) Again, all of these Plan B bequests will take effect only if your child does not survive you by 45 days.

> **EXAMPLE:** Margaret wants to leave all her property to her child, Finn. But thinking about what she would want to happen if Finn were not around to take everything, she decides that she would want to divide her property among several friends, relatives, and charities. When she sits down with WillMaker to make her will, Margaret names Finn to take everything. Then, when it's time to name alternates, she chooses to create a different plan and leaves her china to her sister, some rare books to a neighbor, and $5,000 to the local food bank.

If You Do Not Name Alternates

If you leave your entire estate to one person or a group of people, you do not name alternate beneficiaries, and your primary beneficiaries do not survive you, then your estate will be distributed according to the laws of your state. (See "Dying Without a Will" in Chapter 2.)

Not Married or in a Registered Partnership, No Children

As a single person, your beneficiaries will probably be your loved ones, friends, or organizations you value highly. You can divide your property as you see fit, whether that means leaving it all to one beneficiary or giving specific items to specific people. Or, you might prefer to combine these approaches, leaving most of your assets to one or more beneficiaries and a few unique items to others. In any case, you'll have the opportunity to choose alternate beneficiaries as well.

Choosing Beneficiaries

WillMaker prompts you to choose one of three approaches to leaving your property. You can:

- Leave everything to one or more beneficiaries.
- Leave most of it to one or more beneficiaries, with some specific exceptions.
- Leave your property some other way, making a plan with many specific gifts and then one or more beneficiaries to get "everything else."

If you want to leave specific items of property, be sure that you understand what kinds of property should be left in a will and what might be passed to your survivors in other ways. (See "Property You Should Not Include in Your Will" in Chapter 5.)

EXAMPLE 1: Fernando and Robert have been together for many years but are not officially married or partnered. When Fernando makes his will, he wants all his property to go to Robert. He chooses the first option—leave everything to one person—to make a will that reflects his wishes.

EXAMPLE 2: Theresa, whose husband died several years ago, wants to divide her money and possessions among different friends, relatives, and charities. She chooses the third option. WillMaker then asks her to list specific property items and the person or organization she wants to receive each one. Then she names one person who will receive any other property that she owns at her death.

SKIP AHEAD

When you can skip ahead. If you do not want to name one or more beneficiaries to receive all or most of your property, skip the rest of this section and go to "Making Specific Bequests," below, for a discussion of what comes next.

Choosing Alternates

If you specify that one or more beneficiaries should receive all or most of your property, your next task will be to decide who would get that property if any of your first-choice beneficiaries were to die before you do.

The will you create with WillMaker provides that all beneficiaries must survive you by 45 days to receive the property you leave them. This is a standard will provision, called a survivorship requirement. It is based on the assumption that if a beneficiary survives you by only a few days or weeks, you would prefer the property to go to another beneficiary that you name in your will.

The alternates you choose will receive the property only if your first-choice beneficiaries do not survive for at least 45 days after you die.

WillMaker offers two options for alternates. You can:

- name alternate beneficiaries for each of your first-choice beneficiaries, or
- make a completely new plan that will take effect only if your first-choice beneficiaries do not survive you by 45 days. This way, you can divide your property among several alternate beneficiaries.

Naming Alternates

You can name whomever you want as alternates for each of your first choice beneficiaries. For instance, for each of your first-choice beneficiaries, you can name a charity or a group of friends. If you name more than one person or organization, you can specify the share each is to receive.

If a first-choice beneficiary does not survive you by 45 days, the alternates you name will receive the property the first-choice beneficiary would have received.

EXAMPLE 1: Christine is not married and has no children. She is very close to her sister Karen and wants to leave all her property to her.

In her will, Christine names Karen as her first-choice beneficiary. As alternates, she names Karen's two children.

EXAMPLE 2: Ari leaves all of his property to his two brothers, Seth and David. Because Seth is more financially stable, he indicates that Seth should get one-quarter of his estate and David should get three-quarters. He names his cousin Rachel as an alternate beneficiary for David's share. She will get three-quarters of Ari's estate if David does not survive Ari. Ari names his favorite charity as an alternate for Seth's share. If Seth does not survive Ari, the charity will get one-quarter of the estate.

If you like, you can also name a second level of alternates—that is, alternates to take the property should both your first-choice and alternate beneficiaries not survive you by 45 days or more.

If you name more than one alternate beneficiary but don't name any second alternates for those beneficiaries, the surviving alternate beneficiaries will equally share the property that any deceased beneficiary would have received.

EXAMPLE: In her will, JoEllen leaves all her property to her partner, Katrine. She names her nephews, Jacob and Joseph, as alternates and does not name second alternates. When JoEllen dies, Katrine and Jacob have already passed away. Joseph inherits all of JoEllen's property.

If you name more than one second alternate and one or more of them do not survive you, the surviving second alternates will equally share any property that would have gone to that deceased second alternate.

Making a Different Plan

This option lets you create a whole new plan that takes effect only if your first-choice beneficiary or beneficiaries do not survive you by 45 days. Your alternate plan—Plan B—can include as many specific bequests as you wish. (See "Making Specific Bequests," below.)

After you have made all your specific bequests, you can also name someone to take the rest of your property. This is called your residuary beneficiary. (See "Naming Residuary Beneficiaries," below.)

EXAMPLE: Sven wants to leave all his property to Jeannette, his girlfriend. But thinking about what he would want to happen if Jeannette were to die before him, he decides that he would want to divide his property among relatives and charities.

When he sits down with WillMaker to make his will, Sven names Jeannette to take all of his property. Then, when it's time to name alternates, he chooses the Plan B option and leaves $10,000 to a local food bank, his piano to his niece, and everything else to his brother.

If You Do Not Name Alternates

If you leave your entire estate to one person or a group of people, you do not name alternate beneficiaries, and your primary beneficiaries do not survive you, then your estate will be distributed according to the laws of your state. (See "Dying Without a Will" in Chapter 2.)

Making Specific Bequests

This section discusses how to make specific bequests—that is, leave specific property items to specific people or groups. You should read this section if you:

- left most of your property to one or more main beneficiaries but want to leave some items to others
- want to divide your property among several beneficiaries, without leaving most or all of it to one or more main beneficiaries, or
- left everything to one or more beneficiaries, but instead of naming alternates for those beneficiaries, you want to make a Plan B to take effect if your first-choice beneficiaries don't survive you.

WillMaker lets you make an unlimited number of separate specific bequests. For each one, you must provide this information:

- a description of the item—for example, a house, cash, an heirloom, or a book collection
- the names of the people or organizations you want to get the items, and
- if you wish, the name of an alternate beneficiary who will receive specific property if your first beneficiary does not survive you by 45 days. You can name more than one alternate beneficiary; if you do, you will also decide what share of the property each will receive.

Describing the Property

The first part of making a specific bequest is to describe the property you want to pass to a certain beneficiary or beneficiaries you have in mind. For example, if you want to leave your guitar to your best friend, you would begin by entering a brief description of the guitar, such as "my 1959 Martin guitar."

When describing an item, be as concise as you can, but use enough detail so that people will be able to identify and find the property. Most often, this will not be difficult: "my baby grand piano," "my collection of blue apothecary jars," or "my llama throw rug" are all the description you will need for tangible items that are easy to locate. If an item is very valuable or could be easily confused with other property, make sure you include identifying characteristics, such as location, serial number, color, or some other unique feature.

CAUTION

Do not include property that will pass by other means. Before describing the property you wish to leave in a specific bequest, take a moment to reflect on what property you are legally able to pass in your will. If you have already arranged to leave property outside your will by using legal devices, such as life insurance, pay-on-death bank accounts, a transfer on death deed, or a living trust, you usually should not include that property in a specific bequest. (See "Property You Should Not Include in Your Will" in Chapter 5.)

Naming Beneficiaries

The second step in making a specific bequest is to name one or more beneficiaries. Beneficiaries' names need not be the names that appear on their birth certificates. Just make sure that the names you use clearly identify the beneficiaries.

Tips on Describing Property in Your Will

Here is how to identify different types of property with enough detail to prevent confusion:

- **Household furnishings.** You normally need not get very specific, unless an object is particularly valuable. It is enough to list the location of the property: "all household furnishings and possessions in the apartment at 55 Drury Lane."
- **Real estate.** You can simply provide the street address or, for unimproved property, the name by which it is commonly known: "my condominium at 123 45th Avenue," "my summer home at 84 Memory Lane in Oakville," or "the vacant lot next to the McHenry place on Old Farm Road." You do not need to provide the legal description from the deed.
- **Personal items.** As with household goods, it is usually adequate to briefly describe personal items and group them, unless they have significant monetary or sentimental value. For example, items of extremely valuable jewelry should normally be listed and identified separately, while a drawer full of costume jewelry and baubles could be grouped.
- **Bank, stock, and money market accounts.** List financial accounts using names and partial account numbers: "$20,000 from savings account #XXX-XXX2222 at Independence Bank" or "my money market account #XXXX4567 at Beryl Pynch & Company." For stock, list the company name and the number of shares: "100 shares of General Foods common stock." Do not include accounts for which you've already named a beneficiary in the account's institution's paperwork. If you're not sure, contact the company to check.

TIP

Accounts with online access. Your executor will find it helpful to access your accounts online, but do not leave access information in your will (which will become public). Instead, leave a separate letter for your executor that provides login names and passwords for your accounts. You can do this with the Letter to Survivors. (See Chapter 12.) In the download version of WillMaker, you can use the Information for Caregivers and Survivors form.

Do Not Place Conditions on Bequests

Don't place conditions on any of your bequests; it risks making a confusing and even unenforceable will.

Here are some examples of *what not to do*:

- "I leave my gold Rolex to Andres, but only if he divorces his current wife, Samantha." Such a bequest would not be considered legally valid, because it encourages the breakup of a family.
- "I leave my dental office equipment to Claude, as long as he sets up a dental practice in San Francisco." The reason this bequest is unwieldy becomes obvious once you think ahead to the need for constant supervision. Who would be responsible for tracking Claude's dentistry career and making sure he ends up in San Francisco? What if Claude initially practices in San Francisco, using the equipment he was willed, then moves to grow grapes in the Napa Valley? Must he give up the equipment? To whom?
- "I leave my vintage Barbie doll collection to Collette, if the dolls are still in good condition." Who is to judge whether the dolls are in good condition? What happens if they aren't?

SEE AN EXPERT

When to see a lawyer. If you are determined to place conditions on beneficiaries or property, consult a lawyer who is experienced in drafting bequests that will adequately address these potentially complex arrangements.

Minors or Young Adults

If any of the beneficiaries you name is a minor (younger than 18) or young adult (younger than 35), you will have a chance, in a later part of WillMaker, to choose someone to manage the property for them until they are older. (See Chapter 7.)

Multiple Beneficiaries

If you name two or more beneficiaries to share a specific bequest, you will later be asked to specify each person's share. To avoid possible tiffs among your beneficiaries, the property you plan to leave them should be either property that is easily divided or property that you intend to be sold so that the proceeds can be split. For property that requires discretion to divide, it might be wiser to leave items separately.

Organizations

You might want to leave property to a charity or a public or private organization—for example, the American Red Cross, the Greenview Center for Women's Health, or the University of Illinois Urbana-Champaign.

The organization you name need not be set up as a nonprofit, unless you wish your estate to qualify for a charitable estate tax deduction. (See Chapter 13.) It can be any organization you consider worthy of your bequest. The only limitation is that the organization must not be set up for some illicit or illegal purpose.

The organization you name will receive your gift with no strings attached. You cannot use your will to describe how the property should be used. If you want to do that—for example, if you want a gift to your alma mater to be used as a scholarship for a student who gets a grade point average above 3.5—see an experienced estate planning attorney for advice.

When naming an organization, be sure to enter its complete name, which might be different from the truncated version by which it is commonly known. Several different organizations might use similar names—and you want to be sure your bequest goes to the one you have in mind. Someone at the organization will be more than happy to help you get it right.

Specifying Shares

If you name a group of beneficiaries to receive specific property, WillMaker will ask you whether you want them to receive equal or unequal shares of the property. If you want it shared unequally, the shares must add up to one or 100%. You can choose to use fractions or percentages. WillMaker will warn you if your computations are off.

Gifts to Caregivers in Some States

To guard against abuse by caregivers, California, Illinois, Nevada, and Rhode Island put restrictions on gifts you leave to any nonrelative who has recently helped you with personal or health care. You can leave such a gift—but first you might need to have a lawyer sign a statement, verifying that you're acting freely and aren't being unduly influenced.

If you don't, the gift could be void—meaning the intended recipient won't get it. These states have laws that aim to prevent caregivers from taking advantage of the people who depend on them. However, the laws could easily invalidate perfectly reasonable gifts that you really want to make. For example, a gift to a new neighbor who brings meals and helps you pay bills could be voided, as could a gift to a paid live-in caregiver who has become a good friend.

These laws don't apply to gifts under:

- $5,000 in California (as long as your entire estate is worth at least $208,850)
- $20,000 in Illinois
- $3,000 in Nevada, and
- •$5,000 in Rhode Island (as long as your estate is worth at least $50,000).

Most gifts to family members won't be affected, but gifts to loved ones who are not legally related, like stepchildren or unmarried partners, could be voided if your will is challenged.

Idaho and Missouri have similar laws, but with different parameters:

- In Idaho, gifts to caregivers who work in, own, or operate a residence (including your home, a nursing home, or an assisted living facility) where you've lived in the year before you die are presumed to result from undue influence, and the gift could be voided. There is no dollar threshold.
- In Missouri, if you leave a gift to an in-home health care provider who is not a blood relative, the law presumes that you left the gift under undue influence, and the gift could be voided. This law does not apply to small gifts (those under 5% of the total value of your estate).

Gifts to Caregivers in Some States (continued)

If you think these laws could void gifts that you want to make, see a lawyer who handles estate planning, family law, or elder care matters for help.

(Cal. Prob. Code §§ 13100, 21380–21392; Idaho Code § 15-2-616; 755 Ill. Comp. Stat. §§ 5/4a-5–5/4a-35; Mo. Rev. Stat. § 197.480; Nev. Rev. Stat. §§ 155.093–155.098; R.I. Gen. Laws §§ 33-19.1-1–33-19.1-9.)

EXAMPLE 1: Fred Wagner wants to leave an undeveloped real estate parcel to his three children, Mary, Sue, and Peter. Because he has already paid for Mary's graduate school education, he wants to give Sue and Peter greater percentages of the property. He lists his children and the share of his property to which they are entitled this way: Mary Wagner (1/5), Susan Wagner (2/5), and Peter Wagner (2/5).

EXAMPLE 2: Paola wants to split her estate among her four siblings—one brother from her father's first marriage and three younger sisters. She and her brother were never close, and he doesn't need more money. She wants to give him a share of her estate, but not as much as her three sisters, with whom she is very close. So she leaves her brother 10% of her estate, and then leaves 30% to each of her three sisters.

TIP

Update your will when you gain or lose property. If you leave a specific item of property to a beneficiary and you no longer own that property when you die, that beneficiary will get nothing in its place. For more on this and other reasons to update your will periodically, see Chapter 11.

Naming Alternates

To receive property under your will, a beneficiary must survive you by 45 days. WillMaker assumes that if a beneficiary survives you by only a few days or weeks, you would prefer the property to pass to an alternate or residuary beneficiary named in your will, rather than have the property pass along with the beneficiary's other property.

With WillMaker, you can name one or more alternate beneficiaries to take the bequest if your first choices do not survive you by the required period.

> EXAMPLE: Joan leaves her horse to her brother Pierre. In case Pierre does not survive her by 45 days and so become eligible to receive this bequest, Joan names her sister Carmen as Pierre's alternate beneficiary.

If you name multiple beneficiaries to receive property, you can name an alternate for each beneficiary.

> EXAMPLE: Gideon leaves his house to his three nephews—Aaron, Thomas, and Zeke—in equal shares. In case Aaron does not survive him by 45 days, Gideon specifies that the house should then go to the survivors, Thomas and Zeke. In case Thomas does not survive him by 45 days, Gideon names his brother Horace to take Thomas's share. In case Zeke does not survive him by 45 days, Gideon specifies that Aaron and Horace should take Zeke's share.

If you do not name alternates for specific bequests, and the primary beneficiary dies before you do, the property will become part of your residuary estate.

Reviewing Specific Bequests

When you complete a specific bequest—that is, you have identified the property, named the beneficiary, and named an alternate beneficiary—WillMaker will display the beneficiary's name and the text of the bequest. From this screen you can edit or delete this bequest, or you can add a new one.

Naming Residuary Beneficiaries

WillMaker will ask you to name a beneficiary for your residuary estate only if either of the following is true:

- You chose not to name one or more main beneficiaries to receive most or all of your property.
- After leaving all your property to one or more beneficiaries, you chose to create an alternate plan, or Plan B, in case your first-choice beneficiaries do not survive you. In this case, you name a residuary beneficiary as part of your alternate plan.

If you left all or most of your property to one or more beneficiaries, they will receive property that does not pass in a specific bequest or by means other than your will. In effect, they will automatically become your residuary beneficiaries.

EXAMPLE: When Mikki makes her will, she leaves all her property to her husband, Tyler. By the time she dies, 15 years later, she has acquired a new car, stocks, and other items. Everything goes to her husband.

What a Residuary Beneficiary Receives

Your residuary beneficiary receives anything that does not go, for one reason or another, to the beneficiaries you named to receive specific bequests.

Specifically, the residuary beneficiary receives property that:

- you overlook when making your will
- you acquire after you make your will, or
- does not go to the person you named to get it in a specific bequest—for example, because that person died before you did and you did not name an alternate beneficiary, or the alternate also failed to survive you.

EXAMPLE: In her will, Sara leaves many different items to many different beneficiaries: books to her daughter, jewelry to a friend, a car to her nephew, and so on. She doesn't name alternate beneficiaries for these specific bequests, but she names her daughter as residuary beneficiary.

> When Sara dies some years after making the will, the friend to whom she left the jewelry has already died. The jewelry goes to Sara's daughter, as does any other property that Sara acquired after making her will.

There is no need to describe in your will the property the residuary beneficiary will receive. Your residuary estate is the property that does not pass outside of your will or in a specific bequest, so it is impossible to know exactly what it will include. When inventorying your entire estate after your death, your executor will identify your residuary estate.

How to Name Residuary Beneficiaries

You can name one or more individuals or organizations, or a combination of both, as residuary beneficiaries. If you name more than one residuary beneficiary, WillMaker will ask you what shares you want each to receive.

> EXAMPLE: After making a large number of specific bequests in his WillMaker will, Maurice leaves his residuary estate to his four children, Clara, Heinrich, Lise, and Wiebke. He wants Lise and Wiebke each to receive 30% (3/10) of the property and the other two children to each receive 20% (2/10). So, he indicates that he wants to leave the residuary estate in unequal shares and enters the desired shares on the screen provided for this purpose.

If any of the beneficiaries you name is a minor (younger than 18) or young adult (younger than 35), you will have a chance, in a later part of WillMaker, to choose someone to manage the property for them until they are older. (See Chapter 7.)

Naming Alternates

WillMaker also asks you to choose an alternate residuary beneficiary, in case your first choice does not survive you by 45 days.

If you do not name alternates for specific bequests, and the primary beneficiary dies before you do, the property will become part of your residuary estate.

EXAMPLE 1: After making many specific bequests, Alfredo leaves his residuary estate to his daughter, Vanessa. He then specifies that if Vanessa does not survive him, her share should go to her two children—Alfredo's grandchildren—in equal shares. If Vanessa does not survive Alfredo, and Alfredo does not write a new will, Vanessa's children would each take one-half of Alfredo's residuary estate.

EXAMPLE 2: Jack makes a large number of specific bequests to friends and relatives and then leaves his residuary estate to his friend Joe. He names another friend, Josette, as alternate residuary beneficiary. Josette will be entitled to take property under Jack's will only if Joe does not survive Jack by 45 days and there is property left over after the specific bequests are distributed.

Naming a Trust as Beneficiary

If you like, you can also name a trust as a beneficiary of your will. When you die, the property you leave will be transferred to the trust, rather than directly to a person or organization. This is generally done for one of two reasons—either you want all of the property that passes through your will to "pour" into your living trust, or you want to leave property to a loved one's special needs trust.

Leaving property to a living trust with a pour-over will. If you have a living trust, you can use your will to transfer property to the trust after your death. If the primary purpose of your will is to funnel property to a living trust, the will is called a "pour-over" will.

Making a pour-over will means you don't have to transfer every minor asset into your living trust. Also, if you name your trust as the sole beneficiary or the residuary beneficiary of your will, the pour-over will covers any property that you might have neglected to transfer to the trust during your life. This can be useful if you want to distribute all or most of your property under the terms of your trust, rather than having beneficiary scenarios in both documents.

However, there's one important thing to keep in mind when you make a pour-over will: The property you leave to your trust through the will might have to go through probate when you die. Because living trusts are designed to avoid probate, if you leave too much property through your will, you might end up thwarting your own best intentions—ending up with property in probate and holding up the distribution of property in your trust.

With that important understanding in mind, most people who make pour-over wills leave most or all of their property through the living trust or through other beneficiary designations (such as life insurance), so that very little property ends up passing through the will. Whatever approach you take, before you make a pour-over will, be sure you know how much property your state allows you to pass through your will without triggering probate proceedings. (For more information about probate and how to avoid it, see Chapter 13.)

To use your will to leave property to your living trust, name your trust as beneficiary for that property using the trustee's name and the name of the trust. (For example: "John Doe as trustee of the John Doe Living Trust, dated January 1, 20xx.")

Leaving property to a special needs trust. Special needs trusts allow people with disabilities to receive additional support without risking their eligibility for government benefits. Money or property given directly to people with disabilities is likely to interfere with their ability to receive disability benefits. For this reason, if a loved one has a special needs trust, instead of naming that person as a beneficiary of your will, you might want to name that trust. To name a special needs trust as a beneficiary of your will, enter the name of the trustee and the full legal name of the trust as beneficiary (for example, "Margaret P. Lee as the trustee of The Fredrick M. Lee Special Needs Trust").

RESOURCE

Learn more about special needs trusts. You'll find more information about special needs trusts in *Special Needs Trusts: Protect Your Child's Financial Future,* by Kevin Urbatsch and Jessica Farinas Jones (Nolo). You can access an electronic version of this book online via your WillMaker customer portal or on the Books screen of the download version.

CHAPTER

7

Providing Management for Children's Property

Except for items of little value, minors are not permitted by law to receive property directly. This legal rule is most important if the property is:

- cash or other liquid assets—for example, a savings account that can easily be spent, or
- property that comes with a title document—for example, real estate.

Instead, that property will have to be distributed to and managed by a responsible adult. It is of vital importance—to both your own children and any other young beneficiaries—that you arrange for this management yourself, in your will. If you don't, a court might need to appoint and supervise someone—an expensive and time-consuming alternative. It's better to make your own choice and state it in your will, instead of leaving the decision to someone else.

TIP

Keeping track of children's property. The person you name to take care of your child's property will need access to financial records related to property that the child will own. For help collecting this information, use the Information for Caregivers and Survivors form (in the download version of WillMaker).

Property management consists of naming a trusted adult to care for a young person's property until the minor turns a specific age. The property being managed must be held, invested, or spent in the best interest of the minor. In other words, someone other than the young person will decide if the inheritance will be spent on college tuition or a new car.

With WillMaker you can establish management for two types of property:

- property you pass to minors through your will (they do not have to be your own children), and
- property that your children might acquire outside of your will.

For property received under your will, this management can last until the minor turns an age you choose (up to age 35). For property that your minor children receive outside of your will, the management provided by WillMaker lasts until the children become adults—18 years old in most states.

What Happens If the Minor Does Not Get Property

If you arrange for property management for a minor, but the minor never actually becomes entitled to the property, no harm is done. The management provisions for that minor are ignored. For instance, suppose you identify a favorite niece to take property as an alternate beneficiary and provide management for that property until the niece turns 25. If the niece never gets to take the property because your first-choice beneficiary survives you, no property management will be established for her, since none will be needed.

Property Management for Property That Passes Under Your Will

WillMaker offers three approaches to property management for property that passes to minors under your will:

- the Uniform Transfers to Minors Act
- the WillMaker child's trust, and
- the WillMaker pot trust, an option if you have two or more children and at least one of them is younger than 25 years.

The Uniform Transfers to Minors Act

The Uniform Transfers to Minors Act (UTMA) allows you to name a custodian in your will to manage property you leave to a minor. The management ends when the minor reaches age 18 to 30, depending on state law.

Terminology for This Chapter

This chapter uses a lot of words that sound the same but have different meanings. Here's a cheat sheet for how these terms are used in WillMaker.

	Property management	**UTMA custodianship**	**Child's trust**	**Pot trust**	**Property guardianship**
Lets you…	name an adult to manage a young person's property; an umbrella term for the management of children's property	leave property to a minor under standard "uniform" laws	leave property to young people in individual trusts	leave property to your young children as a group	provide property management for any property your children receive outside of your will
Property covered is…	property transferred to a young person through your will	property transferred to a young person through your will	property transferred to a young person through your will	property left to your children through your will	property your children receive outside of your will, such as income or inheritance
Title of adult who manages the property	property manager	custodian	trustee	trustee	property guardian
The minor gets the property at age…	n/a	18–30, depending on state law	18–35, depending on will maker's choice	18–25 (age of youngest child), depending on will maker's choice	18
Benefits	n/a	low maintenance; familiar to financial institutions	flexible end-age; private	flexible end-age; private; trustee distributes group gift according to the relative needs of the children	allows you to have a say in who should manage property your child receives outside of your will

You may use the UTMA to specify a custodian to manage property you leave to a minor in your will. The custodian will manage the property until the age at which the laws of your state require that it be turned over to the minor. (See the chart below.)

Special Rule for Life Insurance

Often the major source of property left to children comes from a life insurance policy naming the children as beneficiaries. If you want the insurance proceeds for a particular child to be managed, instruct your insurance agent to provide you with the form necessary to name a custodian to manage the property for the beneficiary under the terms of this act.

Florida and Virginia Have Unique UTMA Rules

In Florida and Virginia, you can create an UTMA custodianship that will end when a young beneficiary reaches 25. However, if you choose age 25, the custodian must give the beneficiary the opportunity to terminate the custodianship (and receive custodial property outright) within a month of the beneficiary's 21st birthday. In other words, even if you want a young beneficiary's property management to end at age 25, the beneficiary can choose to take the gift four years earlier. To avoid this possibility, use a child's trust instead, or get help from an experienced Florida or Virginia estate planning attorney. (Fla. Stat. § 710.123; Va. Code §§ 64.2-1908 and 64.2-1919.)

Among the powers the UTMA gives the custodian are the rights to collect, hold, manage, invest, and reinvest the property and to spend it "for the use and benefit of the minor." All of these actions can be taken without getting approval from a court. The custodian must also keep records so that tax returns can be filed on behalf of the minor and must otherwise act prudently in controlling the property.

UTMA Age Limits

State	Age at Which Minor Gets Property	State	Age at Which Minor Gets Property
Alabama	21	Montana	21
Alaska	18 to 25	Nebraska	21
Arizona	21 to 25	Nevada	18 to 25
Arkansas	18 to 21	New Hampshire	21
California	18 to 25	New Jersey	18 to 21
Colorado	21	New Mexico	21
Connecticut	21	New York	21
Delaware	21	North Carolina	18 to 21
District of Columbia	18 to 21	North Dakota	21
		Ohio	21 to 25
Florida	21 or 25*	Oklahoma	18 to 21
Georgia	21	Oregon	21 to 25
Hawaii	21	Pennsylvania	21 to 25
Idaho	21	Rhode Island	21
Illinois	21	South Carolina	21
Indiana	21	South Dakota	18
Iowa	21	Tennessee	21 to 25
Kansas	21	Texas	21
Kentucky	18	Utah	21
Maine	18 to 21	Vermont	21
Maryland	21	Virginia	18, 21, or 25*
Massachusetts	21	Washington	21 to 25
Michigan	18 to 21	West Virginia	21
Minnesota	21	Wisconsin	21
Mississippi	18	Wyoming	21 to 30
Missouri	21		

* In Florida and Virginia, the minor can choose to receive UTMA funds at age 21, even if the account is set to terminate at a later age.

The WillMaker Child's Trust

The WillMaker child's trust, which can be used in all states, is a legal structure you establish in your will. If you create a trust, any property a minor beneficiary gets will be managed by a person or an institution you choose to serve as trustee until the beneficiary turns an age you choose—through age 35. The trustee's powers are listed in your will. The trustee can use trust assets for the education, medical needs, and living expenses of the beneficiary. All property you leave to a beneficiary for whom a trust is established will be managed under the terms of the trust.

When Will Property Management End?

The age at which property management ends depends on the type of management you select:

- **UTMA.** State law determines when property management ends. In some states, you can choose from a limited age range. (See "UTMA Age Limits," above.)
- **WillMaker's child's trust.** The trust ends when the child turns an age you choose, up to age 35.
- **WillMaker's pot trust.** The trust ends when your youngest child turns an age you choose, up to age 25.
- **Other property management.** Property management for property your child receives outside of your will ends when the child becomes a legal adult—age 18 in most states.

Because management under the WillMaker child's trust can be extended through age 35, it is also suitable to use for property left to young adults. (The pros and cons of management options are discussed in "Choosing Among Management Options," below.)

The WillMaker Pot Trust

The WillMaker pot trust is a legal structure you can establish in your will. However, instead of creating a separate child's trust for the property you leave to each child, you create one trust for all the property you leave to your children. You name a single trustee to manage the property for the benefit of the children as a group, without regard to how much is spent on an individual child.

For example, if there are three children and one of them needs an expensive medical procedure, all of the property could be spent on that child, even though the other children would receive nothing. While this potential result might seem unfair, it in fact mirrors the reality faced by many families: Some children need more money than others do.

The pot trust will last until the youngest child turns an age you specify, up to age 25. A word of caution: If there is a significant age gap between your children, the oldest children might have to wait many years past the time they become adults before they receive their shares of the property. For instance, if one of your children is 5 and another child is 17—and you specify that the pot trust should end when the youngest turns 18—the 17-year-old will have to wait at least until age 30 to receive a share of the property left in the trust.

CAUTION

All or none must go in the pot. WillMaker's pot trust option is available only for property you leave to all of your children as a group. If you want to use the pot trust for some but not all of your children, you will need to see a lawyer. (See Chapter 17.)

Choosing Among Management Options

For each minor or young adult to whom you leave property in your will, you must decide which management approach to use: the UTMA, a child's trust, or the pot trust. This section helps you decide which is best.

For other situations described here, get help from an experienced estate planning attorney. (See Chapter 17.)

Using the UTMA

As a general rule, the less valuable the property involved and the more mature the child, the more appropriate the UTMA is, because it is simpler to use than a child's trust or pot trust. There are a couple of reasons for this.

Needs Not Covered by WillMaker's Will

The property management features offered by WillMaker—the UTMA, child's trust, and pot trust—provide the property manager with broad management authority adequate for most minors and young adults. However, they are not designed to:

- provide skilled, long-term management of a business
- provide for management of funds beyond age 35 for a person with spendthrift tendencies or other personal habits that might impede sound financial management beyond young adulthood, or
- meet the special needs of beneficiaries who have disabilities. A physical, mental, or developmental disability will likely require management customized to the beneficiary's circumstances, both to perpetuate the beneficiary's way of life and to preserve the property, while ensuring that the beneficiary continues to qualify for government benefits.

To learn more about trusts for people with disabilities, read *Special Needs Trusts: Protect Your Child's Financial Future,* by Kevin Urbatsch and Jessica Farinas Jones (Nolo). You can access an electronic version of this book online via your WillMaker customer portal or on the Books screen of the download version.

Because the UTMA is built into state law, banks, insurance companies, brokerage firms, and other financial institutions know about it, so it should be easy for the custodian to carry out property management duties. To set up a child's trust or pot trust, the financial institution would have to be given a copy of the trust document and can tie up the proceeding in red tape to be sure the trustee is acting under its terms.

Also, a custodian acting under the UTMA need not file a separate income tax return for the property being managed; it can be included in the young beneficiary's return. However, in a child's trust or a pot trust, both the beneficiary and the trust must file returns.

Because the UTMA requires that management end at a relatively young age, consider using the UTMA if:

- the property you are leaving is likely to run out before the UTMA ends (see the chart "UTMA Age Limits," above), or
- the child is likely to be able to handle their inheritance at a relatively young age.

Using the WillMaker Child's Trust

Generally, the more property is worth and the less mature the young beneficiary, the better it is to use the child's trust, even though doing so creates more work for the property manager than does using the UTMA. For example, in a child's trust, the property manager must keep the beneficiary informed, manage trust assets prudently (meeting the requirements of state law), and file a separate tax return for the trust each year.

However, if a minor or young adult stands to get a fairly large amount of property—a sum that could last into the child's 20s—you might not want it all distributed by your state's UTMA cutoff age. In such circumstances, you might be better off using the WillMaker child's trust. Under the child's trust, management can last until an age you choose, up to age 35 in any state.

Choosing an age for a particular beneficiary to get whatever trust property has not been spent on the beneficiary's needs will depend on:

- the amount of money or other property involved
- how much control you would like to impose over it
- the beneficiary's likely level of maturity as a young adult (for small children, this might be difficult to predict, but by the time youngsters reach their teens, you should have a pretty good indication), and

- whether the property you leave, such as rental property or a small business, needs sophisticated management that a young beneficiary is unlikely to master.

Using the WillMaker Pot Trust

WillMaker's pot trust option is available to you as long as you have two or more children, and at least one of those children is younger than age 25. As a general rule, the pot trust makes the most sense when your children are fairly close in age. This is because the older child will have to wait until the younger child comes of age, so if there is a big age gap, the older child might have to wait too long for their inheritance. For instance, if your children are ages 10 and 20, and you specify that the pot trust should end when the younger child turns 25, the 20-year-old would have to wait until age 35 to receive the property.

Like the trustee of a child's trust, a pot trust trustee must invest trust assets following the rules set out in state law, communicate regularly with the trust beneficiaries to keep them informed, and file annual tax returns. The trustee of the pot trust also has the significant added responsibility of weighing competing claims from the children when deciding how to spend trust assets.

Property Management for Property That Does Not Pass Under Your Will

When you name trustees or custodians to manage property that passes to your minor children through your will, those adults won't automatically have the power to manage property that your minor children acquire from other places. In your will, you can name a person to manage any other property that your children might acquire. If you don't, a court will usually have to step in and appoint a guardian to manage the property under court supervision until the children turn 18.

What property might your children acquire outside of your will? They might receive an inheritance, a life insurance payout, or gifts from relatives. They might also earn money by working, performing, inventing something, or through social media content. Some types of property might come with property management. For example, an inheritance through a trust would be managed by that trust's trustee. And a life insurance payout might be set up to be managed under the UTMA.

It is almost always best to name a property guardian for each of your children in your will, just in case your children do acquire unmanaged property when they are still minors. If needed, a property guardian will manage your child's property until that child turns 18—at that time, the child will receive the property outright. If a property guardian is needed and you haven't named one in your will, a court will likely appoint someone to manage your child's property.

If you are using the WillMaker child's trust, a pot trust, or the UTMA to provide management for property you are leaving to your children in your will, the person you have named as trustee or custodian would also be a good choice for property guardian. Another possible choice is the person you chose to be personal guardian, if you think that person would handle the property wisely for the benefit of the minor. You also might wish to choose someone else entirely. Next are some tips to help you pick the right person.

Naming a Custodian, Trustee, or Property Manager

In WillMaker's will, you can name one person at a time to manage the property of a minor. This is true for each of the property management systems offered—the UTMA, child's trust, pot trust, and general property management for property that passes outside of your will. For each, you can also name one alternate who will take over if your first choice is unable to serve.

Choosing someone to do these jobs is an important decision. Name someone you trust, who is competent with finances and who shares your attitudes and values about how the money should be spent.

CAUTION

Parents do not get the job automatically. You might be surprised to learn that the child's other parent probably will not be able to automatically step in and handle property you leave your children in your will. Rather, unless you provide for management in your will, that other parent usually will have to petition the court to be appointed as the property manager and then handle the property under court supervision until the children turn 18. So, if you want your children's other parent to manage the property you are leaving your children, name that person to manage your children's property.

Keep in mind that you can only name the other parent as custodian or trustee if there is a chance that the other parent will be alive when the child receives the gift. For example, if you leave a gift to the other parent and you name the child as alternate for that gift, you cannot name the other parent to be trustee or custodian of that gift because the child would receive the property only if the other parent were not alive.

Whomever you choose, it is essential to get that person's consent first. This will also give you a chance to discuss, in general terms, how you would like the property to be managed, to be sure the person you select agrees with your vision and fully understands the beneficiary's needs.

As a general rule, name a trusted adult who lives in or near to the state where the property will be managed—or is at least willing to travel there if needed.

You need not worry about finding a financial wizard to be property manager because that person will have the power to hire professionals to prepare accountings and tax returns and to give investment advice. Anyone hired for such help can be paid out of the property being managed. The main job is to manage the property honestly, make basic decisions about how to take care of the assets wisely, and sensibly mete out the money to the trust beneficiary.

It is usually preferable to combine the personal care and property management functions for a particular minor child in the hands of one person. Think first who is likely to be caring for the children if you die, and then consider whether that person is also a good choice for property manager.

Selecting an Institution as Trustee

If you are using the UTMA, you must name a person as custodian; you cannot name an institution. If you're creating a trust, you can name an institution to serve as trustee, but it is rarely a good idea. Most banks will not accept a trust with less than several hundred thousand dollars' worth of liquid assets. Most institutional trustees will accept trustee duties only if a trust includes their own specific trust language, making it unlikely that they would accept appointment as trustee of a trust created by a WillMaker will.

When banks do agree to take a trust, they charge large management and administrative fees. All trustees are entitled to reasonable compensation for their services—paid from trust assets. But family members or close friends who act as trustees often waive payments or accept far less than banks. If you cannot find an individual you think is suitable for handling your assets and do not have enough property to be managed by a financial institution, you might be better off not creating a trust.

Also, it is common for banks to manage the assets of all trusts worth less than $1 million as part of one large fund, while charging fees as if they were individually managed. Any noninstitutional trustee who invests trust money in a conservatively run mutual fund can normally do at least as well at a fraction of the cost.

If you believe that the person who will be caring for the minor is not the best person to handle the minor's finances, consider another adult who is capable and is willing to serve. If you must name two different people, try to choose people who get along well, because they will have to work together.

For property you leave to young adults who are too old to have a personal guardian, select an honest person with business savvy to manage the property.

EXAMPLE: Orenthal and Ariadne agree that Ariadne's sister, Penny, should be guardian of their kids should they both die, but that the $200,000 worth of stock the three kids will inherit might better be handled by someone with more business experience and who will be better able to resist the children's urgings to spend the money frivolously. In each of their wills, they name Penny as personal guardian of the children, but also create trusts for the property they are leaving to their children. They name each other as trustees of the trusts. They name Orenthal's mother as an alternate because she has investment and business knowledge and lots of experience in handling headstrong adolescents. Before finalizing their wills, they talk with her to confirm that she'll do that job and that she'll be able to work well with Penny.

Examples of Property Management

Here are some examples of how WillMaker's property management options might be selected. The following scenarios are intended only as suggestions.

EXAMPLE 1: **Married, adult children age 25 and older.** You want to leave all your property, worth $250,000, to your spouse and name surviving children as alternate beneficiaries. As long as you think the children are all sufficiently mature to handle their shares of the property if your spouse does not survive you, answer no when WillMaker asks if you wish to set up property management.

EXAMPLE 2: **Married, children aged two, five, and nine.** You want to leave all your property, which is worth $250,000, to your spouse and name your children as alternate beneficiaries. You use the property management feature and select the UTMA option to manage the property if it passes to your children. You name your wife's mother—the same person you have named as personal guardian—as custodian and name your brother as alternate personal guardian and alternate custodian. The property will be managed by the custodian until the age set by your state's law.

You also name your wife's mother as property guardian if management is needed for property your minor children receive outside of your will.

Later, when your children are older (and when you might have accumulated more property), you might wish to make a new will and switch from the UTMA management approach to a pot trust so that the property can be used to meet the children's needs as required.

EXAMPLE 3: **Partnered, two minor children from a previous marriage and one minor child with your present partner.** You want to leave all your property, which is worth $250,000, directly to your children. You can use the UTMA, set up a trust for each child, or create a pot trust. You should also name a property guardian to manage any property your minor child might get outside of your will. Consider naming your partner (or the children's other parent, depending on the circumstances) to manage the children's property, and choose another trusted adult as an alternate.

CAUTION

Beware property rights of spouses and registered partners. If you are married or in a registered partnership, your spouse or partner might have a right to claim a portion of your property, so it is usually unwise to leave it all to your children unless your spouse or partner agrees with that plan. (See "Property Ownership Rules for Married People" in Chapter 5.)

EXAMPLE 4: **Second marriage, two adult children from a previous marriage—ages 23 and 27—and one 15-year-old child with your current spouse.** You leave half of your $2 million estate to your spouse and leave the other half to be divided equally among the three children. To accomplish this, you establish a trust for each child from the previous marriage and put the termination age at 30. You name your current spouse, who gets along well with the children, as trustee and a local trust company as alternate trustee. For your third and unusually mature child, you choose the UTMA naming your spouse as custodian and your sister as successor custodian. The UTMA will end at age 25 (an option in your state), and at that time the third child will receive outright any property that remains in the UTMA account.

EXAMPLE 5: **One daughter, age 32, and three minor grandchildren.** You want to leave $50,000 directly to each of your grandchildren. You establish a custodianship under the UTMA for each grandchild and name your daughter as custodian and her husband as successor custodian.

CHAPTER

8

Your Executor

You should name an executor to wrap up your will. After your death, that person will have legal responsibility for safeguarding and handling your property, seeing that debts and taxes are paid, and distributing what is left to your beneficiaries as your will directs.

Some states use the term "personal representative" instead of "executor," but it means the same thing. If you live in one of these states, you will see the term "personal representative" in your will.

TIP

Make your will and records accessible. You can help with the executor's first task: locating your will. Keep the original in a fairly obvious place—such as a desk or file cabinet. Make sure your executor knows where it is and has access to it.

Duties of an Executor

Serving as an executor can be fairly easy, or it can require a good deal of time and patience—depending on the amount of property involved and the complexity of the plans for it.

The Executor's Job

Your executor will have a number of duties, most of which do not require special expertise and can usually be accomplished without outside help. An executor typically must:

- obtain certified copies of the death certificate
- locate will beneficiaries
- examine and inventory the deceased person's safe deposit boxes
- collect the deceased person's mail
- cancel or close credit cards, subscriptions, and accounts
- notify Social Security and other benefit plan administrators of the death

- learn about the deceased person's property—which can involve examining bank account records, deeds, insurance policies, tax returns, and many other records
- get bank accounts released or, in the case of pay-on-death accounts, get them transferred to their new owner
- collect any death benefits from life insurance policies, Social Security, veterans benefits, and other benefits due from the deceased's union, fraternal society, or employer, and
- follow any instructions left by the deceased person about their digital assets.

In addition, the executor will typically have to:

- file papers in court to start the probate process and obtain the necessary authority to act as executor
- handle the probate court process—which involves transferring property and making sure the deceased's final debts and taxes are paid, and
- prepare final income tax forms for the deceased and, if necessary, file estate tax returns for the estate (rare).

For these tasks, it might be necessary to hire outside professionals who will be paid out of the estate's assets—a lawyer to initiate and handle the probate process and an accountant to prepare the necessary tax forms. But in some states, because of simplified court procedures and adequate self-help law materials, it might be possible to accomplish these tasks without outside assistance.

For help with the task of educating your executor, you can print out documents titled Letter to Executor and Letter to Alternate Executor, which you can give to those you name to serve. These documents offer guidance on the executor's duties.

RESOURCE

More help for executors. For a complete guide to an executor's duties and details about how to wrap up an estate, see *The Executor's Guide: Settling a Loved One's Estate or Trust*, by Mary Randolph and Jennie Lin (Nolo).

Note for Texas Residents: Independent Administration

Like many states, Texas offers a simplified probate process. In the Lone Star State, it's called "independent administration" and it gives an executor broad powers to act without supervision of the probate court. For example, an independent executor can pay final bills and distribute property without the court's oversight.

Unlike other states, Texas requires a will to contain a bit of special language to request this simplified process. That's why your WillMaker will refers to your executor as your "independent executor" and includes the required language that permits the independent administration of your estate. (Tex. Est. Code § 401.001.)

SEE AN EXPERT

When to see a lawyer. We've designed your will to request independent administration because it saves money and speeds up probate. If you want your executor to work under the close supervision of a court, see an experienced estate planning attorney for advice.

Posting a Bond

Sometimes, a probate court asks an executor to post a bond—an insurance policy that protects beneficiaries if the executor is dishonest or incompetent. Some probate courts require bonds for all executors, while others require bonds only for out-of-state executors. However, many courts won't demand a bond if the will says that no bond is required.

The will you make with WillMaker expressly states that no bond is necessary. As long as you choose an executor you trust, there's no reason to require your executor to post a bond. Furthermore, the cost of the bond—usually about 10% of its face amount—comes out of your estate, so your beneficiaries receive less than they would if no bond was purchased.

SEE AN EXPERT

If you want to require a bond. If you're less than confident about your executor's competence or you feel that the extra insurance of a bond is worth the cost, see an experienced estate planning attorney for help.

Access to Your Digital Assets

Your executor might need access to your digital assets to pay bills, to distribute property, or to follow any instructions you leave about what to do with your online accounts. Your WillMaker will gives your executor the power to access and control all of your digital assets—including email, social media, blogs, online file storage, and financial accounts. However, your executor's legal authority to handle your digital property might depend on the law in your state, any opt-in arrangements you've made with the company about the fate of your digital assets, why your executor needs access, and each company's terms of service agreement.

The simplest way to ensure that your executor will be able to access your digital assets after you die is for you to leave explicit login information and instructions in a separate letter. Doing this will allow your executor to manage your accounts without relying on government laws or company policies. See Chapter 12 for more about leaving this information.

To learn more about your executor's ability to access your accounts, go to www.nolo.com/legal-encyclopedia/digital-assets.

SEE AN EXPERT

See a lawyer if you want to restrict your executor's access. WillMaker's will gives your executor broad access to your digital assets. So if you have digital files or online accounts that you don't want your executor to see, do not use this will. Moreover, even if you have not given permission, your state's laws might allow your executor to access any digital assets needed to wrap up your estate. If you prefer to limit your executor's access to your digital assets, get help from an attorney.

Getting Paid

The laws of every state provide that an executor can be paid out of the estate. Depending on your state law, this payment can be:

- based on what the court considers reasonable
- a small percentage of the gross or net value of the estate, or
- set according to factors specified in your state's statutes.

An executor who either stands to get a large portion of the estate or is a close family member commonly does the work without being paid. Some will makers opt to leave their executors a specific bequest of money in appreciation for serving.

The will you make with WillMaker won't explicitly state whether your executor will be paid. Instead, your document will say that your executor has all of the powers that your state allows—and this includes the power to pay themself for the work of settling your affairs. So it will be up to your executor to decide whether or not the executor will be paid. This allows your executor to make a decision about this based on the actual circumstances—for example, how much time and effort it takes to settle your estate and whether the estate has enough money to pay the executor. If you would prefer your will to include an explicit payment clause, see a lawyer for help.

Outside experts will almost always be paid out of the estate. The amount experts—including lawyers—are paid is totally under the control of the executor. However, a few states set out fees that can be charged by lawyers and other professionals—usually a percentage of the value of the estate.

CAUTION

Beware of lawyers' fees. Lawyers commonly imply that the fee allowed by statute is the fee that they are required to charge for their services. In fact, lawyers are perfectly free to charge by the hour or to set a flat fee that is unrelated to the size of the estate. One of the most important tasks that your executor can perform is to negotiate a reasonable fee with a lawyer to help probate your estate. Be sure you explain this to your choice for executor.

Naming an Executor

Glancing through the list of the executor's duties mentioned above should tip you off about who might be the best person for the job. The prime characteristics are honesty, skill at organizing, and finesse in keeping track of details. For many tasks, such as collecting mail and finding important records and papers, it might be most helpful to name someone who lives nearby or who is familiar with your business matters.

Choosing Your Executor

The most important guideline in naming an executor is to choose someone you trust enough to have access to your personal records and finances after your death. Many people choose someone who is also named to get a substantial amount of property under the will. This is sensible, because a person with an interest in how your property is distributed—a spouse, partner, child, or close family member—is also likely to do a conscientious job as executor. And that person might also know where you keep your records and why you want your property split up as you have directed.

Following are a few more things you might want to consider when making your choice. Whomever you choose, make sure the person you select is willing to do the job. Discuss with your choice for executor the possible duties involved before naming that person in your will.

SEE AN EXPERT

Avoid naming someone with a criminal history. Many states prohibit people who have committed felonies (or lesser crimes related to the job, like embezzlement or elder abuse) from serving as executor. That said, some states do allow felons to serve under specific circumstances. So if your best choice for executor is a person with a criminal history, get help from an attorney to ensure that your choice will have the best chance to serve. (See these statues as examples of laws that prohibit or limit a felon's qualification to serve as executor: Fla. Stat. § 733.303; 755 Ill. Comp. Stat. § 5/6-13; Ind. Code § 29-1-10-1; and Tex. Est. Code § 304.003.)

Restrictions on Out-of-State Executors	
Arkansas	Nonresident executor must appoint an agent who lives in the county where probate is conducted to accept legal papers. (Ark. Code § 28-48-101(b)(6))
Connecticut	Nonresident executor must appoint in-state probate court judge as agent to accept legal papers. (Conn. Gen. Stat. § 52-60)
Delaware	Nonresident executor must appoint county register of wills as the agent to accept legal papers. (Del. Code tit. 12, § 1506)
District of Columbia	Nonresident executor must appoint the probate register as agent to accept legal papers. (D.C. Code §§ 20-303, 20-343)
Florida	Nonresident can be appointed executor only if related by blood, marriage, or adoption to person making will. (Fla. Stat. § 733.304)
Illinois	Nonresident executor may be required to post bond, even if will expressly states bond not required. (755 Ill. Comp. Stat. § 5/6-13)
Indiana	Nonresident must post a bond and either serve with a coexecutor or appoint an in-state agent to accept legal papers. (Ind. Code § 29-1-10-1)
Iowa	Nonresident can serve as executor only if serving with a resident coexecutor, unless court allows nonresident to serve alone. (Iowa Code § 633.64)
Kansas	Nonresident executor must appoint an agent who lives in the county where probate is conducted to accept legal papers. (Kan. Stat. § 59-1706)
Kentucky	Nonresident can be appointed executor only if related by blood, marriage, or adoption to person making will. (Ky. Rev. Stat. § 395.005)
Maryland	Nonresident executor must appoint an in-state agent to accept legal papers. (Md. Code Est. & Trusts, §§ 5-105, 5-503)
Missouri	Nonresident executor must appoint an in-state agent to accept legal papers. (Mo. Rev. Stat. § 473.117)

Restrictions on Out-of-State Executors (continued)	
New Hampshire	Nonresident executor must be approved by probate judge and must appoint an in-state agent to accept legal papers. (N.H. Rev. Stat. §§ 553:5, 553:25)
New Jersey	Nonresident must post bond unless will waives the requirement. (N.J. Stat. § 3B: 15-1)
New York	Non–U.S. citizen who lives outside of New York can serve as executor only with a resident coexecutor and with court approval. (N.Y. Surr. Ct. Proc. Act § 707)
North Carolina	Nonresident executor must appoint an in-state agent to accept legal papers. (N.C. Gen. Stat. § 28A-4-2)
Ohio	Nonresident can be executor if the nonresident either (1) is related by blood, marriage, or adoption to person making will, (2) is a private trust company, or (3) lives in a state that permits nonresidents to serve. (Ohio Rev. Code § 2109.21)
Oklahoma	Nonresident executor must appoint an agent who lives in the county where probate is conducted to accept legal papers. (Okla. Stat. tit. 58, § 162)
Pennsylvania	Nonresident can serve as executor only with the permission of the register of wills. (Register may refuse to allow a nonresident to serve as administrator.) (20 Pa. Cons. Stat. § 3157)
Rhode Island	Nonresident executor must appoint an in-state agent to accept legal papers. (R.I. Gen. Laws §§ 33-8-7, 33-18-9)
Tennessee	Nonresident executor must appoint secretary of state as agent to accept legal papers and may be required to post bond. Nonresident can also serve with a resident coexecutor. (Tenn. Code § 35-50-107)
Texas	Nonresident executor must appoint an in-state agent to accept legal papers. (Tex. Est. Code § 304.003)
Vermont	Nonresident executor must appoint an in-state agent to accept legal papers. (Vt. Stat. tit. 14, § 904)

Restrictions on Out-of-State Executors (continued)	
Virginia	Nonresident executor can be appointed only with court approval and must appoint an in-state agent to accept legal papers. Bond may be required unless nonresident serves with a resident coexecutor. (Va. Code § 64.2-1426)
Washington	Nonresident executor must post a bond and appoint an agent in the county where probate is conducted to accept legal papers. If nonresident is surviving spouse and sole beneficiary of will, or if will expressly states so, bond is not required. (Wash. Rev. Code §§ 11.28.185, 11.36.010)
West Virginia	Nonresident executor may serve if clerk of the county commission of the county where the probate is conducted serves as nonresident's agent. Nonresident must post bond unless will says otherwise. (W. Va. Code § 44-5-3)
Wisconsin	Nonresident executor must appoint an in-state agent to accept legal papers. At court's discretion, nonresident executor can be removed or refused appointment solely on grounds of residency. (Wis. Stat. § 856.23)
Wyoming	Nonresident executor must appoint an in-state agent to accept legal papers. (Wyo. Stat. § 2-11-301)

Naming Someone Who Lives Out of State

As a practical matter, it's wise to name an executor who lives close to you. It will be more difficult for the executor to handle day-to-day matters from a distance. But if the best person for the job lives far away, there's no law against naming that person in your will. Every state allows out-of-state executors to serve, though many states will require a bond and most states impose special rules on out-of-state executors. The table above sets out the details.

Naming More Than One Person

While you can name two executors or two alternate executors to serve together, doing so is often not wise. Joint executors can act without each other's consent—and if they ever disagree, your estate might be the loser because of lengthy probate delays and court costs.

Naming an Institution

While it is almost always best to choose a trusted person for the job, you might not know anyone who is up to the task of winding up your estate—especially if your estate is large and complicated and your beneficiaries are either very old, very young, or just inexperienced in financial matters. If so, you can select a professional management firm to act as your executor.

If you are considering naming an institution as executor, be sure the one you choose is willing to accept the job—most won't unless your estate is fairly large. Also, institutions charge a hefty fee for acting as executor. They might charge both a percentage of the value of property to be managed and a number of smaller fees for routine services, such as buying and selling property.

If You Do Not Name an Executor

If you do not name an executor in your will, the document will still be valid. But your decision will not have been a wise one. It will most often mean that a court will have to scurry to come up with a willing relative to serve. If that fails, the court will probably appoint someone to do the job who is likely to be unfamiliar with you, your property, and your beneficiaries. People appointed by the court to serve are usually called administrators.

The laws in many states provide that anyone who is entitled under the will to take more than half a person's property has first priority to serve as executor. If no such person is apparent, courts will generally look for someone to serve among the following groups of people, in the following order:

- surviving spouse or registered partner
- children
- grandchildren
- great-grandchildren
- parents
- brothers and sisters
- grandparents

- uncles, aunts, first cousins
- children of a deceased spouse or partner
- other next of kin
- relatives of a deceased spouse or partner
- conservator or guardian
- public administrator
- creditors, and
- any other person.

Naming an Alternate

In case you name someone to serve as executor who dies before you do or for any other reason cannot take on the responsibilities, you should name at least one alternate to serve instead.

You can name up to two levels of alternate executors—called your first alternate and second alternate:

- **First alternate.** Your first alternate will serve only if your primary executor(s) cannot. It's usually best to name just one person to serve as first alternate, but if you feel it is necessary, you can name two people to serve together. (See "Naming More Than One Person," above, for the pitfalls of naming coexecutors.)
- **Second alternate.** Your second alternate will serve only if your executor(s) and first alternate(s) cannot. You can name only one second alternate.

EXAMPLE: Marsha names Bill and Jane as her coexecutors. She then names Susan as first alternate and Keith as second alternate. When Marsha dies, if either Bill or Jane is unavailable to be the executor of her estate, the other will serve alone. If both Bill and Jane are unavailable, Susan will serve. In the unlikely event that Bill, Jane, and Susan are all unavailable, it will be up to Keith to wrap up Marsha's estate.

In choosing an alternate executor, consider the same factors you did in naming your first choice. (See "Choosing Your Executor," above.)

CHAPTER

9

Debts, Expenses, and Taxes

Money matters have a way of living on—even after your death. People might owe you money, you might have debts (including funeral or burial expenses), or your estate might owe taxes when you die. While you're organizing your end-of-life affairs, consider also what will happen with regard to money you owe or money that is owed to you.

TIP

Keeping track of your debts, expenses, and taxes. At your death, your executor and other survivors might need to learn about the debts you owed and that others owed to you during your life. For help collecting and recording this information, use WillMaker's Information for Caregivers and Survivors form (in the download version of WillMaker). See "Organizing Your Records" in Chapter 1.

Debts Others Owe to You

You can release anyone who owes you a debt from the responsibility of paying it back to your estate after you die. You can use your WillMaker will to cancel any such debt—oral or written. If you do, your forgiveness functions much the same as giving a gift; those who were indebted to you will no longer be legally required to pay the money they owed.

One caveat: You might not be able to use your will to forgive debts if your estate is insolvent. In other words, if there isn't enough money in your estate to pay your own debts, you might not be able to forgive debts owed to you. If you think you might die owing large debts, see a lawyer for advice.

Also, keep in mind that releasing people or institutions from the debts they owe you might diminish the property that your beneficiaries receive under your will.

WillMaker prompts you to describe any debt you wish to cancel—including the name of the person who owes it, the approximate date the debt was incurred, and the amount you wish to forgive. This information is important so that the debt can be properly identified.

Explaining Your Intention

If you forgive a debt, it is likely to come as a pleasant surprise to those living with the expectation that they must repay it. And you will probably give the gesture considerable thought before including such a direction in your will. While the final document will contain a brief clause stating your intention, you might wish to explain your reasoning beyond this simple statement. If you wish to do so, it is best to write your explanation in a brief letter that you attach to your will. (See Chapter 12.)

CAUTION

Caution for married or legally partnered people. If you want to use your will to forgive a debt and the debt was incurred while you were married or legally partnered, you might only have the right to forgive half the debt. There is a special need to be cautious about this possibility in community property states. If your debt is a community property debt, you cannot cancel the whole amount due unless your spouse or partner agrees to allow you to cancel their share of the debt—and puts that agreement in writing.

Debts and Taxes You Owe

If you live owing money, chances are you will die owing money. If you do, your executor will be responsible for rounding up your property and making sure all your outstanding debts are satisfied before any of the property is put in the hands of those you have named to get it. The property you own at your death—or your estate—might be liable for several types of debts, expenses, and taxes.

Secured Debts

Secured debts are any debts owed on specific property that must be paid before title to that property fully belongs to its owner.

One common type of secured debt occurs when a major asset, such as a car, an appliance, or a business, is paid for over a period of time. Usually, the lender of credit will retain some measure of legal ownership in the asset—termed a security interest—until it is paid off.

Another common type of secured debt occurs when a lender, as a condition of the loan, takes a security interest in property already owned by the person applying for the money. For instance, most finance companies require their borrowers to agree to pledge "all their personal property" as security for the loan. The legal jargon for this type of security interest is a non-purchase-money secured debt—that is, the debt is incurred for a purpose other than purchasing the property that secures repayment.

Other common types of secured debts are mortgages and deeds of trust owed on real estate in exchange for a purchase or an equity loan, tax liens and assessments that are owed on real estate, and, in some instances, liens or legal claims on personal and real property created as a result of litigation or home repair.

If you are leaving property in your will that is subject to a secured debt, you might be concerned about whether the debt will pass to the beneficiary along with the property or whether it must be paid by your estate.

Your WillMaker will passes all secured debts to the beneficiary of the property.

EXAMPLE 1: Paul owes $50,000 under a deed of trust on his home, signed as a condition of obtaining an equity loan. He leaves the home to his children. The deed of trust is a secured debt on real property and passes to the children along with the property.

EXAMPLE 2: Sonny and Cati, a married couple, borrow $100,000 from the bank to purchase their home and take out a deed of trust in the bank's favor as security for the loan. They still owe $78,000 and are two years behind in property tax payments. In separate wills, Sonny and Cati leave their ownership share to each other and name their children as alternates to take the home in equal shares. The deed of trust is a purchase-money secured debt and, if the children get the property, they will also get the mortgage—and responsibility for paying the past-due amount in taxes.

EXAMPLE 3: Phil owns a Ferrari. Although the car is registered in Phil's name, the bank holds legal title pending Phil's payment of the outstanding $75,000 car note. Phil uses WillMaker to leave the car to his companion, Paula. The car note is a secured debt and will pass to Paula with the car.

Will the Beneficiary Be Able to Make the Payments?

Because the property is usually worth more than any debt secured by it, a person who takes the property at your death but does not want to owe money can sell the property, pay off the debt, and pocket the difference. However, at times, relying on this approach is not satisfactory—especially when it comes to houses.

For example, if you leave your daughter your house with the hope that it will be her home, you will probably not want her to have to sell the house because she cannot meet the mortgage payments. If you think a particular beneficiary will need assistance with paying a debt owed on property, try to leave the necessary money or valuable assets to that person as well.

Unsecured Debts and Expenses

Unsecured debts are all debts not tied to specific property. Common examples are medical bills, most credit card bills, and utility bills. Student loans are also unsecured debts. However, most student loans are canceled when the borrower dies, so the borrower's estate owes nothing.

Even if you have no debt when you die, your estate is likely to incur some unsecured debt following your death. Funeral and burial expenses typically cost several thousand dollars (see Chapter 16), and probate and estate administration fees typically run about 5% of the value of the property you leave to others in your will (see Chapter 13).

Your executor will pay these debts and expenses with money from your estate; see "How Your Debts and Taxes Will Be Paid," below.

Estate and Inheritance Taxes

Most people do not need to worry about estate and inheritance taxes because their estates will not owe them. Whether or not your estate will be required to pay these taxes depends on the value of your estate and your state's laws.

Federal Estate Taxes

Only a tiny fraction of estates end up owing federal estate tax. Primarily, that's because a large amount of property is exempt from the tax. For deaths in 2026, the exemption is $15 million, so only estates worth more than $15 million will owe federal estate taxes. Married spouses can leave estates worth up to $30 million estate tax free. These exemption amounts will rise with inflation. To learn more about the federal estate tax, visit the "Wills, Trusts & Probate" section of Nolo.com.

State Inheritance and Estate Taxes

A handful of states have their own estate and inheritance taxes. If you live or own property in one of these states, you should consider whether your estate might have to pay state estate taxes. Like federal estate tax, state estate tax exempts a large amount of property. However, the exemption amounts for state estate taxes are significantly lower than the federal exemption, varying from $1 million up to the federal exemption amount. So your estate could owe *state* estate tax even if it doesn't owe *federal* tax. (See Chapter 13 for more information.)

SEE AN EXPERT

Getting help with large estates. As you might imagine, financial planning experts have devised many creative ways to plan for paying estate and inheritance taxes. If your estate is large enough to warrant concern about possible federal or state estate taxes, it is large enough for you to afford a consultation with an accountant, an estate planning specialist, or a lawyer specializing in estates and trusts.

How Your Debts and Taxes Will Be Paid

Your WillMaker will directs your executor to pay your debts and taxes as required by the laws of your state. Some states leave the method of payment up to your executor, while others provide that all beneficiaries must share the burden.

Often these debts and expenses will be paid proportionately out of the estate's liquid assets. This means that a beneficiary's property will be reduced by the percentage that the property bears to the total liquid assets. Liquid assets include bank accounts, money market accounts, and marketable securities. Real estate and tangible personal property, such as cars, furniture, and antiques, are not included. This could have unintended consequences if you leave specific liquid assets to certain beneficiaries without considering that those assets will be used to pay your debts and expenses.

However, depending on your financial situation and the laws of your state, there might be many possibilities for how your debts and expenses could be paid. If you have concerns about this issue—or if you would like to use your will to specify sources for payment—see a lawyer for help.

Covering Your Debts With Insurance

One way to deal with the problem of large debts and small assets is to purchase a life insurance policy in an amount large enough to pay your anticipated debts and expenses and have the proceeds made payable to your estate. However, talk with an estate planner or accountant before adopting this sort of plan. Having insurance money paid directly to your estate subjects that amount to probate. A better alternative might be to provide that estate assets be sold, with the proceeds used to pay the debts. Then have the insurance proceeds made payable directly to your survivors free of probate.

CHAPTER

10

Make It Legal: Final Steps

After you have proceeded through all the WillMaker screens and questions, your will is nearly finished. There are just a few more steps you must take to make it legally effective so that the directions you expressed in it can be carried out after your death.

Checking Your Will

Before you sign your will, take some time to scrutinize it and make sure it accurately expresses your wishes. You can do this either by previewing it in WillMaker or by printing out a draft copy.

Having an Expert Check Your Will

You might want to have your will checked by an attorney or a tax expert. This makes good sense if you are left with nagging questions about the legal implications of your choices, or if you own a great deal of property or have a complicated idea of how you want to leave it. But keep in mind that you are your own best expert on most issues and decisions involved in making a will—what property you own, your relation to family members and friends, and your own favorite charities. Also, some attorneys don't support the self-help approach to making a will, so you might have to search a bit to find one who is cooperative. (See Chapter 17.)

Signing and Witnessing Requirements

To be valid, a will must be legally executed. This means that you must sign your will in front of two witnesses. Each witness must sign the will not only in your presence, but also in the presence of the other witnesses.

TIP

Witnessing in Colorado and North Dakota. In these two states, witnessing is still the norm, but you can choose to have your will notarized instead. That said, WillMaker prints your will with witness blocks because witnessing is traditional, familiar, and expected—important, especially if your will might be used in another state that allows only witnessing. If you live in Colorado or North Dakota and want to notarize your will, take it to a notary and ask for a notary "acknowledgment."

Requirements for Witnesses

There are a few legal requirements for witnesses. The witnesses need to be of sound mind. In most states, the witnesses need to be 18 or older. Many states also require that the witnesses not be people who will take property under the will. That's why WillMaker recommends that you not use as a witness someone to whom you leave property in your will, even as an alternate or a residuary beneficiary.

As a matter of common sense, the people you choose to be witnesses should be easily available when you die. While this bit of future history is impossible to foretell with certainty, it is usually best to choose witnesses who are in good health, are younger than you are, and are likely to remain in your geographic area. However, the witnesses do not have to be residents of your state.

RESOURCE

Learn more about your state's requirements. To get details about witnessing and proving wills in your state, read your state's "Making a Will" article at www.nolo.com/legal-encyclopedia/making-will.

The Self-Proving Option

For a will to be accepted by a probate court, the executor must show that the document really is the will of the person it purports to be—a process called proving the will. In the past, all wills were proved by having one or two witnesses either come into court to testify or swear in written, notarized statements called affidavits that they saw you sign your will.

Today, most states allow people to make their wills self-proving—that is, they can be admitted in probate court without the hassle of herding witnesses to appear in court or sign affidavits. This is accomplished when the person making the will and the witnesses all appear before a notary public and sign an affidavit under oath, verifying that all necessary formalities for execution have been satisfied.

In Some States You Don't Need a Self-Proving Affidavit

In California, Illinois, Indiana, Maryland, and Nevada, valid wills are self-proved without an affidavit. The fact that the witnesses sign the will under the oath printed above their signatures is sufficient to have the will admitted into probate. In these states, there is no need to take further steps to make a will self-proving. (Cal. Prob. Code §§ 6222 and 8220; 755 Ill. Comp. Stat. § 5/6-4; Ind. Code § 29-1-5-3.1; Md. Code Est. & Trusts, § 5-303; Nev. Rev. Stat. § 133.050.)

States Without Self-Proving Laws

In the District of Columbia and Ohio, the self-proving option is not available, and your executor will be required to prove your will.

Remote Witnessing and Notarization

In the past few years, electronic signatures have become much more common, even in estate planning. However, the traditional in-person methods for signing, witnessing, and notarizing estate planning documents are still the norm.

Remote Witnessing for Wills

About a third of U.S. states allow remote witnessing for wills, and an increasing number of states are considering legislation to allow it. But until it is widely accepted in practice, with clear guidelines about how to do it right, WillMaker recommends that you follow the traditional practice of having your witnesses physically present when they sign your will.

Remote Notarization

Thankfully, the move to remote notarization is further along than remote witnessing. Currently, most U.S. states allow remote notarizations. If you can gather your witnesses together physically but want to try to use a remote notary to sign your self-proving affidavit, call a few local notaries and ask if remote notarization is allowed in your state. When you ask, remember that you're notarizing the affidavit, not your will.

If remote notarization is not allowed in your state, you might be able to get a mobile notary to come to you. Notaries in your area should know what is permitted and what rules must be followed.

Finally, if you can't find a notary to sign your self-proving affidavit, do not let this stop you from finalizing your will. The affidavit is a good idea if you can do it, but to be legal, your will requires only the signatures of you and your witnesses.

If you live in a state that offers the self-proving option, WillMaker automatically produces the correct affidavit for your state, with accompanying instructions. In all states except New Hampshire, the self-proving affidavit is not part of your will, but a separate document. To use it, you and your witnesses must first sign the will as discussed below. Then, you and your witnesses must sign the self-proving affidavit in front of a notary public. You need three individuals for this (in addition to yourself)—the two witnesses and a notary public. The notary public should not also serve as a witness.

You can notarize your self-proving affidavit any time after the will is signed, but obviously it is easiest to do it while all your witnesses are gathered together to watch you sign your will. Most notaries will charge at least a minimal amount for their services—and will require you and your witnesses to present some identification verifying that you are who you claim to be.

Prevalidating Your Will

In some states, you can have a court validate your will before you die. Doing this significantly reduces the possibility of someone successfully challenging your will after your death. You'll need to have a lawyer help you do it, and you'll also want to prevalidate any wills (or revocations) you subsequently make. Prevalidation is available in these states:

Alaska (Alaska Stat. § 13.12.530)
Arkansas (Ark. Code § 28-40-202)
Delaware (Del. Code tit. 12, § 1311)
Nevada (Nev. Rev. Stat. § 30.040)
New Hampshire (N.H. Rev. Stat. § 552: 18)
North Carolina (N.C. Gen. Stat. § 28A-2B-1)
North Dakota (N.D. Cent. Code § 30.1-08.1-01)
Ohio (Ohio Rev. Code § 5817.02)

You do not have to make your will self-proving. If you don't see the need for it, don't have time for it, or just don't want to hassle with it, your will is still valid as long as it is signed by your two witnesses. If you choose not to use it, file the uncompleted affidavit and instructions in a safe place in case you change your mind later.

Signing Procedure

You need not utter any magic words when signing your will and having it witnessed, but a few legal requirements suggest the best way to proceed:

- Gather all witnesses together in one place.
- Inform your witnesses that the papers you hold in your hand are your last will and testament. This is important, because the laws in many states specifically require that you acknowledge the document as your will before the witnesses sign it. The witnesses need not read your will, however, and there is no need for them to know its contents. If you want to ensure that the contents of the will stay confidential, you can cover all but the signature portion of your will with a separate sheet of paper while the witnesses sign.
- Initial each page of the will at the bottom on the lines provided. The purpose of initialing is to prevent anyone from challenging the will as invalid on the grounds that changes were made to it by someone else.
- Sign the last page on the signature line while the witnesses watch. Use the same form of your name that you stated in your will.
- Ask each of the witnesses to initial the bottom of each page on a line there, then watch as they sign and fill in their addresses on the last page where indicated. Their initials act as evidence if anyone later claims you changed your will without going through the proper legal formalities.

Changing Your WillMaker Will

After you have signed your will and had it witnessed, it is extremely important that you do not alter it by inserting handwritten or typed additions or changes. Do not even correct misspellings. The laws of most states require that after a will is signed, any additions or changes to it, even clerical ones, must be made by following the same signing and witnessing requirements as for an original will.

Although it is legally possible to make handwritten corrections on your will before you sign it, that is a bad idea since, after your death, it will not be clear to the probate court that you made the corrections before the will was signed. The possibility that the changes were made later might throw the legality of the whole will into question.

If you want to make changes after your will has been signed and witnessed, there are two ways to accomplish it: You can either make a new will or make a formal addition, called a codicil, to the existing one. Either approach requires a new round of signing and witnessing.

One of the great advantages of WillMaker is that you can conveniently keep current by simply making a new will. This does away with the need to tack on changes to the will using a codicil. Codicils are not a good idea when using WillMaker because of the possibility of creating a conflict between the codicil and the original will. It is simpler and safer to make a revised WillMaker will, sign it, and have it witnessed. (See "How to Make a New Will" in Chapter 11.)

Making Copies of Your Will

It is sometimes a good idea to make several copies of your finalized will. You might want to give one to your executor or other loved ones, so they know your plans. You can make either hardcopy duplicates or digital copies of your finalized will. If you use a photocopier to make hardcopy duplicates, write "Copy" on the top of each one, just to be very clear that it is not the original. You can also make digital copies (perhaps to send over email) using a scanner or the camera on your cell phone.

Some people are tempted to prepare more than one signed and witnessed original of their wills in case one is lost. While it is legal in most states to prepare and sign duplicate originals, it is never a good idea. Common sense tells you why: If you later want to change your will, it can be difficult to locate all the old copies to destroy them.

Of course, you aren't required to disclose the contents of your will to anyone. If you prefer to keep your will confidential until your death, do not make any copies.

Storing Your Will

When your will is formally completed (signed and witnessed), put the original signed version in a place where your executor can easily locate it at your death. Here are some suggestions:

- Store your printed and witnessed will in an envelope labeled with your name and the word "Will."
- Place the envelope in a fireproof metal box, file cabinet, or home safe. An alternative is to place the original will in a safe deposit box. But before doing that, learn the bank's policy about access to the box after your death. If, for instance, the safe deposit box is in your name alone, the box can probably be opened only by a person authorized by a court, and then only in the presence of a bank employee. In some cases, a court might require an inventory of the box's contents. All of this takes time, and in the meantime, your document will be locked away from those who need it.

Helping Others Find Your Will

Make your will easy to locate at your death. You want to spare your survivors the anxiety of having to search for your will when they are already dealing with the grief of losing you. Make sure your executor and at least one other person you trust know where to find your will.

Should You Register Your Will?

No state requires you to register your will after you write it. However, a few states and some online companies allow you to register basic information about your will, including its location. Additionally, in some counties, you can store the will itself with the probate court.

You might want to register your will if you're worried that your will won't be found when you die. A will registry helps with this because your executor or loved ones can search the registry for information about your will, at least if they know to do so.

However, as long as you are willing to tell your executor or loved ones where you keep your will, there is usually no reason to use a will registry. Will registries—both private and state-run—charge a fee to keep information about your will, and you have to remember to update the registry if you change your will or its location. It's usually better to simply make sure that those who will need it know where to find your will when the time comes.

Also, don't confuse "will registries" with "living will registries," which are more common. Living wills provide instructions about your health care wishes. (See Chapter 15.)

To register your will with a private company, you can find one with an internet search. For example, "find a will registry online" should yield several options. If you prefer to register or deposit your will with your county, check with the probate court for instructions.

Finally, "will registration" is not "will prevalidation." Registration records the location of your will (or stores the will document itself), while prevalidation is a court process that proves to the court that your will is valid before you die. See "Prevalidating Your Will," above.

CHAPTER

11

Updating Your Will

Life wreaks havoc on even the best-laid plans, and changes in your life affect what you include in your will and what laws will be applied to enforce it. You might sell one house and buy another. You might divorce. You might have or adopt children. Eventually you will face the grief of losing a loved one. Not all life changes require you to change your will. However, significant ones often do. This chapter tells you when it's necessary to make a new will.

When to Make a New Will

The following occurrences signal that it is time for you to make a new will.

Marrying or Divorcing

Suppose that, after you use WillMaker to leave all or part of your property to your spouse, you get divorced. Under the law in many states, the divorce automatically cancels the bequest to the former spouse. The alternate beneficiary named for that bequest or, if there is none, your residuary beneficiary gets the property. In some states, however, your former spouse would still be entitled to take your property as directed in the will. If you remarry, state legal rules become even more murky. (In a few states, these rules also apply to registered partners.)

Rather than deal with all these complexities, follow this simple rule: Make a new will if you marry, divorce, are separated and seriously considering divorce, or register or dissolve a registered partnership.

SEE AN EXPERT

Beware of state laws on spouses' shares. If you leave your spouse or registered partner out of your will because you are separated, and you die before you become divorced, it is possible that the spouse or partner could claim a statutory share of your estate. (See "Your Spouse's Right to Inherit From You" in Chapter 5.) Consult a lawyer to find out how the laws of your state apply to this situation. (See Chapter 17.)

Getting or Losing Property

If you leave all your property in a lump to one or more persons or organizations, there is no need to change your will if you acquire new items of property or get rid of existing ones. Those individuals or organizations take all of your property at your death, without regard to what it is.

But if you have made specific bequests of property that you no longer own, it is wise to make a new will. If you leave a specific item—a particular Tiffany lamp, for example—to someone, but you no longer own the item when you die, the person named in your will to receive it might be out of luck. In most states, that person is not entitled to receive another item or money instead. In some states, however, the law presumes that you wanted the beneficiary to have something—and so gives that person the right to a sum of money equal to the value of the gift. While this might be what you want, it could still disrupt your plan for how you want your property distributed. The legal word for a bequest that fails to make it in this way is ademption.

However, in some circumstances, if a specific item has merely changed form, the original beneficiary might still have a claim to it. Examples of this are:

- a promissory note that has been paid and for which the cash is still available, and
- a house that is sold in exchange for a promissory note and deed of trust.

A problem similar to ademption occurs when there is not enough money to go around. For example, if you leave $50,000 each to your spouse and two children, but there is only $90,000 in your estate at your death, the gifts in the will must all be reduced. In legal lingo, this is called an abatement. How property is abated under state law is often problematic.

You can avoid these problems if you revise the type and amount of your bequests to reflect reality—a task that requires the commitment to make a new will periodically.

Adding or Losing Children

Each time a child is born or legally adopted into your family, the new child should be named in the will—where you are asked to name your children—and provided for according to your wishes. If you do not do this, the child might later challenge your will in court, claiming to have been overlooked as an heir, and is entitled to a substantial share of your property. (See "Your Children" in Chapter 4.)

If any of your children die before you and leave children of their own, you should name those grandchildren in your will. If they are not mentioned in your will, they might later be legally entitled to claim a share of your estate. (See "Your Grandchildren" in Chapter 4.)

TIP

Honoring loved ones who have died. If you've lost someone close to you, it might be painful not to be able to mention them in your will. If you want to include them in your estate planning, consider writing about them in a letter instead. See Chapter 12.

Moving to a Different State

WillMaker applies several state-specific laws when it helps you create your will. For example:

- If you have set up property management for young beneficiaries, you might want to update your will if you then move to a different state. This is because the age of distribution under the Uniform Transfers to Minors Act varies between 18 and 30, depending on the state. So the arrangements you make in one state might not be appropriate in another. For details about using the UTMA, see "The Uniform Transfers to Minors Act" in Chapter 7.
- If you are married and do not intend to leave all or most of your property to your spouse, review "Property Ownership Rules for Married People" in Chapter 5, which discusses the rules if you move from a community property state to a common law state or vice versa.

- If you want your will to be self-proving, you might need to make a new will if you move to a different state. State laws vary about how to make a will self-proving—some states require an affidavit, others require witness declarations, and others don't allow self-proving wills at all. Read more about self-proving wills in Chapter 10.

Losing Beneficiaries

If a beneficiary you have named to receive a significant amount of property dies before you, you should make a new will. It is especially important to do this if you named only one beneficiary for a bequest and did not name an alternate—or if the alternate you named is not your first choice to get the property.

Losing Guardians or Property Managers

The first choice or alternate named to serve as a personal guardian for your minor children or those you have named to manage their property might move away, become disabled, or simply turn out to be unsuitable for the job. If so, you will probably want to make a new will naming a different person.

Losing an Executor

The executor of your estate is responsible for making sure your will provisions are carried out. If the executor you originally named is no longer suitable—or dies before you do—you should make a new will in which you name another person for the job.

Losing Witnesses

The witnesses who sign your will are responsible for testifying that the signature on your will is valid and that you appeared capable of making a will when you did so. If two of your witnesses become unable to fulfill this function, you might want to make a new will with new witnesses—especially if you have an inkling that someone might contest your will after you die. But a new will is probably not necessary if you have made your will self-proving. (See "The Self-Proving Option" in Chapter 10.)

How to Make a New Will

It is easy to make a new will using WillMaker. In fact, a subsequent swoop through the questions will proceed even more quickly than the first time through, since you will know what to expect and will likely be familiar with many of the legal concepts you had to learn at first.

If you review your will and wish to change some of your answers, WillMaker will automatically alert you to specific changes that might signal different laws applying to your situation. These include changes in:

- your marital or registered partner status
- your state of residence
- the number of children you have, and
- your general approach to will making—from simple to complex, or vice versa.

If you make a new will, even if it involves only a few changes, you must follow the legal requirements for having it signed and witnessed just as if you were starting from scratch. If you choose to make your will self-proving, you must also complete a new affidavit.

CAUTION

In with the new, out with the old. As soon as you print, sign, and have your new will witnessed, it will legally replace all wills you have made before it. But to avoid possible confusion, you should physically destroy all other original wills and any copies of them.

CHAPTER

12

Letter to Survivors

In addition to the tasks that you can accomplish in a WillMaker will, you might also wish to:

- explain why you are giving property to certain beneficiaries and not to others
- explain disparities in gifts
- explain how shared gifts should be divided
- express wishes about how to care for a pet
- leave instructions for your digital assets
- present support for your relationship, or
- leave a statement about your personal experiences, values, or beliefs.

WillMaker does not allow you to do these things in your will for one important reason: WillMaker has been written, tested, and tested again with painstaking attention to helping you make your own legal and unambiguous will. If you add general information, personal statements, or reasons for making or not making a bequest, you risk the possibility of producing a document with conflicting, confusing, or possibly even illegal provisions.

Fortunately, there is a way you can have a final say about personal matters without seriously risking your will's legal integrity. You can write a letter to accompany your will expressing your thoughts to those who survive you.

Because what you put in the letter will not have legal effect as part of your will, there is little danger that your expressions will tread upon the time-tested legal language of the will or cause other problems later. In fact, if your will is ambiguous and your statement in the letter sheds some light on your intentions, judges might use the letter to help clarify your will. However, if your statements in the letter fully contradict provisions in your will, you might create interpretation problems after your death. For example, if you don't leave anything to your daughter in your will and also state in a letter attached to the will that she is your favorite child and that is why you are leaving her the family home, you are setting the stage for future confusion.

Keeping these cautions in mind, writing a letter to those who survive you to explain why you wrote your will as you did—and knowing they will read your reasoning at your death—can give you a great deal of peace of mind during life. It might also help explain potential slights and hurt feelings of surviving friends and family members.

This chapter offers some guidance on how you can write a clear letter that expresses your wishes without jeopardizing the legality of your will. This chapter also offers some suggestions about topics you might wish to cover.

You can write your letter by hand, type it up on your phone, tablet, or computer, or make it using WillMaker's Letter to Survivors.

An Introduction for Your Letter

A formal introduction to the letter you leave can help make it clear that what you write is an expression of your sentiments and not intended as a will—or an addition to or interpretation of your will. See our suggestion, below.

After the introduction, you are free to express your sentiments, keeping in mind that your estate can be held liable for any false, derogatory statements you make about an individual or organization.

This is the introduction used by WillMaker's Letter to Survivors:

> To My Executor:
>
> This letter is not my will, nor do I intend it to be an interpretation of my will. My will, which I signed, dated, and had witnessed on ______________,
> is the sole expression of my intentions concerning all my property and other matters covered in it.
>
> Should anything I say in this letter conflict with, or seem to conflict with, any provision of my will, the will shall be followed.
>
> I request that you give a copy of this letter to each person named in my will to take property and to anyone else you determine should receive a copy.

Explaining Your Gifts

You don't have to explain why you left your assets the way you did—but you might want to. Especially if you think a particular gift will surprise or disappoint people close to you, a brief explanation of your reasons can head off confusion and bad feelings among survivors.

Why Gifts Were Made

EXAMPLE 1:

> [Introduction]
>
> The gift of my fishing boat to my friend Hank is in remembrance of the many companionable days we enjoyed fishing together on the lake. Hank, I hope you're out there for many more years.

EXAMPLE 2:

> [Introduction]
>
> Julie, the reason I have given you the farm is that you love it as much as I do, and I know you'll do your best to make sure it stays in the family. But please, if the time comes when personal or family concerns mean that it makes sense to sell it, do so with a light heart—and knowing that it's just what I would have done.

EXAMPLE 3:

> [Introduction]
>
> The reason I left $10,000 to my physician, Dr. Buski, is not only that she treated me competently over the years, but that she was unfailingly gentle and attentive. I always appreciated that she made herself available—day or night—and took the time to explain my ailments and treatments to me.

Why Gifts Weren't Made

EXAMPLE 1:

> [Introduction]
>
> I am leaving nothing to my brother Malcolm. I wish him no ill will. But over the years, he has decided to isolate himself from me and the rest of the family and I don't feel I owe him anything.

EXAMPLE 2:

> [Introduction]
>
> I have left nothing to my son Anthony because he has been well provided for during my life. I have not given similar financial help to his siblings and think this is the fairest way to leave my estate.

Disparities in Gifts

EXAMPLE 1:

> [Introduction]
>
> I love all my children equally. The reason I gave a smaller ownership share in the house to Tim than to my other children is that Tim received family funds to purchase his own home, so it is fair that my other two children receive more of my property now.

EXAMPLE 2:

> [Introduction]
>
> I am giving the bulk of my property to my son Jason for one reason: Because of his health problems, he needs it more.
>
> Ted and Ellen, I love you just as much, and I am extremely proud of the life choices you have made. But the truth is that you two can manage fine without a boost from me, and Jason cannot.

Offering Suggestions for Shared Gifts

If you are leaving a shared gift that contains a number of specific items—such as "my household furnishings" or "my art collection"—you might have some thoughts on how you'd like your beneficiaries to divide up the property. Of course, you can use your will to control the size of the share that each beneficiary gets, but that still leaves your survivors to figure out who gets which specific assets. For example, if you leave your entire estate to be shared equally by your three children, how should they decide who gets the house, who gets the bank accounts, and who gets the cars?

You can use a letter to make suggestions to your beneficiaries about how they might go about dividing up shared gifts. Your suggestions will not have any legal weight, but you can give beneficiaries helpful guidance. For example, you might want to suggest a fair way of figuring it out, such as a lottery for the highly coveted items.

Whatever suggestions you give, be very careful not to contradict any of the gifts you make in your will. Doing so could cause confusion and promote conflicts and hurt feelings among beneficiaries. Worse, it could lead to a legal challenge to your will.

EXAMPLE:

> [Introduction]
>
> I have left my library equally to my grandchildren. I know each of them has enjoyed many of the books over the years and I want to make sure that each receives a few favorites. I suggest that you hold a drawing to determine the order in which each grandchild will choose a book, with each then taking a volume in turn until their favorites are spoken for. The rest of the library can be distributed—taken or given away—in whatever manner they choose.

Explaining Decisions About Your Pets

As discussed in Chapter 4, the best way to provide a home for your pet is to use your will to name a caretaker for your pet and leave some money to that person to cover the costs of your pet's care. If you like, you can use your letter to say why you chose a particular person to watch over your animals after your death.

EXAMPLE:

> [Introduction]
>
> I have left my dog, Cessna, to my neighbor Belinda Mason because she has been a loving friend to him, taking care of him when I was on vacation or unwell. I know that Belinda and her three children will provide a caring and happy home for Cessna when I no longer can.

Leaving Details About Your Pet's Care

You might want to provide your pet's caretaker with information and suggestions about your pet's habits and needs. To do this, you can use the Information for Caregivers and Survivors form (in the download version of WillMaker). It allows you to leave specifics about each animal, including health needs, food and exercise requirements, and sleeping habits. You can also use the document to describe memorial plans or final arrangements for your pet.

Instructions for Your Digital Assets

As discussed in Chapter 5, you might want to leave instructions about your digital assets—your online accounts, information, identities, and files—that will be left when you die. If you know what you want to happen with them, you can leave guidance and login information in your letter.

EXAMPLE 1:

[Introduction]

For many years I have been blogging about my experiences as a stay-at-home mom. I am thankful to have a large online following, I consider many of the people in that community to be my friends, and I would like them to be notified of my death. Please log in to my account and post a brief message about my passing. Also, please leave the blog live for at least a year (it's paid for) and save as much of the content as you can—I hope the kids might enjoy reading it someday. You can access the account at http://homemakerglenda.blogspot.com. My login name is my email address—homemakerglenda@gmail.com—and the password is 8tle1oAK.

EXAMPLE 2:

> [Introduction]
>
> I don't like the idea of my online accounts lingering after I die. In fact, as much as it's possible, I would like you to erase all traces of me from the internet. I've listed all of my known online accounts and identities in a document called Information for Caregivers and Survivors—kept in the same folder as this letter. Please access and close all listed accounts. Then search the internet for my name to see if there are any other traces that could be removed. I know this might be tedious and difficult, but I feel much better knowing that you'll do what you can in this regard.

To provide your survivors with a thorough and detailed inventory of your online accounts and passwords, consider using the Information for Caregivers and Survivors form (in the download version of WillMaker). The Information for Caregivers and Survivors interview elicits access information about many types of online accounts—from email and financial accounts to photo storage and blogs. Leaving this detailed information can save your executor and other survivors time and headaches when wrapping up your affairs.

You can use the Letter to Survivors and the Information for Caregivers and Survivors form together: Leave your inventory of online accounts in the Information for Caregivers and Survivors form and leave instructions for what to do with those accounts in the Letter to Survivors.

In the download version of WillMaker, start the Information for Caregivers and Survivors form from the Your Documents screen.

See "Organizing Your Records" in Chapter 1 for other ideas about how to pass on important information to your loved ones.

RESOURCE

Get more information about leaving your digital assets. Visit Nolo's digital assets page at www.nolo.com/legal-encyclopedia/digital-assets to learn more about the executor's powers, what happens to your online accounts, and how you can control what happens to your online presence after you die.

Writing About Relationships

In some situations, you might want to leave a note providing information about a relationship. For example, if you have loved ones who don't know about or approve of your partner, leaving a note that clearly describes the importance of your relationship can clear up any possible confusion. Or you might describe the relationship you have with a good friend to explain to your family why you left that person part of your estate.

The information you provide in your letter won't change how your property is distributed by your will, but it will make your intention clear. Be very careful not to contradict the decisions you made in your will or other estate planning documents.

EXAMPLE 1:

[Introduction]

Although Sam and I never married, he is my life partner and best friend. For eight years we have shared every aspect of our lives together, I love him dearly, and our relationship has brought me immeasurable happiness. Mom and Dad, this is why I left him a portion of my retirement accounts—I hope you understand. Also, it is my wish that you continue to treat Sam as family after I am gone. He is a good and caring person, and I think you will all find comfort in your shared grief.

EXAMPLE 2:

[Introduction]

I have left Cole Jones a substantial part of my estate because, although legally I am not his parent, he is my biological child and I want to help provide for his future. Mom and Dad, I know it might come as a shock that you have a biological grandchild but I never felt comfortable telling you about it. I wasn't sure that you would understand or accept my decision to help my friends Alex and Julie have a child. I know you might be curious about Cole, but please understand that you have no legal right to get to know him. Whether you meet him is completely up to Alex and Julie, his legal parents.

Thoughts About Life

Many people are interested in leaving behind more than just property. If you wish, you can also leave a statement about the experiences, values, and beliefs that have shaped your life. This kind of letter or document is often known as an "ethical will," and it can be of great worth to those who survive you.

As long as you don't contradict the provisions of your legal will, your options for expressing yourself are limited only by the time and energy you have for the project. You could do something as simple as use your letter to set out a concise description of your basic values. Or, if you feel inspired, you can leave something much more detailed for your loved ones. Many survivors are touched to learn about important life stories, memories, and events.

EXAMPLE 1:

> [Introduction]
>
> When I was young, I was very close to my Aunt Jinny—my mom's sister—and she taught me a lot about how to make the most of life. She once told me, "Life isn't about what happens to you; it's about what you make happen." Throughout my life, I found her words comforting and encouraging. Hope you all think of those words through your lives as well and that you find comfort in them as I have.

EXAMPLE 2:

> [Introduction]
>
> I know our family does not have a shared understanding of what happens to us when we die. But I want each of you to know that if there is an afterlife, I will be waiting for you there. And as for this life, I have loved you all more than I could ever express.

You might also consider including photographs or other mementos with your letter. If writing things down seems like too much effort, you could use audio or video to talk to those who are closest to you. A little thought will surely yield many creative ways to express yourself to those you care for.

RESOURCE

More information about ethical wills. If you want to go beyond writing down some of your experiences and values in your letter, there is a growing body of websites and literature that can help you explore different ways of making an ethical will. You might begin by searching "ethical will" online and exploring some of the resources available.

Signing and Storing Your Letter

Sign and date your letter. Then store it where it can be found easily after your death—for example, with your other estate planning documents like your will, living trust, or final arrangement documents.

During your life, you can share your letter with loved ones, or you can keep it private, with the intention of your loved ones reading it after you die. If you later update your letter, destroy any outdated versions or clearly indicate that they've been revised.

CHAPTER

13

When You Might Need More Than a Will

If you have little to leave your survivors you probably don't need to do any planning beyond making a basic will, powers of attorney, and health care directives (all of which you can make with WillMaker). If that's your situation, you can skip this chapter altogether.

On the other hand, you might want to take another look at your situation and possibly do some additional estate planning to:

- avoid probate
- reduce estate taxes, or
- control how property left to one or more beneficiaries can be used.

If your estate is moderate to large, you should think about planning to avoid probate. Putting to work even a few simple probate avoidance devices can save your inheritors a bundle. Tax planning is more complicated, but it's also something you probably won't need to worry about unless you have a very, very large estate. Finally, if you have reason to want to place controls on the property you leave, you'll most likely want to see a good estate planning lawyer. At the end of this chapter, we'll talk a bit about your options.

Avoiding Probate

You might have heard or read that you ought to avoid probate—and that if you don't take steps to do so, your survivors will surely waste a lot of time and money after your death. This section will help you understand what probate is and why you might want to steer your estate away from it.

What Is Probate?

Probate is the legal process that includes filing a deceased person's will with a court, locating and gathering assets, paying debts and taxes, and eventually distributing what's left as the will directs. Most estates that pass by wills must go through probate to take care of these tasks.

However, there are many non-will ways to transfer property, and many of those do not require probate. Also, estates that qualify as "small" under the terms of a state's law can avoid probate even if a will is used. If there is no will and no probate avoidance devices are used, property is distributed according to state law—and it must go through probate.

Fortunately, there are many non-probate devices you can use to pass your property after your death, including revocable living trusts, joint tenancy, transfer on death deeds, pay-on-death beneficiary designations, and others. Property transferred by any of these methods can be given directly to the people slated to get it at your death—no court proceedings required.

Why Avoid Probate?

Probate has many drawbacks and few advantages. It's usually costly, involving fees for attorneys, appraisers, accountants, and the probate court. The cost of probate varies widely from state to state, but fees can eat up about 5% of your estate, leaving that much less to go to the people you want to get it. If the estate is complicated, the fees can be even larger.

The Cost of Probate

If you leave property worth:	Probate might cost about:
$200,000	$10,000
$500,000	$25,000

At least as bad as the expense of probate is the delay it causes. In many states, probate can take a year or two, during which time beneficiaries generally get nothing unless the judge allows the immediate family a small "family allowance."

If you own real estate in more than one state, it's usually necessary to have a separate probate proceeding in each state. In that case, surviving relatives will need to find and hire a lawyer in each state and pay for multiple probate proceedings.

From the family's point of view, probate's headaches are rarely justified. If the estate contains common kinds of property—a house, stocks, bank accounts, a small business, cars—and no relatives or creditors are fighting about it, the property merely needs to be handed over to the new owners. In the vast majority of cases, the probate process entails nothing more than tedious paperwork, and the attorney is nothing more than a very highly paid clerk.

TIP

Probate isn't always bad. In some circumstances, the benefits of probate can outweigh the burdens and costs. For example, probate court might be the best place to deal with an estate with substantial debt or numerous creditors. Similarly, if there is insurmountable fighting among beneficiaries, the probate court can serve as a neutral party to make final distributions. Also, if no one in the deceased person's life is available to do the work as executor or trustee, then the probate court will be there to do the job.

Living Trusts: A Popular Way to Avoid Probate

If you've heard something about living trusts but wonder exactly what they are and how they work, this section will give you a quick lesson.

A trust is an arrangement under which one person, called the trustee, owns property on behalf of someone else, called the beneficiary. You can create a trust simply by preparing and signing a document called a declaration of trust.

A *living* trust is a trust that you set up during your lifetime—usually to avoid probate. Living trusts sometimes go by "inter vivos trusts" because they're created while you're alive, not at your death like some other kinds of trusts. They're also sometimes called "revocable living trusts" because you can revoke or change them at any time.

You can make an individual living trust or a trust that is shared with your spouse or partner.

How a Living Trust Works

A basic living trust does, essentially, what a will does: leaves your property to the people you want to inherit it. But because a trustee owns your property, your assets don't have to go through probate at your death.

When you create a living trust, you appoint yourself trustee, with full power to manage trust property. Then you transfer ownership of some or all of your property to yourself as trustee. You keep absolute control over the property held in trust. You can:

- sell, mortgage, or give away property held in trust
- put ownership of trust property back in your name
- add property to the trust
- change the beneficiaries
- name a different successor trustee, or
- revoke the trust completely.

If you and your spouse or partner create a trust together, both of you must consent to changes, although either of you is permitted to revoke the entire trust.

After you die, the person you named in your trust document to be "successor trustee" takes over. This person transfers the trust property to the relatives, friends, or charities you named as the trust beneficiaries. No probate is necessary for property that was held in trust. In most cases, the whole thing can be handled within a few weeks. When the property has all been transferred to the beneficiaries, the living trust ceases to exist.

If any of your beneficiaries inherit trust property while still young, the successor trustee (or the surviving grantor of a shared trust) will probably have more responsibility, following instructions you leave in the trust to manage the property until the beneficiaries are old enough to inherit it outright.

TIP

WillMaker now offers a quitclaim deed. You can use the quitclaim deed to transfer your home or other property into your living trust. To get started or learn more, go to the WillMaker screen that lists all of WillMaker's documents and look for Quitclaim Deed in the Estate Planning section.

More Advantages of Living Trusts

In addition to avoiding probate, a living trust offers other benefits.

Avoiding the need for a conservator or guardianship. A living trust can be useful if you become incapacitated and unable to manage your own financial affairs. That's because the person you name as trustee (or the other grantor, if you make a shared trust) can take over management of trust assets, watching over the property for your benefit.

If there is no living trust and you haven't made other arrangements for someone to take over your finances if you become incapacitated, such as preparing a durable power of attorney for finances, a court will have to appoint someone to do the job. Typically, the spouse or adult child of the person seeks this authority and is called a conservator or guardian.

Keeping your estate plan confidential. When your will is filed with the probate court after you die, it might become a matter of public record. A living trust, on the other hand, is a private document in most states. Because the living trust document is never filed with a court or other government entity, what you leave to whom remains private. (There is one exception: Records of real estate transfers are always public.)

Some states require you to register your living trust with the local court, but there are no penalties if you don't. The only way your trust might become public is if—and this is very unlikely—someone files a lawsuit to challenge the trust or collect a court judgment you owe.

Do You Really Need a Living Trust?

Here are some factors to think about when deciding whether a living trust is right for you.

Your proximity to death. If you're youngish and expect to live many more years, it often makes sense to prepare a will, use simple probate-avoidance devices, such as joint tenancy and pay-on-death bank accounts, for some property, and leave the more complicated estate planning until later.

The size of your estate. The bigger your estate, the bigger the potential probate cost and the less likely that your estate will qualify for simplified probate proceedings, discussed below. Often it makes good sense to concentrate effort on making sure that major assets, such as real estate or business assets, are owned in a way that will avoid probate.

The type of property you own. You don't need a trust to avoid probate for assets like your bank and retirement accounts and many other types of property. Take some time to learn a little bit about other types of probate avoidance devices before you jump into preparing a living trust; see "Other Ways to Avoid Probate," below.

Why You Still Need a Will

A living trust cannot completely replace a will. Even if you want to use a living trust to pass all of your property, there are reasons why you need a will, too.

Naming a guardian for minor children. You can't nominate a personal guardian for your young children in a living trust; you need a will in which to do this. (See "Personal Guardians for Your Minor Children" in Chapter 4.)

Passing property not included in the trust. A living trust works to pass only property you transfer into the trust. Property you might receive after you make the trust won't be transferred unless you add it to the living trust later. For example, if you have inherited property from a relative that is still tied up in probate, or you expect to receive money from the settlement of a lawsuit, you need a will in case something happens to you tomorrow. And because you cannot accurately predict what property you might receive shortly before death, it's smart to back up a living trust with a will.

RESOURCE

How to make your own living trust. You can use WillMaker's Living Trust to create an individual or shared basic trust for you or a member of your family.

Other Ways to Avoid Probate

Here are some methods you might want to investigate, to use with or instead of a living trust.

Pay-on-Death Bank Accounts

Pay-on-death bank accounts offer one of the easiest ways to keep money—even large sums of it—out of probate. All you need to do is fill out a simple form, provided by the bank, naming the person you want to inherit the money in the account at your death.

As long as you are alive, the person you named to inherit the money in a pay-on-death (POD) account has no rights to it. You can spend the money, name a different beneficiary, or close the account. At your death, the beneficiary just goes to the bank, shows identification and proof of death, and collects whatever funds are in the account. The probate court is never involved.

Transfer on Death Registration of Securities

In the process of setting up or managing your securities accounts, you can name someone to inherit your stocks, bonds, or brokerage accounts without probate. It works very much like a pay-on-death bank account. When you register your ownership, either with the stockbroker or the company itself, you make a request to take ownership in "beneficiary form."

After you register ownership this way, the beneficiary has no rights to the stock as long as you are alive. You are free to sell it, give it away, or name a different beneficiary. But when you die, the ownership of the securities will transfer to the beneficiary you named without probate. To claim them, the beneficiary will present identification and proof of your death to the broker or transfer agent, who will then reissue the securities in the name of your beneficiary. (A transfer agent is a business that is authorized by a corporation to handle stock transfers.)

Transfer on Death Deeds for Real Estate

In Alaska, Arizona, Arkansas, California, Colorado, Delaware, District of Columbia, Georgia, Hawaii, Illinois, Indiana, Kansas, Maine,

Maryland, Minnesota, Mississippi, Missouri, Montana, Nebraska, Nevada, New Hampshire, New Mexico, New York, North Dakota, Ohio, Oklahoma, Oregon, South Dakota, Texas, Utah, Virginia, Washington, West Virginia, Wisconsin, and Wyoming you can prepare a deed now but have it take effect only at your death. These transfer on death (TOD) deeds must be prepared, signed, notarized, and recorded (filed in the county land records office) just like a regular deed. But unlike a regular deed, you can revoke a transfer on death deed. The deed must expressly state that it does not take effect until death.

RESOURCE

You can make a transfer on death deed with WillMaker. If you own property in one of the states that allows transfer on death deeds, WillMaker can help you make the deed that is correct for your state. If you live in a state that does not yet offer TOD deeds, do not fret. Additional states continue to adopt them, and when your state offers them, WillMaker will too. You can read more about transfer on death deeds at www.willmaker.com/legal-manual/transfer-on-death-deeds.

Transfer on Death Registration for Vehicles

Arizona, Arkansas, California, Colorado, Connecticut, Delaware, District of Columbia, Illinois, Indiana, Kansas, Kentucky, Maryland, Minnesota, Mississippi, Missouri, Montana, Nebraska, Nevada, New Jersey, Ohio, Oklahoma, South Carolina, South Dakota, Texas, Vermont, Virginia, and Wyoming offer vehicle owners the sensible option of naming a beneficiary, right on the certificate of title or title application, to inherit a vehicle. If you do this, the beneficiary you name has no rights as long as you are alive. You are free to sell or give away a car or name someone else as the beneficiary.

Look for instructions for naming a beneficiary on the website of your state's motor vehicle department. You might need to apply for registration in "beneficiary form," or there might be an online or hard-copy form you fill out and submit. The beneficiary will automatically own the vehicle after your death.

Retirement Plans

Retirement plans, such as IRAs, 401(k)s, and Keoghs, don't have to go through probate. All you need to do is make sure you have provided the plan administrator with the names and contact information for your beneficiaries, and they will receive the funds at your death without probate. You should be able to review or change your beneficiary designations at any time.

Life Insurance

Life insurance proceeds are subject to probate only if the beneficiary named in the policy is your estate. That's done occasionally if the estate will need immediate cash to pay debts and taxes, but it's usually counterproductive because doing so could greatly increase probate fees. More commonly, in the policy paperwork you name the people who should receive the payout. You should be able to review or change your beneficiary designations at any time.

Joint Tenancy

Joint tenancy is an efficient and practical way to transfer some kinds of property without probate.

Joint tenancy is a way two or more people can hold title to property they own together. In most states, joint owners (called joint tenants) must own equal shares of the property. When one joint owner dies, the surviving owners automatically get complete ownership of the property. This is called the "right of survivorship." The property doesn't go through probate court—there is only some simple paperwork to fill out to transfer the property into the name of the surviving owner.

A will doesn't affect who inherits joint tenancy property. So, even if your will leaves your half-interest in joint tenancy property to someone else, the surviving owners will still inherit it.

This rule isn't as ironclad as it might sound. You can, while still alive, break the joint tenancy by transferring your interest in the property to someone else (or, in some states, to yourself, but not as a joint tenant).

Joint tenancy often works well when couples acquire real estate or other valuable property together. If they take title in joint tenancy, probate is avoided when the first owner dies—though not (unlike a living trust) when the second owner dies.

Joint tenancy is usually a poor estate planning device when an older person, seeking only to avoid probate, puts solely owned property into joint tenancy with someone else. If you make someone else a co-owner, in joint tenancy, of property that you now own yourself, you give up half-ownership of the property. The new owner has rights that you can't take back. For example, the new owner can sell or mortgage their share. And federal gift tax might be assessed on the transfer.

There can also be serious problems if one joint tenant becomes incapacitated and cannot make decisions. The other owners must get legal authority to sell or mortgage the property. That might mean going to court to get someone (called a conservator or guardian, in most states) appointed to manage the incapacitated person's affairs. (This problem can be dealt with if the joint tenant has signed a durable power of attorney. See Chapter 14.) With a living trust, if you (the grantor) become incapacitated, the successor trustee (or the other spouse, if you made a trust together) takes over and has full authority to manage the property. No court proceedings are necessary.

State Restrictions on Joint Tenancy	
Alaska	No joint tenancies for real estate, except for spouses, who may own property as tenants by the entirety. (See below.)
Oregon	A transfer of real estate to spouses creates a tenancy by the entirety, not joint tenancy. All other transfers in joint tenancy create a tenancy in common, unless the deed clearly and expressly states a right of survivorship. (See "Property You Own With Others" in Chapter 5.)
Tennessee	A transfer of real estate to spouses creates a tenancy by the entirety, not joint tenancy. All other transfers in joint tenancy create a tenancy in common. (See "Property You Own With Others" in Chapter 5.)
Wisconsin	No joint tenancies between spouses after January 1, 1986. If spouses attempt to create a joint tenancy, it will be treated as community property with right of survivorship. (See below.)

Generally, to create a joint tenancy, the title document must clearly demonstrate that the owners want to hold the property as joint tenants. In some states, holding the deed "in joint tenancy" is enough. However, in other states, the property must be held "in joint tenancy, with right of survivorship" (JTWROS) or it must be created through a written document that specifies a right to survivorship. And a few states have abolished or restricted joint tenancy; see above.

Tenancy by the Entirety

"Tenancy by the entirety" is a form of property ownership that is similar to joint tenancy. About half the states offer it, and it is limited to married couples or same-sex couples who have registered with the state (in states that allow this).

States That Allow Tenancy by the Entirety		
Alaska[1]	Maryland	Oklahoma
Arkansas	Massachusetts	Oregon[1,2]
Delaware	Michigan	Pennsylvania
District of Columbia[2]	Mississippi	Rhode Island[1,2]
Florida	Missouri	Tennessee
Hawaii[2]	New Jersey[2]	Vermont[2]
Illinois[1,2]	New York[1]	Virginia
Indiana[1]	North Carolina[1]	Wyoming
Kentucky[1]	Ohio[3]	

1 For real estate only.

2 Also available to registered domestic partners (DC, OR), civil unions (IL, HI, NJ, RI, VT), or reciprocal beneficiaries (HI).

3 For real estate only, and only if created before April 4, 1985.

Tenancy by the entirety has many of the same advantages and disadvantages of joint tenancy and is most useful in the same kind of situation: when a couple acquires property together. When one owner dies, the surviving co-owner inherits the property. The property doesn't go through probate.

If property is held in tenancy by the entirety, neither spouse or partner can transfer their one-half of the property alone, either while alive or by will or trust. It must go to the survivor. (This is different from joint tenancy; joint tenants are free to transfer their shares to someone else.)

> **EXAMPLE:** Fred and Ethel hold title to their house in tenancy by the entirety. If Fred wanted to sell or give away his half-interest in the house, he could not do so without Ethel's signature on the deed.

Community Property With Right of Survivorship

Most states that allow married couples to own property as community property also allow them to agree that when one spouse dies, the deceased spouse's community property should automatically transfer to the surviving spouse without probate.

In some states, you can create this type of ownership by using the phrase "community property with right of survivorship" (or something similar, depending on the state) on a deed, a transfer document, or an account registration. In other states, you can agree to leave community property to a surviving spouse without probate by making a written agreement.

If this interests you, get help from a knowledgeable estate planning attorney who can help you weigh the pros and cons of survivorship in community property. A good attorney will also know the correct terminology and formalities required by your state.

You can learn more about community property in Chapter 5.

WillMaker's Washington CPA

If you and your spouse or partner live in the State of Washington, WillMaker can help you make a community property agreement (CPA) that leaves all of your property to your surviving spouse without probate. When you make a will with WillMaker, if you indicate that you live in Washington and that you want all of your property to go to your spouse or partner, a Washington CPA (and detailed instructions for completing it) will print out with your will document. You don't have to use it, but it's there for you if you want it.

If you choose to use the CPA, you still need your will. The CPA will transfer all of your property to your spouse without probate, but you need your will to name an executor, guardians for children, and beneficiaries for the unlikely possibility that you and your spouse or partner die at the same time.

Simplified Probate Proceedings

Many states have simplified some of the more onerous parts of probate by creating categories of property and beneficiaries that don't have to go through a full-blown probate court proceeding. If your family can take advantage of these procedures after your death, you might not need to worry too much about avoiding probate.

Almost every state has some kind of simplified (summary) probate or out-of-court transfer process for one or more of these categories.

Small estates. Most states offer streamlined probate court procedures for small estates; what qualifies as a small estate varies widely from state to state. In many states, even if your total estate is too large to qualify as a small estate, your heirs can still make use of the simplified procedures if the amount that actually goes through probate is under the limit.

Personal property. If the estate is small, many states also let people collect personal property (that's anything but real estate) they've inherited by filling out a sworn statement (affidavit) and giving it to the person who has the property. Typically, the beneficiary must also provide some kind of proof of the right to inherit, such as a death certificate and copy of the will.

Property left to the surviving spouse. In some states, if a surviving spouse inherits less than a certain amount of property, no probate is necessary.

RESOURCE

More information about avoiding probate. To learn more about saving your family the costs and hassles of probate, see *8 Ways to Avoid Probate*, by Mary Randolph (Nolo). You can also learn more about avoiding probate on Nolo.com. Go to www.nolo.com/legal-encyclopedia/ways-avoid-probate.

Reducing Estate Taxes

Estate taxes are imposed after your death, on property you leave at your death. Because everyone is entitled to a very large federal estate tax exemption, only a small number of estates end up owing it. However, some states impose their own estate taxes, and those exemptions can be significantly lower.

The Federal Estate Tax

The vast majority of Americans do not need to worry about federal estate tax, because under the current rules, only very, very large estates owe this tax. Here's why.

The personal estate tax exemption. The personal exemption allows a set dollar amount of property to pass tax free, no matter who inherits it. For deaths in 2026, the personal exemption is $15 million. So if you die in 2026 and your estate is worth less than $15 million, it won't owe federal estate tax. This exemption will rise annually with inflation. Also, if you have made taxable gifts during your life, the amount of the personal exemption will be reduced by the amount of those taxable gifts.

The marital deduction. All property left to a surviving spouse passes free of estate tax. (The marital deduction does not apply to noncitizen spouses.)

The charitable deduction. All property left to a tax-exempt charity is also free of estate tax.

An additional option for married couples. Through "portability," married couples can share their personal exemptions. This allows a surviving spouse to claim any unused portion of the deceased spouse's exemption. In effect, this gives married couples a shared $30 million exemption in 2026.

EXAMPLE: Juan dies in 2026 and leaves $18 million to his widow, Janice. Because property left to a spouse is tax free, no estate tax is owed and none of Juan's personal exemption is used.

Later that year Janice dies, leaving $26 million (her own $8 million plus the $18 million she inherited from her husband) to her children. Her estate won't owe any estate tax either. Here's why: The first $15 million is covered by her own personal exemption. The remaining $11 million is covered by Juan's completely unused personal exemption. Janice's estate would owe tax only if it had grown to over $30 million.

Unless you plan to leave many million dollars' worth of property, you don't need to give federal estate taxes a second thought. If you do expect to leave a very large estate, consult a tax professional or an estate planning attorney to discuss tax planning. (See Chapter 17.)

For more information about federal estate taxes go to the "Estate and Inheritance Taxes" section of Nolo.com at www.nolo.com/legal-encyclopedia/estate-tax.

State Estate and Inheritance Taxes

Even if your estate isn't big enough to owe federal estate tax, you could owe *state* estate or inheritance taxes, if you live in one of the few states that impose them.

Estate tax. A handful of states collect their own estate taxes. Like the federal government, states exempt a large amount of property from each estate. For deaths in 2026, state exemption amounts range between about $1 and $15 million, many increasing over time with inflation. A few of the state exemptions are significantly lower than the federal exemption (like Oregon, which has a $1 million exemption). So, depending on which state you live in and how much property you own, your estate could end up owing state estate taxes, even if it doesn't owe federal estate tax. To find out whether your state has an estate tax and to learn the amount of the personal exemption if it does, go to www.nolo.com/legal-encyclopedia/state-estate-taxes.html.

Inheritance tax. Several states impose a separate tax on a deceased person's property, called an inheritance tax. The tax rate depends on who inherits the property; usually, spouses and other close relatives pay nothing or at a low rate. Learn more about state inheritance taxes in your state at www.nolo.com/legal-encyclopedia/state-inheritance-taxes.html.

If you're worried that your estate might owe state estate or inheritance taxes, see an experienced estate planning lawyer or tax professional to find out whether you can make a plan to avoid or reduce these taxes.

Ways to Reduce Federal Estate Tax

If you have a very large estate, here are some tax-saving strategies you might want to talk about with a tax adviser or an estate planning attorney. Each can be used alone or in combination with other methods.

Annual Tax-Exempt Gifts

If you don't need all your income and property to live on, making sizable gifts while you're alive can be a good way to reduce eventual federal estate taxes. Currently, only gifts larger than $19,000 made to one person or organization in one calendar year count toward the personal estate tax exemption. You can give smaller gifts tax free.

> EXAMPLE: Allen and Julia each give each of their two daughters $19,000 every year for four years. They have transferred $304,000 without becoming liable for gift tax.

Other Tax-Exempt Gifts

Other gifts are exempt regardless of amount, including:

- gifts between spouses who are U.S. citizens (gifts to spouses who are not U.S. citizens are exempt only up to $194,000 per year)
- gifts paid directly for medical bills or school tuition, and
- gifts to tax-exempt charitable organizations.

AB Living Trusts

AB living trusts are designed to help couples with very large estates reduce or eliminate estate tax. However, for married couples, the current federal estate tax rules (see above) make this type of trust useful only if their combined estate is greater than $30 million. Needless to say, most married couples do not need an AB trust under these rules.

That said, you might still consider making an AB trust if:

- **You and your spouse or partner have a large estate** and are worried that changes to estate tax laws might cause you to owe taxes. In this case, you might consider making an AB *disclaimer* trust. AB disclaimer trusts provide flexibility under changing tax laws.
- **You and your partner aren't legally married.** Unmarried couples won't qualify for the special rules for married couples described above, and an AB trust could be useful if you and your partner have a combined estate worth more than $15 million.
- **You might owe state estate tax.** If you live in a state that has an estate tax with an exemption that's lower than the federal exemption, you might owe state estate tax, even if you don't owe federal estate tax. (See above.) An AB disclaimer trust could help you and your spouse or partner avoid or reduce these state taxes.

Keep in mind that AB trusts limit the surviving spouse's ability to use trust property, can be expensive to create, and in some situations can cause stress among family members. So, if you think that an AB trust might be useful for you, do some more research on your own or discuss your options with an experienced estate planning attorney. To learn more about AB trusts, visit the "Wills, Trusts & Probate" section at Nolo.com.

Charitable Trusts

If you want to make a big contribution to a charitable cause you care about—and, at the same time, cut your income taxes now and guarantee some income for life—then a charitable trust might be for you. They're not just for the very rich; some charitable trusts have minimum contributions of a few thousand dollars, and others have no minimum at all.

QTIPs and QDOTs

These trusts, known by their catchy acronyms (easier to say than qualified terminable interest property trust or qualified domestic trust, you have to admit), are mainly used by married couples concerned about estate tax. A QTIP lets couples postpone paying estate tax until the second spouse's death and also locks in, while both are still alive, who inherits the property at the second spouse's death. A QDOT is useful when a spouse who is not a U.S. citizen stands to inherit a large amount of property.

Life Insurance Trusts

Although the proceeds of a life insurance policy don't go through probate, they are included in your estate for estate tax purposes. You can reduce the tax bill by giving ownership of the policy to a life insurance trust (or to the beneficiary directly) at least three years before your death. But like other estate tax-saving strategies, this one will have to be reassessed in light of any changes in estate tax law.

Using Trusts to Control Property

Most people are content to leave their property to their survivors outright, without trying to control what they do with it. However, there are times, especially for people with very large estates, when it can make sense to impose controls on what people can do with property you leave them.

Children and Young Adults

Many people who leave property to children or young adults want to delay the age at which the beneficiaries will receive the property. You can set up this kind of property management in your will. (See Chapter 7.)

Second or Subsequent Marriages

Some people enter into second, third, or fourth marriages unconcerned about estate planning. If each spouse has enough separate property to live comfortably, there might be no need to combine assets and create the problems that can arise as a result. In such cases, the simplest solution is often to make a prenuptial agreement making it clear that separate property stays separate; then each can make an independent estate plan for that property.

But in many second or subsequent marriages, one or both spouses might feel conflicted about estate planning. On one hand, a surviving spouse might need the income from, or the use of, the other spouse's property to live comfortably. On the other hand, either spouse might want to provide an inheritance for children from a former marriage. This situation becomes even more complicated when a current spouse and children from a former marriage don't get along well.

One possible solution is to set up a trust—often called a "marital property control trust"—to try to balance the interests and needs of all concerned. Essentially, this type of trust gives the surviving spouse some use of or income from the trust property, then leaves the property outright to children from a prior marriage when the surviving spouse dies.

A marital property control trust is different from an AB trust (discussed above), which aims only to reduce estate taxes. With an AB trust, the surviving spouse is usually granted the maximum rights allowed under IRS rules to use trust property. In contrast, a marital property control trust is designed to protect the trust principal, so that most of it still exists when the surviving spouse dies.

Trusts like these are tricky, and you'll need an experienced lawyer to help you set one up.

Beneficiaries With Special Needs

Gifts left directly to a beneficiary with special needs will jeopardize that person's access to public benefits. The solution is often to establish a trust—called a "special needs trust"—to manage the property while preserving the beneficiary's eligibility for government benefits. You can learn more about this kind of trust by reading *Special Needs Trusts: Protect Your Child's Financial Future*, by Kevin Urbatsch and Jessica Farinas Jones (Nolo). An electronic version of this book is available online in your WillMaker portal and in the Books section of your WillMaker software.

Big Spenders

If you want to leave a substantial amount of property to someone who is known to be irresponsible with money, a good estate planning lawyer can help you establish a "spendthrift trust." In it, you can empower a trusted person or institution to dole out the money a little at a time.

Groups of Beneficiaries

For any number of reasons, you might want the exact division of your estate to be determined after your death, instead of directing the division in a will or trust.

The usual way to accomplish this is to create what is called a "sprinkling trust." Usually, the trust creator names the beneficiaries of the trust during life, but does not specify what share each is to receive. That is done by the trustee, after the creator dies, under whatever terms the trust dictates. Again, you'll need an experienced lawyer to set up this kind of trust.

SEE AN EXPERT

How to find a good lawyer. Many of the estate planning strategies discussed in this chapter require a lawyer's help. For tips on finding the expert you need, see Chapter 17.

CHAPTER

14

Durable Power of Attorney for Finances

Many people fear that they might someday become seriously ill and unable to handle their own financial affairs—that they might be unable to pay bills, make bank deposits, watch over investments, or collect insurance and government benefits. As you grow older or face the possibility of an incapacitating illness, it's wise to plan for such a contingency. Fortunately, there's a simple way to do so: preparing a durable power of attorney for finances.

About Durable Powers of Attorney for Finances

A durable power of attorney for finances is a reliable legal document in which you name someone who will make your financial decisions if you become unable to do so yourself.

This person is called your agent, or in some states, your attorney-in-fact. (Your WillMaker document will include the correct term for your state.)

If you ever do become incapacitated, the durable power of attorney will likely appear as a minor miracle to those who are close to you.

TIP

Keeping track of information for your agent. The agent you name might need to know a vast number of details about your property and how you deal with it. With the download version of WillMaker, you can make an Information for Caregivers and Survivors form to help with this task. With this document, you can provide a comprehensive guide to the details of your life—ranging from information about your property and your financial accounts to the names and addresses of people you want contacted in the event of your illness—to the person who will care for you in the event of your incapacity. To find out more, open the download version of WillMaker, click "Your Documents," and select "Information for Caregivers and Survivors" from the list.

CAUTION

The perils of forging a signature. If someone becomes incapacitated, panicky family members might consider just faking the signatures necessary to carry on routine financial matters. It might seem perfectly acceptable to sign Aunt Amanda's name to a check if the money is used to pay her phone bill.

But this is forgery—and it's a crime. The law is strict in this area to guard against dishonest family members who might loot a relative's assets.

Forging a signature on checks, bills of sale, tax returns, or other financial documents might work for a while, but it will probably be discovered eventually. And then the court proceeding everyone was trying to avoid will be necessary—and a judge will not be eager to put a proven liar in charge of a relative's finances.

Important Terms

- **Principal.** The person who creates and signs the power of attorney document, authorizing someone else to act for them. If you make a durable power of attorney for finances, you are the principal.
- **Agent (Attorney-in-Fact).** The person who is authorized to act for the principal.
- **Alternate Agent (Alternate Attorney-in-Fact).** The person who takes over as agent if your first choice cannot or will not serve.
- **Durable Power of Attorney.** A power of attorney that will remain in effect even if the principal becomes incapacitated. This is the kind of power of attorney you make with WillMaker.
- **Incapacitated.** Unable to handle one's own financial matters or health care decisions. Also called disabled or incompetent in some states. Usually, a physician makes the determination.

About WillMaker's Form

WillMaker allows you to create your own durable power of attorney for finances. Using this power of attorney, you can:

- name your agent
- appoint a backup in case your agent cannot serve, and
- state exactly how much authority you want your agent to have over your finances.

In addition to your durable power of attorney for finances, WillMaker prints out a number of related documents. The first of these is an information sheet for you to give to your agent, explaining what the agent's responsibilities will be. There are also several forms designed to make your agent's job easier—including forms for delegating tasks to others and resigning from the job if that becomes necessary. Finally, WillMaker provides a form that you can use to revoke your durable power of attorney if you change your mind.

When Not to Use This Form

A durable power of attorney is not the right solution for every problem. In some cases, a different form is needed. In other cases, a conservatorship might be a better idea. Do not use a durable power of attorney for finances in these situations:

- **You can't think of someone you trust enough to appoint as your agent.** In this case, you're probably better off without a durable power of attorney. A conservatorship, with the safeguard of court supervision, might be worth the extra cost and trouble.
- **You anticipate family fights.** If you expect that family members will challenge your document or make continual trouble for your agent, a conservatorship might be preferable. Your relatives might still fight, but at least the court will be there to keep an eye on your welfare and your property. If family discord is a concern, hire an attorney to help you decide whether a durable power of attorney is the right choice for you.

- **You want to authorize health care decisions.** A durable power of attorney for finances does not give your agent legal authority to make health care decisions for you. To make sure that your wishes for health care are known and followed, create a health care directive. (See Chapter 15.)

Avoiding Conservatorship Proceedings

If you don't have a durable power of attorney, or if there is no one available to serve as your agent, a judge will name someone to manage your financial affairs. This process is commonly known as "conservatorship proceedings," and the person appointed is usually called a "conservator."

State law generally provides a priority list for who should be appointed. This might be your spouse, adult child, parent, or sibling. In many states, the law allows the court to appoint whoever it determines will act in your best interests.

Conservatorship proceedings can be a complex and costly affair. They are also a matter of public record, potentially exposing your personal financial matters to the public. In addition, family disagreements over the choice of conservator can make things even more complicated, leading to considerable strain and expense, particularly if legal representation is required.

That said, in some cases, a conservatorship could be useful or even desirable—for example, when a judge is the best person to resolve family infighting or when a court is needed to keep an eye on your finances. But more often, the hassles of a conservatorship do not justify the benefits, and you should do what you can to avoid a conservatorship.

Thankfully, you can use your durable power of attorney to give your agent full legal authority to handle your financial affairs. If you do that, a conservatorship proceeding would be necessary only if no one were willing to serve as agent, if the agent wanted guidance from a court, or if a close relative thinks the agent isn't acting in your best interests.

- **You want to authorize decisions about marriage, adoption, voting, or wills.** You cannot authorize your agent to marry, adopt, vote in public elections, or make a will on your behalf. These acts are considered too personal to delegate to someone else.
- **To give powers delegated to others.** If you've already given someone legal authority to manage some or all of your property, you cannot delegate that authority to your agent. For example, you cannot use your durable power of attorney to give your agent the authority to manage your interest in a partnership business if you have a signed agreement giving that authority to your partners.
- **To create, modify, or revoke a trust.** The power of attorney you make with WillMaker doesn't allow you to give your agent permission to create, modify, or revoke a trust on your behalf—with one exception. If you've already set up a revocable living trust, you can give your agent the power to transfer property to that trust.

About Your Agent

This section explains more about the responsibilities the person you name as agent will have toward you and your property.

Possible Powers

Commonly, people give an agent broad power over their finances. But it's up to you. Using WillMaker's durable power of attorney, you can give your agent authority to do some or all of the following:

- use your assets to pay your everyday expenses and those of your family
- handle transactions with banks and other financial institutions
- buy, sell, maintain, pay taxes on, and mortgage real estate and other property
- file and pay your taxes
- manage your retirement accounts
- collect benefits from Social Security, Medicare, or other government programs or civil or military service

- invest your money in stocks, bonds, and mutual funds
- buy and sell insurance policies and annuities for you
- operate your small business
- access and control your digital assets
- claim or disclaim property you get from others
- make gifts of your assets to organizations and individuals that you choose
- transfer property to a living trust you've already set up, and
- hire someone to represent you in court.

(These powers are discussed in detail a little later in this chapter.) You can tailor your durable power of attorney for finances to fit your needs by choosing which powers you grant and placing certain conditions and restrictions upon the agent. For example, you can give your agent authority over your real estate, with the express restriction that your house cannot be sold.

Legal Responsibilities

The agent you appoint in your durable power of attorney is a fiduciary—someone who holds a position of trust and must act in your best interests. The law requires your agent to:

- handle your property honestly and prudently
- avoid conflicts of interest
- keep your property completely separate from their own, and
- keep adequate records.

These standards do not present problems in most simple situations. For example, if you just want your agent to sign for your pension check, deposit it in your bank account, and pay for your basic needs, there is little possibility of uncertainty or dispute.

Sometimes, however, these rules impose unnecessary hardships on an agent. For example, your property might already be mixed with that of your agent, and it might make good sense for that to continue. WillMaker allows you to insert clauses in your power of attorney document that permit your agent to deviate from some of the rules above, so that the agent's freedom isn't unnecessarily fettered. (See "Additional Duties and Responsibilities," below.)

When Court Supervision Might Be Required

An agent is not directly supervised by a court; that's the whole point of naming one. The agent is not required to file reports with any courts or government agencies.

But a court might become involved if someone close to you fears that the agent is acting dishonestly or not in your best interests. It's rare, but close relatives or friends might ask a court to order the agent to take certain actions. Or they might ask the court to terminate the power of attorney and appoint a conservator to look after your affairs. If a conservator is appointed for you, the agent will have to account to the conservator—or the conservator might revoke your durable power of attorney altogether.

Some states have statutes that set out specific procedures for such court actions. For example, a California statute authorizes any interested person, including relatives and friends of the principal, to ask a court to resolve questions relating to the durable power of attorney. Tennessee law provides that the next of kin can petition a court to require an agent to post a bond—something like an insurance policy, generally issued by a surety company.

Even if your state does not have a statute specifically authorizing court actions, someone interested in your welfare and upset with the agent could still go to court and ask for a conservator to be appointed.

Liability for Mistakes

Your agent must be careful with your money and other property. State laws require an agent to act as a prudent person would under the circumstances. That means the primary goal is to not lose your money.

The agent can, however, make careful investment moves on your behalf. For example, if your money is in a low-interest bank account, the agent might invest the money in government bonds, which pay higher interest but are still very safe.

Because most people choose a spouse, close relative, or friend to be agent, your power of attorney makes your agent liable only for losses resulting from intentional wrongdoing or extreme carelessness—not for a well-meaning decision that turns out badly.

Record-Keeping Responsibilities

Your agent is legally required to keep accurate and separate records for all transactions made on your behalf. Good records are particularly important if the agent ever wants to resign and turn the responsibility over to another person.

Record keeping isn't an onerous requirement. The agent must simply be able to show where and how your money has been spent. In most instances, it's enough to have bank records and receipts for bills paid and claims made. And because the agent will probably file tax returns on your behalf, income and expense records might be necessary.

> **EXAMPLE:** Keiji appoints Kathryn, his niece, to serve as his agent. Keiji receives income from his savings, two IRAs, Social Security, and stock dividends. Kathryn must keep records of the income.

You and your prospective agent should discuss and agree on what record keeping is appropriate. The agent might also want to review your current records now to make sure they're in order. If you don't have clear records, the agent might have to spend a lot of time sorting things out later.

As part of managing your finances, the agent might hire a bookkeeper, an accountant, or another financial adviser and pay for the services from your property.

TIP

Getting help with organizing. If, like many people, you keep records in haphazardly labeled shoeboxes and file folders, this might be a good time to get organized. For help, use the Information for Caregivers and Survivors form in the download version of WillMaker.

The Basics of Your Durable Power of Attorney

In almost every state, you can create a valid power of attorney if you are at least 18 years old and of sound mind. This mental competency requirement isn't hard to meet. Generally, you must understand what a durable power of attorney for finances is and does—and you must understand that you are making one.

To make WillMaker's durable power of attorney, you must enter some basic identifying information about yourself. This section explains the questions WillMaker poses, in the order they appear.

Your Name

If you have already used WillMaker to prepare your will, living trust, health care directives, or final arrangements, your name will automatically appear on the screen that requests this information.

If it does not, enter your name the way it appears on formal business documents, such as your driver's license, bank accounts, or real estate deeds. This might or might not be the name that appears on your birth certificate.

If you have used different names in important documents, you can list all of them on the screen, separated by a.k.a., which stands for "also known as." Be sure to enter all names in which you hold bank accounts, stocks, bonds, real estate, and other property. This will make it far easier for your agent to get the job done.

If you use more than one name and you're up for some extra work, you might also consider settling on one name for your power of attorney document, and then changing your other documents to conform. That will clean up your records and save your agent some trouble later on. To change your name on official documents and records—for example, bank accounts, deeds, or Social Security records—you'll have to contact the appropriate government office or financial institution to find out what documentation they'll need.

Your Social Security Number

Your Social Security number can be very useful for your agent. It can help your agent to obtain your financial information and take care of your affairs. WillMaker does not ask you to include the number in your document. Concerns about identity theft make it important for you to protect this sensitive piece of information. Some states even forbid Social Security numbers on documents that will be placed in the public records. That said, you should be sure that your agent knows your Social Security number. Write it down and ask your agent to keep it safe.

Your Address

Enter the complete address of your residence. If during the course of the year you live in more than one state, use the address in the state where you vote, register vehicles, own valuable property, have bank accounts, or run a business. If you've already made other estate planning documents, be consistent: Use the same address for every document.

When Your Document Takes Effect

Your WillMaker durable power of attorney for finances is effective as soon as you sign it. This means that your agent can start acting on your behalf whenever you choose. If you need someone to help you keep an eye on your finances, you might want your agent to start acting for you right away. On the other hand, you might prefer that your agent use the document only if you are unable to handle matters yourself, either because you are temporarily ill or injured or because of long-term incapacity.

If you want your agent to use the document only if you become incapacitated and unable to take care of your finances, be sure to clearly convey those wishes to the person you name. If you don't trust that your agent will refrain from using the document unless and until you are incapacitated, consider naming someone else to do the job.

Springing Powers of Attorney

You might have heard of "springing" powers of attorney—that is, powers of attorney that "spring" into effect when you become incapacitated. Many people like the idea of these documents because they prefer not to make their power of attorney effective while they can still manage their own affairs. However, in practice, using a springing power of attorney often causes more problems than it solves. For example:

- **Delay.** Instead of being able to use the power of attorney as soon as the need arises, the agent must get a "determination" of your incapacity before using the document. In other words, someone—usually a doctor—must certify that you can no longer make your own decisions. This could take days or weeks and disrupt the handling of your finances.
- **HIPAA/privacy issues.** State and federal laws, including the Health Insurance Portability and Accountability Act (HIPAA), protect your right to keep medical information private. This means that doctors can release information about your medical condition only under very limited conditions. To certify your incapacity, your agent will need to provide proof that the doctor can legally release information about you to your agent. You might be able to resolve this issue by completing a release form before you become incapacitated. However, your agent could still run into problems caused by bureaucracy or by the doctor's confusion about what is legally required. Navigating these issues could cause serious headaches and delays for your agent.
- **Definition of incapacity.** A springing power of attorney must define incapacity. Then, when it comes time for the determination, your doctor will have to agree that you meet that definition. But how do you know now what health changes will cause you to need help managing your finances? What if you want help before you become incapacitated as defined by your document? What if you have some good days and some bad days? What if your agent or your lawyer believes you no longer have capacity, but your doctor disagrees? These gray areas might make it difficult, if not impossible, for your agent to help you when you need it.

Springing Powers of Attorney (continued)

Making a durable power of attorney that takes effect as soon as you sign it avoids these problems. Just make sure your agent understands exactly when and how you want the document to be used. This degree of trust is a basic requirement for naming an agent. If you don't trust your agent to handle the power of attorney exactly as you intend, you should choose someone else to handle your finances.

If you still feel that you want a springing power, see a lawyer for help. An experienced lawyer can draft a power of attorney that is more closely tailored to your specific situation and concerns.

Choosing Your Agent

WillMaker asks you to name your agent. This is the most important decision you must make when you create a durable power of attorney. Depending on the powers you grant, the agent can have tremendous power over your property. You need to choose someone you trust completely. Fortunately, most of us know at least one such person—usually a spouse, relative, or close friend. If there's no one you trust completely with this authority, a durable power of attorney isn't for you.

Remember that you can't count on anyone else to keep an eye on your finances after your agent takes over. If your agent handles your affairs carelessly or dishonestly, the only recourse would be a lawsuit—usually not a satisfactory approach. Lawsuits are burdensome and expensive and would entangle your loved ones in all the legal red tape a power of attorney is designed to avoid. And there's no guarantee that money an incompetent agent lost would ever be recovered. This reality is not intended to frighten you needlessly, but simply to underscore the need to make a careful choice about who will represent you.

Any competent adult can serve as your agent; the person most definitely doesn't have to be a lawyer. But don't appoint someone without first discussing it to make sure that person will accept this serious responsibility.

If you don't, you might well cause problems down the line. The person you've chosen might not want to serve, for a variety of reasons. And even if the person would be willing, if your choice doesn't know about the document, confusion and delay are inevitable if you become incapacitated.

TIP

A printout of your agent's tasks. Your power of attorney prints out with an information sheet you can give to your agent explaining the responsibilities of the job. You can use this document to help you remember the main issues when talking with your agent.

In most situations, the agent does not need extensive experience in financial management; common sense, dependability, and complete honesty are enough. If necessary, your agent can get professional help—from an accountant, a lawyer, or a tax preparer, perhaps—and pay for it out of your assets.

Sometimes it's tough to know whom to choose. Perhaps your spouse or partner is ill or wouldn't be a good choice for other reasons. Or you might not know anyone whom you feel entirely comfortable asking to take over your financial affairs. Or, if you have an active, complex investment portfolio or own a business, you might decide that your agent needs business skills, knowledge, or management abilities beyond those of the people closest to you.

If you're not sure who your agent should be, read the rest of this section and discuss the issue with those close to you. If you can't come up with a family member or close friend to name, you might want to consider asking your lawyer, business partner, or banker to serve as agent. If you really know and trust the person, it might be a good option for you. Keep in mind that it's better not to make a durable power of attorney than to entrust your affairs to someone in whom you don't have complete confidence.

Discussing Your Wishes

Set aside time to talk with your agent about when to start taking care of financial tasks for you. You can agree that your agent should not exercise any authority under the document unless you become completely unable to take care of yourself and your property—or unless you otherwise direct. With respect to exercising authority under the document, your agent is legally required to follow your wishes.

If you become dissatisfied with your agent's actions and you are still of sound mind, you can revoke the durable power of attorney and end your agent's power to act for you.

CAUTION

Addressing family conflict. If there are long-standing feuds among family members, they might object to your choice of agent or the extent of the authority delegated. If you foresee any such conflicts, it's wise to try to defuse them in advance. A discussion with the people who are leery of the power of attorney might help. If you still feel uncomfortable after talking things over, you might want to discuss the troubles with a knowledgeable lawyer. A lawyer can review your estate planning documents and might help you feel reassured that your plans will be carried out as you wish.

CAUTION

Residents of medical facilities in Utah or Nevada. In Nevada and Utah, if you live (or will soon live) in a hospital, an assisted living facility, or a skilled nursing facility, your agent cannot be the facility itself, the owner or operator of the facility, or an employee of the facility. This rule does not apply if the agent is your spouse, next of kin, or legal guardian. If you have questions or concerns about this issue, see an attorney for help. (Utah Code § 75A-2-105; Nev. Rev. Stat. § 162A.220.)

Avoiding Poor Choices for Your Agent

When choosing an agent:

Avoid naming someone who lives far away. To carry out duties and responsibilities properly and promptly, it's usually best that the agent live nearby. Although overnight mail, email, smartphones, video calls, and other technology have made it easier to conduct business long-distance, it's still best for your agent to be close at hand—or at least willing to travel and spend time handling your affairs when needed. After all, this is the person who will be responsible for day-to-day details of your finances: opening your mail, paying bills, looking after property, and so on. Of course, many families are spread across the country these days. If there's only one person you trust enough to name as agent, and that person lives far away, you might have to settle for the less-than-ideal situation.

Don't name an institution, such as a bank, as agent. Naming an institutional agent isn't legal in some states, and it's definitely not desirable. Serving as agent is a personal responsibility, and there should be personal connection and trust between you and your agent. If the person you trust most happens to be your banker, appoint that person, not the bank.

If You Are Married or Partnered

If you're married or partnered, you'll probably want to name your spouse as your agent unless there is a compelling reason not to do so. There are powerful legal and practical reasons, in addition to the emotional ones, for appointing your spouse. The main one is that naming anyone else creates the risk of conflicts between the agent and your spouse over how to manage property that belongs to both spouses.

EXAMPLE: Henry and Amelia, a married couple, each create a durable power of attorney for finances. Henry names Amelia as his agent, but Amelia names her sister Anna. Later, Amelia becomes unable to manage her financial affairs, and Anna takes over as her agent. Soon Anna and Henry are arguing bitterly over what should be done with the house and investments that Henry and Amelia own together. If they can't resolve their differences, Henry or Anna might have to go to court and ask a judge to determine what is in Amelia's best interests.

However, if your spouse is ill, quite elderly, or simply not equipped to manage your financial affairs, you might have to name someone else as agent. The wisest course is for you and your spouse to agree on whom the agent should be, perhaps one of your grown children.

SEE AN EXPERT

Divorce might not end your spouse's authority. In many states, if your spouse is your agent, that designation does not automatically end if you get divorced. Wherever you live after a divorce, you should revoke the power of attorney and create a new one, naming someone else as your new agent.

If You Have a Living Trust

If you have created a revocable living trust, the successor trustee you named in the trust document will have power over the trust property if you become incapacitated. If you and your spouse made a living trust together, the trust document almost certainly gives your spouse authority over trust property if you become incapacitated.

Creating a durable power of attorney for finances doesn't change any of this. Your agent will not have authority over property in your living trust. To avoid conflicts, it is usually best to have the same person managing both trust property and nontrust property if you become incapacitated. So, normally, you'll name the same person as successor trustee and as your agent.

EXAMPLE: Carlos, a widower, prepares a revocable living trust to avoid probate and a durable power of attorney for finances in case he becomes incapacitated. He names his son, Jeffrey, as successor trustee of the living trust and agent under the durable power of attorney.

Several years later, Carlos has a stroke and is temporarily unable to handle his everyday finances. Jeffrey steps in to deposit his father's pension checks and pay monthly bills, using his authority as agent. As successor trustee, he also has legal authority over the property Carlos transferred to his living trust, including Carlos's house.

Appointing More Than One Person

In general, it's a bad idea to name more than one agent, because conflicts between them could disrupt the handling of your finances. Also, some banks and other financial institutions prefer to deal with a single agent.

Still, it is legal to name more than one person—and WillMaker allows you to name up to three people to serve together. But if you're tempted to name more than one person simply so that no one feels hurt or left out, think again. It might be better to pick one person for the job and explain your reasoning to the others now. If you name more than one person and they don't get along, they might wind up resolving their disputes in court. The result might be more bad feelings than if you had just picked one person to be agent and explained your choice in the first place.

Making Decisions

If you name more than one agent, you'll have to grapple with the question of how they should make decisions. You can require coagents to carry out their duties in one of two ways:

- they must all reach agreement before they take any action on your behalf, or
- they can make decisions independently of one another.

Both methods have strengths and pitfalls, and there's no hard-and-fast rule on which is better. Choose the approach that feels more comfortable to you.

Requiring your agents to act jointly ensures that decisions are made carefully and with the knowledge of everyone involved, but coordinating multiple decision makers can be burdensome and time-consuming. On the other hand, allowing your agents to act separately makes it easy to get things done, but allowing two or three people to make independent decisions about your finances can lead to poor record keeping and general confusion. For example, your agents might independently take money out of your bank accounts or buy and sell stock without full knowledge of what the others are doing to manage your investments.

If There Is a Disagreement

If your agents get into a dispute that interferes with their ability to represent you properly, they might need help working things out. Getting help could mean submitting the dispute to mediation or arbitration—or going to court to have a judge decide what's best. Your agents can decide how they want to handle the matter, keeping in mind that their foremost responsibility is to act in your best interest. The downside of all this is not just that there could be confusion and delays in handling your finances, but that you'll probably be the one to pay the costs of settling the dispute. All these are reasons to name just one agent.

If One or More Cannot Serve

If you name more than one agent, and one of them can't serve, the others will continue to serve. If none of them can serve, an alternate can take over.

SEE AN EXPERT

If you want to name more than three people. The best approach is usually to choose just one agent. But WillMaker allows you to name up to three people to serve together. Asking two or three people to manage your finances can prove unwieldy enough—counting on more than three to coordinate their actions on your behalf would be a logistical nightmare. If you want to name more than three agents, get help from a lawyer.

Naming Alternates

It's a good idea to name someone to take over as your agent in case your first choice can't serve or needs to resign. Using WillMaker's financial power of attorney, you can name up to two alternate agents, officially called successors. Your first alternate would take over if your initial choice can't serve. The second alternate would take the job only if your first and second choices can't keep it.

When naming alternates, use the same criteria that you used to make your first choice for agent. Your alternates should be every bit as trustworthy and competent. If you don't know anyone you trust well enough to name as a first or second alternate, skip the matter altogether.

Someone who is asked to serve as an alternate agent might be worried about possible liability for the acts of the original agent. To protect against this, your power of attorney will state that a successor agent is not liable for any acts of a prior agent.

You can also authorize your agent to appoint someone to serve if all those you named cannot. You do this by giving your agent permission to delegate tasks to others. (See "Additional Duties and Responsibilities," below.) Allowing your agent to delegate the job to someone else eliminates the risk that the position might become vacant because of the original agent's disability or resignation. If this occurs, and you haven't named a successor or none of your successors is available, your durable power of attorney would be useless. There would have to be a conservatorship proceeding to find someone to manage your finances.

If You Name More Than One Agent

If you name more than one agent, the person you name as a first alternate will take over only if all of your agents are unable to do the job. If any number of your first choices can continue to serve, they can do so alone, without the addition of your alternate.

If you name a second alternate, that person will take over only in the extremely unlikely event that all of your named agents and your first alternate cannot serve.

Specific Financial Powers

Using WillMaker's financial power of attorney, you can give your agent up to 16 specific financial powers. The powers can put an enormous amount of control over your finances into the hands of your agent, and it's important that you understand exactly what each power authorizes your agent to do. To that end, the next sections walk you through each power, one at a time, asking whether you want to grant it or not.

If you grant all the powers, your agent will be able to handle your investments, real estate, banking, and other financial tasks. The agent can use your assets to pay your debts and expenses—including home maintenance, taxes, insurance premiums, wage claims, medical care, child support, alimony, and your personal allowance. The agent can sign deeds, make gifts, pay school expenses, and endorse and deposit checks.

Restricting the Sale of Your Home

Losing your home, especially if you've lived there many years, can be a disturbing prospect. Some people feel strongly that the agent should not sell their home—no matter what happens. If you want to grant the real estate power but forbid your agent from selling or mortgaging your home, WillMaker allows allow you to include that restriction.

But think carefully before you tie the hands of your agent in this way. You certainly don't want to lose your home—but a financial emergency might make it necessary. Ideally, you'll trust the person you name as your agent to use discretion to make the decision based on your best interests—particularly if you have named your spouse or other co-owner of your home to serve as your agent.

As you go through the list of powers, you might find yourself feeling concerned about how much power you're putting in someone else's hands. These feelings are not unusual, as the lists of actions your agent can take are long, exhaustive, and perhaps a bit overwhelming. As reassurance, keep in mind your agent's overriding legal duty to act carefully—and always with your best interests at heart. (See "About Your Agent," above.) If you still find yourself feeling uncomfortable, take some time to reflect on your choice of agent; be sure you've chosen the best person for the job.

Each of the financial powers is explained here. They are presented as they appear in the interview.

Real Estate Transactions

This power puts the agent in charge of any real estate you own. Your agent must, for example, use your assets to pay your mortgage and taxes and arrange for necessary repairs and maintenance to your home. Most important, this power allows the agent to sell, mortgage, partition, or lease your real estate.

The agent can also take any other action connected to real estate. For example, your agent can:

- buy or lease real estate for you
- refinance your mortgage to get a better interest rate
- pay off legal claims on your property
- buy insurance for your property
- build, remodel, or remove structures on your property
- grant easements over your property, and
- bring or defend lawsuits over real estate.

If you grant this power, in addition to signing your power of attorney and having it notarized, you must record it with the local land records office. See "Recording," below.

Personal Property Transactions

Personal property here means physical items of property—for example, cars, furniture, jewelry, computers, and tools. It does not include real estate or intangible kinds of property such as stocks or bank accounts.

If you grant this power, your agent can buy, sell, rent, or exchange personal property on your behalf. Your agent can also insure, use, move, store, repair, or pawn your personal things. Again, all actions must be taken in your best interest.

EXAMPLE: Paul names his wife, Gloria, as his agent for financial matters. When he later goes into a nursing home, his old car, which he can no longer use, becomes an expense Gloria cannot afford. As Paul's agent, she has legal authority to sell the car.

Stock, Bond, Commodity, and Option Transactions

This power gives your agent the power to manage your securities—including stocks, bonds, mutual funds, certificates of deposit, commodities, and call and put options. If you grant this power, your agent can buy or sell securities on your behalf, accept or transfer certificates or other evidence of ownership, and exercise voting rights.

CAUTION

Brokers might use different forms. Many brokerage houses have their own durable power of attorney forms. If yours does, it's a good idea to use it in addition to the power of attorney you make with WillMaker. Using your broker's form will make things easier for your agent, because your broker will have no need to investigate your power of attorney and quibble over its terms. The broker will already have its form on file and will understand exactly what your agent is authorized to do. If you do use a broker's form in conjunction with WillMaker's power of attorney, be consistent; name the same agent for both documents.

Banking and Other Financial Institution Transactions

One of the most common reasons for making a durable power of attorney is to arrange for someone to handle banking transactions. If you give your agent authority to handle your bank accounts, your bills can be paid, and pension or other checks can be deposited in your accounts even if you can no longer take care of these matters yourself.

EXAMPLE: Virginia, who is in her 70s, is admitted to the hospital for emergency surgery. She's too weak to even think about paying her bills or making sure that her Social Security check is deposited into her checking account. Fortunately, she earlier created a durable power of attorney for finances, naming her niece Marianne as her agent. Marianne can use her power as Virginia's agent to check the balance of Virginia's bank account and to pay the bills that come while Virginia is in the hospital.

With this power, your agent can open and close accounts with banks, savings and loans, credit unions, or other financial institutions on your behalf. The agent can write checks on these accounts, endorse checks you receive, and receive account statements. The agent also has access to your safe deposit box, to withdraw or add to its contents.

In most states, the agent can also borrow money on your behalf and pledge your assets as security for the loan.

Signing Checks and Other Documents

Many people wonder how the agent signs checks and other documents on behalf of the principal. Exact procedures vary depending on both local custom and the procedures of a particular financial institution or government agency. In some places, after establishing authority with a particular institution or agency, the agent will sign the agent's own name to checks and documents, followed by "POA" or other language such as "under power of attorney dated June 15, 2024." In other locations, the agent will first sign your name and then the agent's own name, followed by the "POA" designation. The agent should ask the institution or agency for its preference before signing.

CAUTION

Financial institutions might use different forms. Many banks and other financial institutions have their own durable power of attorney forms. Even though granting the banking power in your WillMaker power of attorney will give your agent authority to act on your behalf at any financial institution, it's a good idea to use the financial institution's form in addition to the form you make with WillMaker. Using the form that your financial institution is most familiar with will make it easier for your agent to get things done. If you do use their form in conjunction with WillMaker's power of attorney, be consistent; name the same agent for both documents.

Business Operating Transactions

This power gives your agent authority to act for you in operating a business that you own yourself or that you run as a partnership, limited liability company, or corporation. Subject to the terms of a partnership agreement, an operating agreement, or corporate rules set out in the bylaws and shareholders' agreements, this power allows your agent to:

- sell or liquidate the business
- merge with another company
- prepare, sign, and file reports, information, and returns with government agencies
- pay business taxes
- enforce the terms of any partnership agreement in court, and
- exercise any power or option you have under a partnership agreement.

If your business is a sole proprietorship, the agent can also:

- hire and fire employees
- move the business
- change the nature of the business or its methods of operation, including selling, marketing, accounting, and advertising
- change the name of the business

- change the form of the business's organization—that is, enter into a partnership agreement or incorporate the business
- continue or renegotiate the business's contracts
- enter contracts with lawyers, accountants, or others, and
- collect and spend money on behalf of the business.

If you're a sole proprietor, a durable power of attorney is a very useful way to let someone else run the business if you become unable to do so. No court proceedings are required for the agent to take over if you become incapacitated, so there should be no disruption of your business. If you grant this power, be sure to work out a business plan with the person you plan to appoint as your agent; explain what you want for your business and how you expect it to be managed.

CAUTION

Check your existing agreements. If you operate your business with other people as a partnership, limited liability company, or closely held corporation, your business agreement should cover what happens if a partner or shareholder becomes incapacitated. Typically, the other business owners can operate the business during the incapacitated person's absence or even buy out that person's share. A durable power of attorney will not affect these rules you already have in place.

EXAMPLE: Mike wants his wife, Nancy, to be his agent to manage his finances if he becomes incapacitated. Mike, a housepainter, runs the M-J Painting Co. with his equal partner, Jack. Their agreement provides that if one partner becomes incapacitated, the other has exclusive authority to operate the business.

If Jack and Nancy have conflicts over money, however, there could be some problems. Mike, Jack, and Nancy should think through the arrangement carefully and might want to consult a lawyer. Whatever they decide on should be spelled out in detail in the partnership agreement. They might also want to create a customized durable power of attorney, with the lawyer's help, that sets out the details of the business arrangements.

Digital Assets and Accounts

This power gives your agent the ability to manage your digital assets, including email, blogs, online financial accounts, social media, and any other electronic accounts or files.

If you include this power, your document will provide very broad rights for your agent, including the right to access, control, distribute, duplicate, deactivate, or delete your accounts or records. Of course, like all authority you grant in your power of attorney, your agent can do these things only in your best interest and according to your instructions.

Ideally, this power will allow your agent to handle tasks such as paying bills using your online bank account, posting a note to your blog, or renewing your auto insurance online. But stating this power in your document might not be enough. Your agent's ability to get into your accounts will depend on:

- whether your agent has your username and password information
- whether you have made any prior arrangements with the company about your agent's ability to access your account
- possibly, the company's terms of service agreement
- why your agent needs access, and
- your state's law.

The easiest way to make sure that your agent will be able to access your accounts is to give your agent a list of your usernames and passwords. That way, your agent will immediately have the same control over the accounts that you would have. You can include this information in a separate letter to your agent, like WillMaker's Letter to Survivors. Or you can use the Information for Caregivers and Survivors form (available in the download version of WillMaker), which prompts you to leave username and password information for a variety of accounts. Of course, as discussed above in "Choosing Your Agent," providing this sensitive information to your agent underscores the need for you to trust that person completely. Be sure to store it in a safe place and tell your agent where to find it.

If your agent doesn't have your username and password information, getting access to your digital assets will probably be difficult. Most states now give agents the legal power to access digital assets when the power of attorney provides for such power. However, even where access is theoretically permitted by law, in the practical matter of actually getting access or information from the businesses that control the accounts, agents are likely to face bureaucracy (at best) and obstruction (at worst).

If you want your agent to have maximum access to your digital assets, include this power and also leave instructions about how to access the accounts in a separate document. You might also want to provide some guidance on what you'd like your agent to do with your digital property. For example, you could ask your agent to respond to certain emails, update the amount of your automatic online payments to reflect the annual increase of your insurance premium, or close your Facebook account. For more help thinking about how your agent could help with your digital assets, go to www.nolo.com/legal-encyclopedia/digital-assets.

If, on the other hand, you don't want your agent to have access to your online accounts and other digital assets, skip this power. But also keep in mind that you might need to take further steps to protect your privacy. Depending on state law, your agent might be able to access some of your digital assets even if you leave this power out of your document. To restrict your agent's authority to access your online accounts, see a lawyer for help.

Insurance and Annuity Transactions

This power allows your agent to buy, borrow against, cash in, or cancel insurance policies or annuity contracts for you and your spouse, children, and other dependent family members. Under this power, the agent's authority extends to all your policies and contracts, whether they name you or someone else as the beneficiary—that is, the person who will receive any proceeds of the policy when you die.

The one exception to this rule covers insurance policies you own with your spouse. Under these policies, your spouse must consent to any transaction that affects the policy. So, if your agent is not your spouse, your agent will have to obtain your spouse's permission before taking action. Especially in community property states, even policies that are in one spouse's name might, in fact, be owned by both spouses. (See "Property Ownership Rules for Married People" in Chapter 5.) If you have questions about who owns your insurance policies, consult a lawyer. (See Chapter 17.)

If you already have an insurance policy or annuity contract, this power allows your agent to keep paying the premiums or cancel it—whichever is in your best interests.

With this power, your agent is also permitted to change and name the beneficiaries of your insurance policies or annuity contracts. This is a broad power, and it's a good idea to discuss your wishes about it with your agent. If you don't want your agent to change your beneficiary designations, make that clear. If you have strong feelings about whom the designated beneficiary of any new policies should be, you can discuss that as well.

Estate, Trust, and Other Beneficiary Transactions

This power authorizes your agent to act on your behalf to claim or disclaim property you get from any other source. For example, if you were entitled to money from a trust fund, this power would allow your agent to go to the trustee—the person in charge of the trust—and press a claim on your behalf. Or, if for any reason it would be in your best interest to disclaim the inheritance, your agent could turn down the cash.

Transferring Property to Your Living Trust

If you've already set up a living trust, this power gives your agent the authority to transfer items of your property to that trust. But your agent can transfer property into your living trust only if you've given your agent authority over that type of property elsewhere in your document. For example, if you want your agent to be able to transfer real estate into the living trust, you must also grant the real estate power. And if you want your agent to transfer bank accounts to your living trust, you must also grant the banking transactions power.

This power doesn't allow you to give your agent permission to create, modify, or revoke a trust.

Legal Actions

This provision allows your agent to act for you in all matters that involve courts or government agencies. For example, with this power your agent can bring or settle a lawsuit on your behalf. Your agent can also accept court papers intended for you and hire an attorney to represent you in court, if necessary. Unless your agent is a lawyer, your agent cannot actually represent you in court but must hire someone to do so. If you lose a lawsuit, the agent can use your assets to pay the winner whatever you owe.

Personal and Family Care

This is an important power. It gives the agent the authority to use your assets to pay your everyday expenses and those of your family. With this power, the agent can spend your money for your family's food; shelter; education; cars; medical and dental care; membership dues for churches, clubs, or other organizations; pets; vacations; and travel. The agent is allowed to spend as much as it takes to maintain the standard of living to which you, your spouse, children, and anyone else you usually support are accustomed.

If you regularly take care of others—for example, you are the primary caretaker for a disabled sibling or parent—this power would allow your agent to use your assets to continue to help those people.

Pet Care

A properly executed power of attorney that includes the standard powers discussed in this section—for example, the banking power and the personal and family care power—should permit your agent to spend money to take care of your pets. But because the law isn't explicit about pets, you can grant this special pet care power to ensure that your agent has complete authority to provide care for your animals.

This power guarantees that your agent can pay for the ongoing care of your pets or animals, including food, veterinary care, grooming, toys, day care, and temporary boarding or pet-sitting fees. Your agent will be permitted to care for your pets or animals in the same way as you have done.

Government Benefits

This power allows your agent to apply for and collect any benefits you might be entitled to from Social Security, Medicare, Medicaid, or other government programs or civil or military service. To collect most government benefits, your agent must send the government office a copy of the durable power of attorney to prove the agent's authority. Social Security is an exception, however. (See below.)

Retirement Plan Transactions

This power gives your agent authority over retirement plans such as IRAs and Keogh plans. Under this power, your agent can select payment options and designate beneficiaries—the people who will take any money left in the fund at your death. Your agent can also change current beneficiary designations, make voluntary contributions to your plan, change the way the funds are invested, and roll over plan benefits into other retirement plans. The agent can also perform any other actions authorized by the plan, including borrowing from it.

The power to change the beneficiaries of your retirement funds is a drastic one. Make sure your agent understands your wishes with respect to this power.

Social Security Benefits

If you collect your Social Security benefits by direct deposit, your agent will have access to those funds as long as you've given that person access to the bank account where the funds are deposited.

However, if you receive Social Security payments through a debit card, your agent will need to take your power of attorney to the local Social Security office to be named the official "representative payee" of your Social Security benefits. This will establish your agent as someone entitled to receive your Social Security benefits on your behalf.

If you're creating a power of attorney that's effective immediately, you can save your agent some work by simply contacting the Social Security Administration (SSA) and naming your agent as your representative payee. However, that means your agent will start receiving your Social Security payments right away, and you might not want that. If it's not yet time for the agent to take control under your power of attorney, you're better off granting the government benefits power and letting the agent deal with the SSA when the time comes.

In addition to granting the government benefits power, you might consider receiving your Social Security payments through direct deposit into a bank account where your agent will have access to the funds without the hassles of dealing with the SSA. You can set up a direct deposit arrangement at any time, as long as you are of sound mind.

To appoint a representative payee or arrange for direct deposit of your benefits, contact the SSA at 800-772-1213.

Tax Matters

This provision gives your agent authority to act for you in all state, local, and federal tax matters. With this power, your agent can prepare and file tax returns and other documents, pay tax due, contest tax bills, and collect refunds. To file a tax return on your behalf, the agent must include a copy of the power of attorney with the return. The agent is also authorized to receive confidential information about you from the IRS.

The IRS Power of Attorney Form

The IRS has its own power of attorney form, but you don't need to use it. It is primarily designed to allow attorneys, accountants, and other professionals to receive confidential tax information on behalf of clients. It is not a comprehensive, durable power of attorney for tax matters. This document gives your agent the power to receive confidential information from the IRS, plus the authority to handle any tax matters that arise.

Making Gifts

This last financial power allows your agent to make gifts of your property. You might already know that you want your agent to be able to give away your property under some circumstances. On the other hand, allowing your agent to make gifts might feel like giving up too much control.

Reasons to Allow Gifts

There are many reasons why you might want to permit your agent to make gifts of your property. Here are a few of the most common.

Continuing gift-giving plans. There are lots of reasons to give gifts during your lifetime. You might, for example, want to donate regularly to your church or a favorite charity. Or perhaps you've made a commitment to help a family member with college or starting up a business.

Family emergencies. All of us are occasionally caught off guard by unexpected financial troubles. You might want your agent to be able to help out if a loved one faces such an emergency.

Estate tax savings. If you have substantial assets (many millions of dollars) and are concerned about your eventual estate tax liability, you might be planning to reduce estate taxes by giving away some of your property while you are still alive. If you have set up this sort of gift-giving plan, you'll probably want to authorize your agent to continue it.

Possible Gift Tax Consequences

Except for gifts to your agent, you cannot use WillMaker's power of attorney to limit the size of the gifts that your agent makes. If your agent gives away more than a certain amount—currently $19,000—to any one person or organization in one calendar year, a federal gift tax return will probably have to be filed.

Several kinds of gifts, however, are not taxable regardless of amount: gifts to your spouse, gifts that directly pay for medical expenses or tuition, and gifts to tax-exempt charities. Even when gift tax must be paid, unless you make millions of dollars' worth of taxable gifts during your life, no tax will actually be due until after your death. Because your agent is required to act in your best interest, making large gifts could create a conflict. On one hand, your agent might feel that you would want to make a sizable gift—even if it's a taxable one—to a particular person or organization. On the other hand, if you have a very large estate that is likely to owe estate tax at your death, your agent won't want to increase your eventual tax liability.

For these reasons, if you do permit your agent to make gifts, it's particularly important that you explain, ahead of time, what you intend and whether you have any limits.

RELATED TOPIC

More information about estate taxes. If you want to learn more about estate and gift taxes, see Chapter 13. For help beyond this book, see *Nolo's Guide to Estate Planning*, by Liza Hanks (Nolo). It's a detailed guide to estate planning, including all major methods of reducing or avoiding estate and gift taxes. If you still have questions, talk with a knowledgeable attorney.

Gifts to the Agent

In the WillMaker interview, you must first decide whether you want to allow your agent to make gifts to themself. Because this raises some unique issues, you must consider it separately from the question of gifts to other people.

If you want to allow gifts to your agent, you must place an annual limit on them. This is because of a tricky legal rule called a general power of appointment. If your agent has an unlimited power to give your property to themself and happens to die before you do, the agent could become the legal owner of all your property. In this case, your agent would be subject to taxes based not only on the agent's own assets, but on yours as well.

Gifts to the Alternate Agent

You might want to allow your primary agent to receive gifts of your property, but not your alternate agent. WillMaker allows you to include this restriction in your power of attorney document. If you allow gifts to your first-choice agent and you've also named an alternate agent, WillMaker will ask you whether your alternate is allowed to receive gifts of your property.

If you wish to allow your alternate to accept gifts of your property, that's fine, too. If you do allow gifts to your alternate, the annual gift limit will be the same as the amount you set for your first-choice agent.

To avoid this problem, you must limit the amount of money your agent can accept in any given year. To avoid trouble with gift taxes, you might want to let the current gift tax threshold be your guide and set the limit at $19,000 or less. Whatever amount you choose, be sure it's far less than what you're worth. If you set the limit too high, you might inadvertently create a general power of appointment.

Gifts to Others

After you've decided whether you want to allow gifts to your agent, WillMaker asks you about gifts to other people and organizations. If you're comfortable giving your agent broad authority, you can allow gifts to anyone your agent chooses. Or, you can specify the people and organizations to which your agent can give your property.

Talk With Your Agent

It's critically important that you talk with your agent, not just to be sure your choice is willing to take on the job of handling your finances, but to be sure your representative understands what that job entails. Sit down and discuss the list of powers you grant, being especially careful to cover those areas where your agent might exercise a lot of personal discretion.

Now is the time to clarify any special needs or concerns that you have. For example, if there are certain items of personal property you'd never want your agent to sell, note them down and let your agent know how you feel. Or, if you are allowing your agent to make gifts to help out family members or other loved ones who need help, talk frankly about whom you'd feel comfortable helping, as well as when and to what extent.

There is one caveat here: While it is wise to let your agent know what your wishes are, it's generally a bad idea to create a lot of complicated restrictions. There is no way to know what the future will bring—and, ideally, your agent will have enough flexibility to take whatever actions are necessary to take care of you. It is important to let your agent know what you want, but also to trust your choice enough to make the right decisions when the time comes.

You can't use your power of attorney to limit the size of gifts to others, so if you give your agent broad authority to make gifts, be sure to discuss your intentions. Your agent should have a sound understanding of your plans for giving gifts—including the recipients you have in mind, under what circumstances gifts should be made, and in what amounts.

Remember that any gifts your agent makes must be in your best interest or according to your explicit instructions. For example, your agent can make annual gifts to each of your three children to reduce your estate tax liability—or periodic gifts to your niece because you promised to help her with college costs. Your agent should follow the guidelines you have set out in the power of attorney document.

Forgiving Loans

When you give your agent the power to make gifts, you also give the power to forgive or cancel debts others owe you. If anyone owes you money and you've authorized your agent to make gifts to them, be sure you let your agent know which debts you want to be paid and which can be forgiven.

If you've authorized power over gifts, and your agent owes you money, your agent can forgive those debts, too. But for these debts, your agent can't cancel amounts worth more than the maximum gift amount in any calendar year. For example, your son, whom you've named as agent, owes you $20,000. You've placed the annual gift limit at $7,000. He can forgive his debt to you at the rate of $7,000 per year.

Additional Duties and Responsibilities

After you've named your agent and decided which financial powers to grant, you have just a few more choices to make about how your agent will carry out the job. These last few questions ask whether you want:

- your agent to make periodic reports to anyone about your finances
- your agent to be able to delegate tasks to others
- your agent to be able to benefit financially from actions taken on your behalf
- your agent to keep their own property strictly separate from yours, and
- to pay your agent.

Periodic Reports

WillMaker's power of attorney lets you require the agent to issue reports to people you name. Unless you require it, your agent doesn't have to report to anyone about your finances. In most cases, that arrangement is fine.

But in some circumstances, you might want to require reports. For example, if the agent is in charge of your business, investors might need to receive periodic financial statements, audited or reviewed by an accountant. Or perhaps you want to defuse a potentially explosive personal conflict by reassuring suspicious family members that they'll receive regular reports about your finances. WillMaker allows you to require quarterly or semiannual reports to people whom you name. (If you live in New York, this works a little differently. See the note below.)

EXAMPLE: Theodore, who is ill, appoints his son Jason as his agent for finances. Theodore's two other children, Nancy and Ed, live out of state and aren't on the best of terms with Jason.

To prevent conflict between his children over Jason's handling of Theodore's finances, Theodore decides to require Jason to give Nancy and Ed semiannual reports of all financial transactions he engages in as agent.

About Reports

The idea of making your agent accountable to people might appeal to you. But before you enter a long list of names of people to whom your agent must make reports, ask yourself whether these reports are truly necessary.

One of the most important reasons for making a durable power of attorney is to give control of your finances to someone you trust completely, bypassing the court system. One big advantage of this tactic is that you spare your agent the hassle and expense of preparing reports and accountings for a court.

If you want someone to keep tabs on your agent, think again about whether you truly trust the person you've named.

WillMaker's power of attorney document requires that all reports include income received by you and expenses incurred. If you want other details included, be certain your agent knows what they are.

Unless the timing of reports is governed by a business agreement or other legally binding document, you are free to require quarterly or semiannual reports. Weigh the need for the reports against the inconvenience to your agent and the expense of preparing the reports. If you have a very anxious relative, for example, you might want to authorize quarterly reports. Making these reports could be less hassle for your agent than dealing with constant interference from your family members. If the situation is not so tense, semiannual reports will probably do fine.

Note for New York Readers

In New York, instead of requiring reports, WillMaker will ask you whether you want to designate one or more "monitors." If you do, any monitor can ask your agent for a copy of the power of attorney document and a record of all transactions your agent makes on your behalf.

As with requiring reports, naming monitors can place a substantial burden on your agent. (See "About Reports," above, for help determining whether you really need to monitor your agent.)

Delegating Powers

If your agent resigns from the job, the alternate you named will take over. But if there is no alternate available, or if your agent is only temporarily unavailable, the agent will need to find another person to do the job.

If you allow it, your agent can turn over all or part of the agent's duties to someone else in this situation. This reassignment of duties is called delegation.

An agent with the power to delegate tasks is free to turn over any or all of the job to a competent third person. This person may step in temporarily or permanently, depending on the situation.

EXAMPLE 1: Caroline names her son, Eugene, as her agent for finances, effective immediately. She names a close friend, Nicole, as alternate agent. A year later, Eugene goes on vacation for three weeks, so he delegates his authority over Caroline's bank accounts to Nicole until he returns.

EXAMPLE 2: Anthony names his wife, Rosa, as his agent; his son Michael is the alternate agent. When Rosa declines to serve because of her own poor health, Michael takes over but soon finds that other responsibilities make it impossible to continue. He delegates all his authority to his sister, Theresa.

If You Named More Than One Agent

Delegation becomes more complicated if you've named more than one agent.

Agents Who Must Act Jointly

If you require your agents to act together in all that they do, it's a good idea to give them the power to delegate responsibilities. This is to avoid trouble in the event that one or more of your agents becomes unable to act on your behalf. If this happens, the unavailable agent can use the delegation form to give their authority to the remaining agents, temporarily or permanently. Your remaining agents can use the delegation form to prove that they are permitted to act alone. If you don't grant the delegation power, an agent who will be unavailable will have to execute an affidavit—a sworn, notarized statement—ending or pausing the power to act for you. (An agent who permanently resigns can sign a resignation form; the remaining agents can use that form to prove their authority.)

In the unlikely event that all of your agents will be temporarily unavailable, they can get together to choose a person to take over.

Agents Who Can Act Separately

If you've authorized your agents to act independently, allowing them to delegate tasks is probably not necessary or wise. The main reason for allowing delegation is to ensure that someone will always be on hand to take care of your finances. In your situation, if just one of your agents is temporarily unable to act on your behalf, the others can simply act alone, without any special documents or fuss. And you can name up to two alternate agents to take over if all of your agents must step down. (See "Naming Alternates," above.)

Allowing delegation in your situation could, in fact, create much unnecessary confusion. Because your agents can act independently, they could each delegate tasks to individuals that they choose—without consulting each other. When it comes to your finances, it's better not to open the door to that sort of chaos.

WillMaker produces a form that your agent can use to delegate authority to someone else. The new representative will use the signed form, along with your power of attorney document, to act on your behalf.

Exceptions to Legal Responsibilities

As discussed, your agent must always act in your best interests, must act honestly and prudently when managing your property, and must keep good records. However, you might want to allow your agent to deviate from some standard legal duties, including:

- avoiding conflicts of interest, and
- keeping your property completely separate from the agent's own property.

Conflicts of Interest

In most states, an agent has no right to engage in activities from which the agent personally stands to benefit. Such activities, which create conflicts of interest between the principal and agent, are called self-dealing. The agent's motive is irrelevant. If the transaction is challenged in court, it is presumed fraudulent until the agent proves otherwise.

EXAMPLE: David is the agent for his elderly mother, Irene. After Irene's failing eyesight makes it impossible for her to drive, David decides to buy her car from her. He looks up the car's fair market value to make sure he is paying a fair amount, writes a check, and deposits it in Irene's bank account.

This transaction is forbidden, even though David isn't cheating Irene, unless Irene's power of attorney specifically allows David to benefit from his management of her property and finances.

The ban on self-dealing is intended to protect you; after all, the agent is supposed to be acting on your behalf. However, it's quite sensible to give the agent permission to self-deal if the agent is your spouse, a close family member, a business partner, or another person whose finances are already intertwined with yours. WillMaker allows you to grant this permission in your power of attorney document.

> EXAMPLE: Maurice wants Alice, his best friend, to serve as his agent. They have been involved in many real estate transactions together—including several current projects. Maurice doesn't want to risk disrupting these projects or curtailing Alice's ability to do business, so he specifically states in his durable power of attorney that Alice may benefit from transactions she undertakes on Maurice's behalf as his agent.

Gifts and Conflicts of Interest

When you grant financial powers to your agent, you can allow your agent to receive gifts of your property. (See "Making Gifts," above.) If you explicitly grant the gift-making power in your document, receiving permitted gifts is not considered a conflict of interest. In other words, it's perfectly fine to forbid your agent from using your power of attorney document for personal benefit while also allowing your agent to receive some of your property as a gift.

Mixing Funds

An agent is never allowed to mix or commingle your funds with the agent's own unless the power of attorney specifically authorizes it. You will probably want to grant that authority if you appoint your spouse or immediate family member as agent and your finances are already thoroughly mixed together in joint bank or security accounts.

EXAMPLE: Jim and Eduardo have been living together for 25 years. They have a joint checking account and share all basic living expenses. Each names the other as his agent. To avoid any possible problems, Jim and Eduardo both include, in their powers of attorney, specific provisions that allow commingling of funds.

Different Powers for Alternate Agents

While you might want to give your first-choice agent full power to benefit personally from transactions conducted on your behalf or to mix your funds with theirs, you might not feel comfortable giving an alternate agent the same authority. This is often the case for those who name a spouse or partner as agent and then name alternates with whom they are not so close or financially entwined. WillMaker allows you to specify whether an alternate agent should have the same power as your first choice, or whether you want to restrict the alternate's authority when it comes to personal benefit and mixing funds.

Paying Your Agent

You can decide whether you want to pay your agent. If you do, you can specify your payment arrangement.

In family situations, an agent is normally not paid if the duties won't be complicated or burdensome. If your property and finances are extensive, however, and the agent is likely to devote significant time and effort managing them, it seems fair to offer compensation for the work. Discuss and resolve this issue with the proposed agent before you finalize your document.

If you decide to pay your agent something for managing your financial affairs, you can set your own rate—for example, $10,000 per year, $20 per hour, or some other figure on which you agree. Or, if you don't want to decide on an amount right now, you can allow your agent to determine a reasonable wage at a later time. No single strategy works best for everyone. Choose the approach—and the amount—that feels right to you.

EXAMPLE 1: Frederick is quite wealthy. He owns and operates a successful chain of convenience stores in a large city. He also owns a house, several pieces of investment property, and a wide array of stocks. When he is diagnosed with a life-threatening illness, he creates a durable power of attorney for finances appointing his close friend Barbara as his agent. Because he expects Barbara to watch over his business as well as tend to his other financial affairs, he feels it's appropriate to pay her for her services. Frederick and Barbara settle on a rate of $20,000 per year for her services.

EXAMPLE 2: Martin creates a durable power of attorney naming his brother, Andrew, as agent. Martin owns a complex investment portfolio, and the brothers agree that Andrew should be paid if he has to manage Martin's finances. They consider an hourly wage but decide not to be that specific now. In his durable power of attorney, Martin states that Andrew can pay himself "reasonable" fees for his services.

If You Name More Than One Agent

In WillMaker's power of attorney, if you name more than one agent and you want to pay them, the amount you enter—for example, $5,000 per year or $18 per hour—applies to each one. If you want to allow your agents to determine a reasonable amount for their services, each is allowed to set their own fee.

Nominating a Conservator or Guardian

It is possible, though highly unlikely, that a court proceeding could be brought to invalidate or overrule your durable power of attorney for finances. (See "Invalidation," below.) If your document is invalidated for any reason, a judge will appoint someone to manage your finances. This person is usually called a "guardian of your estate" or "conservator of your estate."

You can nominate your agent to serve as your financial guardian or conservator, if a court must appoint someone to that position. The court will follow your recommendation unless there is a compelling reason not to do so—for example, if someone has proved that your agent is mishandling your money. (Again, this type of outcome is very rare.)

If you do not nominate your agent to serve as the guardian or conservator of your estate, your power of attorney document will not mention the issue at all. In this case, the court would appoint a guardian or conservator by determining what would be in your best interests, but would do so without input from you.

Making It Legal

After you've done the hard work of putting together a durable power of attorney, you must carry out some simple tasks to make sure the document is legally valid and will be accepted by the people with whom your agent might have to deal. This section explains what to do.

Signing and Notarizing

A durable power of attorney is a serious document, and to make it effective you must observe certain formalities when you sign the document.

In almost all states, you must sign your durable power of attorney in the presence of a notary public. (In just a few states, you can choose to have your document witnessed or notarized. See "For California, Indiana, Michigan, or Washington Residents: Making the Choice," below.) In many states, notarization is required by law to make the durable power of attorney valid. But even where law doesn't require it, custom usually does. A durable power of attorney that isn't notarized might not be accepted by people with whom your agent tries to deal.

The notary public watches you sign the durable power of attorney and then signs it, too, and stamps it with an official seal. The notary will want proof of your identity, such as a driver's license that bears your photo and signature. The notary will charge a fee, usually based on the number of signatures they are witnessing. You can ask the notary ahead of time how much it will cost.

Before You Sign

Before you finalize your power of attorney, you might want to show it to the banks, brokers, insurers, and other financial institutions you expect your agent to deal with on your behalf.

Discussing your plans with people at these institutions before it is final—and giving them a copy of the durable power of attorney after you sign it, if you wish—can make your agent's job easier. An institution might require that you include specific language in your durable power of attorney, authorizing the agent to do certain things on your behalf. You might have to go along if you want cooperation later. If WillMaker's power of attorney doesn't satisfy their requirements, you can either find another bank that will accept the document as it is, or use a different power of attorney document that can give them what they want.

Another option is to use a power of attorney that your financial institution provides in addition to your WillMaker power of attorney. However, if you do this, it is essential that you are consistent. Name the same agent for both documents and be sure that the provisions of the two documents don't conflict.

Finding a notary public shouldn't be a problem; many advertise online. Your bank, mailbox stores, real estate offices, and title companies might also have notaries.

If needed, you might be able to find a notary who will come to your home or hospital room, and in some states, you might be able to have your document notarized on a video call. (Read more about this in Chapter 10.) To find out what is possible in your area, call a few local notaries and ask what services they provide. Expect to pay a reasonable extra fee for mobile and remote notary services.

TIP

In Florida, you must put your initials next to certain powers you grant to your agent. Florida requires this extra initialing to make extra clear that you want your agent to have those powers. When you print your document, read the instructions and carefully look through the power of attorney for the lines where you should put your initials.

If you are physically unable to sign your document, the notary public can sign it for you. At your direction, the notary can also initial all required provisions in your power of attorney. The notary must sign and initial the document in front of you and two witnesses. (For more about the witnessing requirement, see below.) After each signature or initial, the notary must write "signature or initials affixed by the notary pursuant to s. 709.2202(2), Florida Statutes."

TIP

In Nevada, there's an extra requirement for residents of hospitals and nursing homes. A medical professional must state in writing that the person signing the document is competent. If this applies in your situation, read the signing instructions that print with your document for directions on what to do. (Nev. Rev. Stat. § 162A.220.)

Witnessing

Unless your state requires witnesses (see chart below), WillMaker will ask you whether you want to have witnesses sign your document. Most states don't require witness signatures, but it doesn't hurt to have a witness or two watch you sign, and sign the document themselves.

Witnesses' signatures can make the power of attorney more acceptable to lawyers, banks, insurance companies, and other entities the agent might have to deal with. Part of the reason is probably that some other legal documents with which people are more familiar—including wills and some health care directives—must be witnessed to be legally valid.

States That Require Witnesses		
State	**No. of Witnesses**	**Other Requirements**
Arizona	1	Witness cannot be your agent, the spouse or child of your agent, or the notary public who acknowledges your document.
California	2	Witnesses are required only if your document is not notarized. The agent cannot be a witness.
Connecticut	2	Witnesses cannot be your agent.
Delaware	1	Witness cannot be your agent, be related to you by blood, marriage, or adoption, or be entitled to inherit a portion of your estate under your will or trust.
Florida	2	Witnesses cannot be your agent.
Georgia	1	Witness cannot be your agent or the notary public who acknowledges your document.
Illinois	1	Witness cannot be your agent, someone related to you or your agent by blood, marriage, or adoption, a person who provides health services to you, or an owner or operator of a health care facility where you are a resident.
Indiana	2	Witnesses are required only if your document is not notarized. Neither witness can (1) be your agent or successor agent, (2) stand to benefit from your power of attorney document—for example, by receiving gifts you have authorized your agent to make, or (3) be your spouse, child, or grandchild.
Maryland	2	Witnesses cannot be your agent.
Michigan	2	Witnesses are necessary only if (1) your power of attorney is not notarized or (2) another person signs the power of attorney on behalf of and at the direction of the principal. The agent cannot be a witness.

States That Require Witnesses (continued)

State	No. of Witnesses	Other Requirements
New York	2	Witnesses should not be your agent, and neither witness should be a person who stands to benefit from your power of attorney document—for example, by receiving gifts you have authorized your agent to make.
Pennsylvania	2	Witnesses cannot be your agent, the notarial officer who provides the certification of acknowledgment, or the person who signs the document for you, if you can't sign it yourself.
South Carolina	2	Witnesses cannot be your agent.
Washington	2	Witnesses are required only if your document is not notarized. Witnesses cannot be (1) your agent, (2) related to you by blood, marriage, or state-registered domestic partnership, or (3) a care provider for you at your home, at an adult family home, or at a long-term care facility, if you live there. After you have signed your document, the witnesses should carefully read the witness statement at the end of the document and sign their names, too.

Witnesses can serve another function, too. If you're worried that someone might challenge your capacity to execute a valid durable power of attorney later, it's prudent to have witnesses. If necessary, they can testify that in their judgment, you knew what you were doing when you signed the document.

The witnesses must be present when you sign the document in front of the notary. Witnesses must be mentally competent adults, preferably ones who live nearby and will be easily available if necessary. The person who will serve as agent should not be a witness. In some states, the agent must sign the durable power of attorney document. (These states are listed below.)

For California, Indiana, Michigan, or Washington Residents: Making the Choice

If you live in California, Indiana, Michigan, or Washington, your durable power of attorney is valid if you have it notarized *or* if you sign it in front of two witnesses. Some people feel most comfortable using both methods together, but you are legally required to choose only one. In the Finalizing Your Document section of the interview, WillMaker prompts you to indicate how you want to finalize your document.

When choosing a method, there's one important consideration to keep in mind. If your power of attorney grants your agent authority over your real estate, you should absolutely have your document notarized. This is because you will have to put a copy of your document on file in the county recorder's office (see "Recording," below)—and in order to record your document, it must be notarized.

There is one exception in Michigan: If you will have someone else sign your power of attorney at your direction, the document must be witnessed.

(Cal. Prob. Code § 4121; Ind. Code § 30-5-4-1; Mich. Comp. Laws § 556.205; Wash. Rev. Code § 11.125.050.)

TIP

Your notary public should not also be a witness. If you must also have your power of attorney witnessed, the notary should not serve as a witness, even if your state does not explicitly prohibit it. Find separate individuals to witness and notarize your document.

Obtaining the Agent's Signature

In the vast majority of states, the agent does not have to agree in writing to accept the job of handling your finances. The exceptions to this rule are California, Delaware, Michigan, Minnesota, New

Hampshire, New York, and Pennsylvania. In these states, the agents (and alternates) do not need to sign the document unless or until they need to use it.

California

In California, your agent must date and sign the durable power of attorney before taking action under the document. Ask the agent to read the Notice to Person Accepting the Appointment as Agent at the beginning of the form. An agent who will begin using the power of attorney right away should date and sign the designated blanks at the end of the notice. If you've asked your agent not to use the document unless or until you become incapacitated, there's no need to obtain the signature now. Your agent can sign later, if it's ever necessary. (Cal. Prob. Code § 4128.)

Delaware, Michigan, Minnesota, New Hampshire, and Pennsylvania

In Delaware, Michigan, Minnesota, New Hampshire, and Pennsylvania, your agent must complete and sign an acknowledgment form. (Delaware calls it a certification.) This simple form ensures that your agent understands the legal responsibilities involved in acting on your behalf. When you print out your durable power of attorney, it will be accompanied by an acknowledgment form for your agent to sign.

If your agent will begin using the power of attorney right away, give the acknowledgment form to your agent along with the finalized, original power of attorney document. Your agent must complete the form and attach it to the power of attorney before taking action under the document.

If you've asked your agent not to use the power of attorney unless or until you become incapacitated, keep the acknowledgment form together with the original power of attorney document. Your agent can complete it later, if it ever becomes necessary to use the power of attorney. (Del. Code tit. 12, § 49A-105; Mich. Comp. Laws § 556.213; Minn. Stat. § 523.23; N.H. Rev. Stat. § 564-E: 113; 20 Pa. Cons. Stat. § 5601.)

New York

If you live in New York, your agent must sign the power of attorney before taking action under the document. If your agent will begin using the power of attorney right away, ask the agent to print and then sign their full name in the designated blanks at the end of the form. (In New York, the agent must also have this signature notarized.) If you've asked your agent not to use the document unless or until you become incapacitated, there's no need to obtain the agent's signature now. The agent can sign the document later, if it's ever necessary. (N.Y. Gen. Oblig. Law § 5-1513.)

Preparation Statement

At the end of the power of attorney interview, WillMaker asks you to enter the name and address of the person who is preparing the power of attorney. WillMaker uses this information to add a "preparation statement" to the end of your power of attorney document. Some states or counties require a preparation statement to record a document. But even where the law doesn't require it, tradition (or a county recorder's habit) often does, so WillMaker includes a preparation statement on every durable power of attorney for finances.

The preparation statement is a simple listing of the name and address of the person who prepared the document. In most cases, the name of the principal and the name of the person who prepared the document will be the same: your own. Occasionally, however, someone might use WillMaker to prepare a form for another person—an ailing relative, for example. In that case, use the name and address of the person who stepped in to help.

Recording

You might need to put a copy of your durable power of attorney on file in the land records offices of the counties where you own real estate. Only South Carolina requires you to record a power of attorney for it to be durable—that is, for it to remain in effect if you become incapacitated.

(S.C. Code § 62-8-109.) In other states, you must record the power of attorney only if it gives your agent authority over your real estate. Essentially, *this means you must record the document if you granted the real estate power.* If the document isn't recorded, your agent won't be able to sell, mortgage, or transfer your real estate.

Recording makes it clear to all interested parties that the agent has power over the property. County land records are checked whenever real estate changes hands or is mortgaged; if your agent attempts to sell or mortgage your real estate, there must be something in the records that proves that the agent has authority to do so.

There is no time limit on when you must record a durable power of attorney. So if you've created a document that won't be used unless and until you become incapacitated, you might not want to record it immediately. Your agent can always record the document later, if it's ever needed.

Even if recording is not legally required, you can do so anyway; officials in some financial institutions might be reassured later on by seeing that you took that step.

Where to Record

In most states, each county has its own land records office, often called the recorder's office or register of deeds. If you're recording to give the agent authority over real estate, take the durable power of attorney to the office in the county where the real estate is located. If you want your agent to have authority over more than one parcel of real estate, record the power of attorney in each county where you own property. If you're recording for any other reason, take the document to the office in the county where you live.

How to Record

Recording a document shouldn't be complicated, though some counties can be quite fussy about their rules. (See below.) You might even be able to record your document by mail, but it's safer to go in person. Typically, the clerk makes a copy of your document for the public records and assigns it a reference number, and you pay a per-page fee to have the document recorded.

CAUTION

Check your county's recording procedures before you finalize your document. Some counties will ask you to meet very particular requirements before they will put your power of attorney on file. Or, if you don't adhere to their rules, they will charge you an extra fee for filing the document.

For example, in some counties, you might be required to file an original document, rather than a photocopy, with the land records office. In this case, you'll need to make a second original, being sure to have it signed, notarized, and witnessed (if necessary), just like the first.

And some counties require a margin of a certain number of inches at the top of the first page of a power of attorney. This is where they put the filing stamp when you record the document. Local customs vary widely here; some counties will accept a standard one-inch margin while others ask for a margin of two, three, or even four inches. When you make your document, you can set the correct number of inches for the top margin of the first page. This option is available in the last chapter of the document interview, Finalizing Your Document.

To avoid hassles and extra expenses, before you finalize your power of attorney, check the land records office (of the county where you own real estate) to make sure you're prepared to meet any special requirements for putting it on file.

What to Do With the Signed Document

Your agent will need the original power of attorney document, signed and notarized, to act on your behalf. So, if you want your agent to start using the document right away, give the original document to the agent.

If you named more than one agent, give the original document to one of them. Between them, they will have to work out the best way to prove their authority. For example, they might decide to visit some financial institutions or government offices together to establish themselves as your agents. Or they might need to take turns with the document. Some agencies, such as the IRS, will accept a copy of the document, rather than the original: Such flexible policies make things easier on multiple agents who need to share the original document.

Making and Distributing Copies

If you wish, you can give copies of your durable power of attorney to the people your agent will need to deal with—in banks or government offices, for example. If the durable power is in their records, it might eliminate hassles for your agent later because these institutions will be familiar with the document and expecting your agent to take action under it.

If your power of attorney won't be used unless and until you become incapacitated, however, it might seem premature to contact people and institutions about a document that might never go into effect. It's up to you.

Be sure to keep a list of everyone to whom you give a copy. If you later revoke your durable power of attorney, notify each institution of the revocation. (See "Revoking Your Durable Power of Attorney," below.)

Keeping Your Document Up to Date

If you make a power of attorney that your agent won't use unless and until you become incapacitated, it's a good idea to revoke it and create a new one every five to seven years, especially if your circumstances have changed significantly. A durable power of attorney never expires, but if the document was signed many years before it is used, the agent might have more difficulty getting banks, insurance companies, or people in government agencies to accept it.

It's especially important to review your durable power of attorney if significant changes occur in your life. For example, if the person you named as your agent moves far away, becomes ill, or is no longer closely involved with your life, you should appoint someone else to serve. To do that, revoke the old power of attorney and prepare a new one.

Revoking Your Durable Power of Attorney

After you make a power of attorney, you can revoke it at any time, as long as you are of sound mind. But to make the revocation legally effective, you must carefully follow all the procedures set out in this section.

Who Can Revoke

Only you, or someone a court appoints to act for you, can revoke your power of attorney.

When You Can Revoke

You can revoke your durable power of attorney as long as you are of sound mind and physically able to do so. The sound mind requirement is not difficult to satisfy. If someone challenged the revocation, a court would look only at whether you understood the consequences of signing the revocation. (The competency requirement is the same as that required to create a valid power of attorney in the first place; see "Possible Challenges to Your Document," below.)

SEE AN EXPERT

If you and your agent can't agree. An agent who refuses to accept a revocation can create serious problems. If you get into such a dispute with your agent, consult a lawyer. (See Chapter 17.)

If a Conservator or Guardian Is Appointed

If your agent is satisfactorily handling your financial affairs while you can't, it's very unlikely that a court will need to appoint a conservator for you. And if it does become necessary, you can use your document to name your agent to the post. (See "Nominating a Conservator or Guardian," above.)

If, however, you or a family member objected to the agent's actions, a court might appoint someone else as conservator. In a few states, appointment of a conservator automatically revokes a durable power of attorney. In that case, the conservator would become solely responsible for your property and financial matters.

In many states, the conservator would have the legal authority to revoke your durable power of attorney. Someone appointed to take physical care of you—usually called a guardian or guardian of the person—not your property, can also, depending on state law, have the power to revoke a financial power of attorney.

What to Do With the Additional Documents

WillMaker produces several additional documents along with your durable power of attorney form. These are discussed throughout the chapter, but here is a quick summary of these documents and what you should do with them.

Information for an Agent

This sheet is intended to help your agent understand the job. It discusses the agent's duties and responsibilities, including the duties to manage your property honestly and prudently and to keep accurate records. You should give a copy to the person you name in your document and take some time to talk together about the responsibilities involved.

Delegation of Authority

If you allow your agent to delegate tasks to others, your agent might want to use the Delegation of Authority form. Give a copy to your agent. Or, if your power of attorney won't be used right away, keep the form with your power of attorney document so your agent will have easy access to it later.

Resignation of Agent

Your agent can use the Resignation of Agent form to step down from the job. The agent should fill out the form and send it to the alternate agent. If you name more than one agent, the one who resigns can send the form to the others. Give a copy of this form to your agent along with your power of attorney document. Or, if your power of attorney won't be used right away, keep the forms together in a safe place known by your agent, who can obtain them if it becomes necessary.

Notice of Revocation of Durable Power of Attorney

If you ever want to revoke your power of attorney, prepare and sign a Notice of Revocation. Keep a copy of this form on file in case you need it later.

Notice of Revocation of Recorded Power of Attorney

If you record your power of attorney, then change your mind and want to cancel the document, you must also record a Notice of Revocation. To do this, you can use the Notice of Revocation of Recorded Power of Attorney form. Keep a blank copy on file for future use.

When to Revoke

If you've prepared a power of attorney that won't be used unless you're incapacitated, years might elapse between the time you sign the durable power of attorney and when it is put to use. During that interval—or even after your agent starts using the document, as long as you are mentally competent—you might decide you need to revoke the durable power of attorney. Here are the most common situations in which you should revoke a power of attorney and start over.

Changing the Terms

There is no accepted way to amend a power of attorney. If you want to change or amend a durable power of attorney, the safe course is to revoke the existing document and prepare a new one. Don't go back and modify your old document—you could throw doubt on the authenticity of the whole thing.

> EXAMPLE: Tom signed a durable power of attorney several years ago. Now he is in declining health and wants to add to the authority he gave his agent, Sarah, giving her the power to sell his real estate if necessary. Tom should revoke his old durable power of attorney and create a new one, granting the additional authority.

Similarly, you should revoke your durable power of attorney if you change your mind about your choice of agent. If you create a durable power of attorney that won't be used until later, the person you named to be your agent might not be available when the power of attorney is eventually needed. Or you might simply change your mind. If that's the case, you can revoke the durable power of attorney before it is ever used.

Moving to Another State

If you move to another state, it's best to revoke your old durable power of attorney and create a new one, complying with all regulations of your new state. This is true even though your old power of attorney might be acceptable under your new state's laws.

If you don't make a new document, your agent might run into problems that are more practical than legal. For example, the document might need to be recorded with the local land records office in the new state. If the document does not meet certain requirements, the recorder's office in the new state might not accept it. Making a new document will ensure that things will go smoothly for your agent.

Losing the Document

If you lose your signed power of attorney document, it's wise to formally revoke it, destroy any copies, and create a new one. Very few people are likely to accept your agent's authority if they can't look at the document granting the authority. By officially revoking the lost version, you reduce chances that the old power of attorney might someday resurface and confuse matters.

Marrying or Divorcing

If you get married after signing a durable power of attorney, you'll probably want to designate your new spouse to be your agent, if your spouse wasn't the person you named originally.

In most states, your spouse's designation as agent ends automatically if you later divorce. In that case, any alternate you named would serve as agent in place of your ex. However, after a divorce would be a good time to revoke that power of attorney and make a new one that doesn't mention your former spouse and lets you name another alternate agent.

How to Revoke

There are two ways to revoke your power of attorney. You can:

- prepare and sign a document called a Notice of Revocation, or
- destroy all existing copies of the document.

The first method is always preferable, because it creates proof that you really revoked the power of attorney.

Some states might allow you to revoke your power of attorney simply by preparing a new one. It's still advisable, however, to prepare a separate Notice of Revocation and notify everyone who needs to know about the revocation.

Preparing a Notice of Revocation

The purpose of a Notice of Revocation is to notify the agent and others that you have revoked the durable power of attorney.

Your power of attorney document comes with two kinds of Notice of Revocation forms for you to use. If you didn't record your durable power of attorney in the county land records office, choose the Notice of Revocation for an unrecorded document. If you did record the original durable power of attorney, you must also record the revocation; choose the Notice of Revocation for a recorded document.

Signing, Notarizing, and Witnessing the Revocation

You must sign and date the Notice of Revocation in front of a notary public. It need not be witnessed, but witnessing might be a prudent idea—especially if you have reason to believe that someone might later raise questions regarding your mental competence to execute the revocation. WillMaker provides lines for witnesses' signatures in case you want them. In WillMaker, if you use the stand-alone power of attorney revocation (as opposed to the one that prints with your power of attorney), you can choose whether to print witness lines and whether to print lines for recording. If you want to have your revocation notarized and witnessed, have your witnesses present when you sign the revocation in front of a notary. (For more on notarization, see "Making It Legal," above.)

Recording the Revocation

If you recorded the original durable power of attorney at your local recorder of deeds office, you must also record the revocation.

But even if the original durable power of attorney was not recorded, you can record a revocation if you fear that the former agent might try to act without authorization. If the revocation is part of the public records, people who check those records in dealing with the real estate later will know that the former agent is no longer authorized to act on your behalf.

Who Needs to Know?

When you're ready to send out revocation notices, try to think of everyone with whom the agent has had, or might have, dealings. These might include:

- banks
- mortgage companies
- title companies
- stockbrokers
- insurance companies
- Social Security offices
- Medicare or Medicaid offices
- military or civil service offices
- the IRS
- pension fund administrators
- post offices
- hospitals
- doctors
- schools
- relatives
- business partners
- landlords
- lawyers
- accountants
- real estate agents, and
- maintenance and repair people.

Note for North Carolina Readers

In North Carolina, if you register the revocation in the register of deeds office, it must be accompanied by a document showing that a copy of the revocation notice has been delivered to—or served on—the former agent. This document is called a proof of service. The revocation must be served on the agent by the county sheriff or someone else authorized by law to serve legal papers. (N.C. Gen. Stat. § 32C-1-110.)

Notifying Others

It's not enough to sign a revocation, or even to record it, for it to take effect; there's one more crucial step. You must notify the former agent and all institutions and people who have dealt or might deal with the former agent. Each of them must receive a copy of the Notice of Revocation.

If you don't give this written notification, people or institutions who don't know the durable power of attorney has been revoked might still enter into transactions with the former agent. If they do this in good faith, they are legally protected. You might well be held legally liable for the acts of your agent, even though you have revoked the agent's authority. In other words, once you create a durable power of attorney, the legal burden is on you to be sure everyone knows you have revoked it.

> EXAMPLE: Before Michael undergoes a serious operation, he makes a durable power of attorney. After his convalescence, Michael revokes the power of attorney in writing. He sends a copy of the revocation to Colette, his agent, but neglects to send a copy to his bank. Colette, fraudulently acting as Michael's agent, removes money from Michael's accounts and spends it. The bank isn't responsible to Michael for his loss.

When the Power of Attorney Ends

A durable power of attorney for finances is valid until you revoke it, you die, or there is no one to serve as your agent. A court can also invalidate a power of attorney, but that happens very rarely.

Revocation

As long as you are mentally competent, you can revoke a power of attorney for finances at any time, whether or not it has taken effect. In most cases, all you need to do is fill out a simple form, sign it in front of a notary public, and give copies to the agent and to people or institutions with whom the agent has been dealing. (See "Revoking Your Durable Power of Attorney," above.) You can use WillMaker to print out a revocation form.

EXAMPLE: Susan prepares a durable power of attorney naming her closest friend, Tina, as her agent. Three years later, they have a bitter fight. Susan prepares a one-page document that revokes the durable power of attorney, and she gives Tina a copy. She destroys the old document and then prepares a new one, naming her sister Joan as her agent.

Invalidation

Even if you sign a durable power of attorney for finances, if you become incapacitated there is a remote possibility that a disgruntled relative could ask a court to appoint a conservator to manage your financial affairs.

It's rare, but a power of attorney could be ruled invalid if a judge concludes that you were not mentally competent when you signed the durable power of attorney or that you were the victim of fraud or undue influence. The power of attorney could also be invalidated for a technical error, such as the failure to sign your document in front of witnesses if your state requires it. If that happens, the judge could appoint a conservator to take over management of your property.

In most states, if a court appoints a conservator, the agent becomes accountable to the conservator—not just to you—and the conservator has the power to revoke your durable power of attorney if the conservator doesn't approve of the way your agent is handling your affairs. In a few states, however, your durable power of attorney is automatically revoked, and the conservator assumes responsibility for your finances and property.

Divorce

In most states, if your spouse is your agent and you divorce, your ex-spouse's authority is immediately terminated. If you named an alternate agent in your power of attorney, that person takes over as agent. If you didn't name an alternate, your power of attorney ends.

In any state, however, others can question the validity of a document created before a divorce that names the ex-spouse as agent. For this reason, if you get divorced you should revoke your durable power of attorney and make a new one. For complete clarity, make a new durable power of attorney even if you still want your ex to be your agent.

No Agent Is Available

A durable power of attorney must end if there's no one to serve as the agent. To avoid this, WillMaker lets you name up to two alternate agents, so someone will be available to serve if your first choice can't do the task.

For a bit of extra insurance, you can also allow the alternate agent to delegate duties to someone else. (See "Delegating Powers," above.)

Death

A durable power of attorney ends when the principal dies. In most states, however, if the agent doesn't know of your death and continues to act on your behalf, those actions are still valid.

If you want your agent to have any authority over winding up your affairs after your death, grant that authority in your will by naming that person as your executor. (See Chapter 8 for information about executors.) To grant your agent authority over what happens to your body after you die, in most states you can use your durable power of attorney for health care, like the one you can make with WillMaker's Health Care Directive. (See Chapter 15.)

Possible Challenges to Your Document

A common fear is that your durable power of attorney for finances will not be accepted by those around you. While rare, challenges are sometimes raised by people who feel you were not of sound mind when you signed the document or who fear that the document is not legally valid.

Your Mental State

You must be of sound mind when you create your durable power of attorney for finances. When you sign the document, no one makes a determination about your mental state. The issue will come up only if someone goes to court and challenges the durable power of attorney, claiming that you weren't mentally competent when you signed it. That kind of lawsuit is very rare.

Even in the highly unlikely event of a court hearing, the competency requirement is not difficult to satisfy. If you understood what you were doing when you signed your durable power of attorney, that's enough. To make this determination, a judge would probably question any witnesses who watched you sign the document and others who knew you well at the time. There would be no general inquiry into your life. It wouldn't matter, for example, that you were occasionally forgetful or absentminded around the time when you signed your power of attorney document.

The Document's Validity

It's reasonable for someone to want to make sure that your durable power of attorney is still valid and hasn't been changed or revoked. To reassure other people, your agent can show that person the power of attorney document. To lay any fears to rest, it clearly states that any person who receives a copy of the document may accept it without the risk of legal liability—unless that person knows that the document has been revoked.

Laws in most states also protect people who rely on apparently valid powers of attorney. For example, many states have laws stating that a written, signed power of attorney is presumed valid, and a third party may rely on it.

As a last resort, the agent can sign a sworn statement or affidavit in front of a notary public, stating that as far as the agent knows, the durable power of attorney has not been revoked and that you are still alive. Most states have laws that make such a statement conclusive proof that the durable power of attorney is in fact still valid.

Heading Off Problems

If you think someone is likely to challenge the legitimacy of your durable power of attorney, you can take several steps to head off problems:

- **See a lawyer.** An experienced estate planning lawyer can answer questions about your durable power of attorney and about your other estate planning documents as well. For example, you might also be expecting challenges to your will, a trust, or your health care wishes. A lawyer can:
  - put your fears to rest by answering your questions and reviewing or modifying your documents
  - help to ensure that your estate plan will hold up under the challenges of your stubborn relatives, and
  - testify about your mental competency, should the need arise.
- **Sign your document in front of witnesses.** You can sign your document in front of witnesses, even if your state does not require it. (See "Making It Legal," above.) After watching you sign, the witnesses themselves sign a statement that you appeared to know what you were signing and that you signed voluntarily. If someone later challenges your competency, these witness statements will be strong evidence that you were of sound mind at the time you signed your document.
- **Get a doctor's statement.** You might also want to get a doctor's statement around the time you sign your durable power of attorney. The statement should say that the doctor has seen you recently and believes you to be mentally competent. The doctor should sign and date the statement, and you can attach it to your power of attorney document. Then, if necessary, your agent can produce the statement as evidence that you were of sound mind when you signed your power of attorney.
- **Record a video.** You can also use video to record a statement of your intent to make and sign the durable power of attorney. However, using video could work against you if it shows any visible quirks of behavior or language that could be used as evidence that you were not in fact competent when you made your document. If you do make a video, keep a copy of it with your power of attorney document.

The Powers Granted

Any other person who relies on a durable power of attorney must be sure that the agent has the power the agent claims to have. That means the person must examine the document to see what power it grants.

WillMaker's power of attorney document is very specific about the agent's powers. For example, if you give your agent authority over your banking transactions, the document expressly states that the agent is empowered to write checks on your behalf. Your agent can point to the paragraph that grants that authority, so a doubting bank official can read it in black and white.

An agent who runs into resistance should seek, politely but insistently, someone higher up in the bureaucracy.

CHAPTER

15

Health Care Directives

Every adult can benefit from making health care directives—that is, documents in which you express your health care wishes and appoint a person to make decisions for you if, someday, you can no longer speak for yourself. If you're looking to name someone to act on your behalf or to document your health care preferences, you're in the right place. WillMaker can help you make a power of attorney for health care and a living will, two types of health care directives.

If you're older or in ill health, you surely understand why these documents are important. But if you're younger—perhaps using WillMaker to help prepare health care documents for a loved one—consider making documents for yourself now, even if you don't think it's necessary.

You Have the Legal Right to Direct Your Own Care

Your right to direct your own health care is well established. But that wasn't always the case. Just a few decades ago, heart-wrenching legal battles were fought to win permission to create a document stating that life-prolonging treatments should be terminated—or continued—at the end of life.

Landmark cases involving Karen Ann Quinlan and Nancy Cruzan—two young women who experienced severe injury to their brains and became unable to communicate their wishes—opened the way to laws supporting health care documents.

In the *Cruzan* case, decided in 1990, the U.S. Supreme Court established the constitutional right to end life-sustaining treatment if a patient's wishes to do so are clear. The next year, the federal Patient Self-Determination Act (PSDA) took effect, requiring any facility that participates in Medicare or Medicaid to ask patients whether they have an advance directive and to inform them about their health care decision-making rights.

Now, every state has a law that permits you to express your health care wishes and requires medical personnel to follow those wishes—or transfer you to the care of someone else who will do so.

While the elderly and the seriously ill should make health care directives to smooth the way for decision making at the end of life, we tend to avoid another disturbing truth: Younger, healthy adults should also have health care directives, because an incapacitating accident or unexpected illness can occur at any time. In fact, if you look at the painful stories that make headlines, you'll quickly notice that the bitterest family fights over end-of-life health care don't happen when a patient is very old or has a long illness. The worst disputes arise when tragedy strikes a younger adult who never clearly expressed any wishes about medical treatment.

The sections below walk you through the process of making your own customized health care directives. It won't take long to make your preferences known: You can most likely prepare your documents in less than an hour. That hour might save your family days, months, or even years of confusion and grief.

What Happens If You Don't Make Documents

If you do not prepare health care documents, state law tells your health care providers what to do. In some states, your health care providers can decide what kind of medical care you will receive. Most states, however, require them to consult your spouse or an immediate relative. The person entitled to make decisions on your behalf is usually called your "surrogate." A few states allow a "close friend" to act as surrogate. If there is a dispute about who should be your surrogate, it might have to be resolved in court.

Whether required by law or not, if there is a question about whether surgery or some other serious procedure is authorized, health care providers will usually turn for guidance to a close relative—a spouse, parent, or child. Friends and unmarried partners, although they might be most familiar with your wishes for medical treatment, are rarely consulted or—worse still—are sometimes purposely left out of the decision-making process.

Problems arise when loved ones and family members disagree about what treatment is proper and everyone takes sides, claiming they want what is best for the patient. Battles over medical care might even end up in court, especially now that some religious organizations finance lawsuits to block the removal of feeding tubes from permanently unconscious patients. In court, a judge, who usually has little medical knowledge and no familiarity with the patient, must decide the course of treatment. Such battles—which are costly, time-consuming, and painful to those involved—are unnecessary if you have the care and foresight to prepare a formal document to express your wishes for health care.

What You Can Do With WillMaker's Health Care Directive

With WillMaker, you can create comprehensive health care documents that are valid for your state. With these documents, you can clearly express your preferences for medical care if you become unable to communicate your wishes. Specifically, you can:

- appoint a trusted person, called your "health care agent" in most states, to oversee your medical care if you become unable to speak for yourself
- name the doctor or other health care professional you'd like to supervise your care
- specify whether you want your life prolonged with medical treatments and procedures
- identify specific medical treatments and procedures that you want provided or withheld, and
- provide instructions for donating your organs, tissues, or body after death.

TIP

Keep track of other health care information. In addition to your health care directives, caregivers need other medical information as well. In the download version of WillMaker you can use the Information for Caregivers and Survivors form to help with this task. Among other details, the form includes the names of and contact information for your health care providers and information about your insurance coverage. This important information will be a great help to those who take care of you in the event of your incapacity. To find out more, open the download version of WillMaker, go to the Your Documents screen, and select Information for Caregivers and Survivors from the list. See "Organizing Your Records" in Chapter 1 for other ideas about gathering information for your loved ones.

You can also state any general wishes you have about your care, such as where you would like to be cared for (for example, in a particular hospice facility or at home, if possible) or any special directions that might affect your comfort or awareness (for instance, whether you would like to receive full doses of pain medication even if it makes you unaware of the presence of family and friends).

The Basics of Health Care Directives

This section explains what you need to know about health care directives before you start making yours, including:

- the different types of health care directives you might need to make
- what your state's documents are called
- who is legally permitted to make health care directives
- how to help someone else make health care directives
- when the documents take effect, and
- how to make sure your documents cover all the issues that are important to you.

Types of Health Care Directives

A health care directive is any document in which you set out instructions or wishes for your medical care. WillMaker provides two basic documents for this purpose:

- A durable power of attorney for health care, in which you name someone you trust to oversee your health care and make medical decisions should you become unable to do so.
- A living will, in which you spell out any wishes about the types of care you do or do not wish to receive if you are unable to speak for yourself. Your doctors and the person you name as your agent in your durable power of attorney for health care must do their best to follow any instructions you leave.

The exact names of these documents vary from state to state, and some states combine the two into a single form, usually called an "advance health care directive." The table below shows how your state handles it. In most states, you can make two additional types of health care directives that are used in emergencies, DNR orders and POLST forms, discussed below. Those you make with the help of a medical professional.

The Five Wishes Document: Does It Help or Hurt?

You might have heard of Five Wishes, an easy-to-prepare advance health care directive said to be legally valid in almost every state. While a single, straightforward health care document that would pass legal muster in all states is a good idea, it is not, unfortunately, an idea whose time has come.

The laws governing health care directives include plenty of state-specific provisions, including terms, definitions, and procedures that state health care providers know and trust. The generic language in Five Wishes could create confusion, delays, or—at worst—legal tussles, which is exactly what health care directives should seek to avoid.

While WillMaker provides a more effective health care directive, Five Wishes helps you as you think through the issues involved in end-of-life care—and discuss them with your loved ones. You can preview and print a sample copy of the document at www.fivewishes.org.

What Your Documents Are Called

State	Number of Documents	Living Will	Durable Power of Attorney for Health Care
Alabama	1	Advance Directive for Health Care	
Alaska	1	Advance Health Care Directive	
Arizona	2	Living Will	Health Care Power of Attorney
Arkansas	2	Living Will	Durable Power of Attorney for Health Care
California	1	Advance Health Care Directive	
Colorado	2	Declaration as to Medical Treatment	Medical Durable Power of Attorney
Connecticut	1 or 2	Document Concerning Health Care and Withholding or Withdrawal of Life Support Systems	Appointment of Health Care Representative
	If you name a health care agent and leave health care instructions, your wishes will be combined into a single form called Health Care Instructions and Appointment of Health Care Representative. Your document might have several additional titles, depending on the choices you make.		
Delaware	1	Advance Health Care Directive	
District of Columbia	2	Declaration	Durable Power of Attorney for Health Care
Florida	2	Living Will	Designation of Health Care Surrogate
Georgia	1	Advance Directive for Health Care	
Hawaii	1	Advance Health Care Directive	
Idaho	1	Advance Care Planning Document	
Illinois	1 or 2	Declaration	Durable Power of Attorney for Health Care
	If you name a health care agent and leave health care instructions, your wishes will be combined into a single Durable Power of Attorney for Health Care form.		

What Your Documents Are Called (continued)			
State	**Number of Documents**	**Living Will**	**Durable Power of Attorney for Health Care**
Indiana	1	Advance Directive	
Iowa	2	Declaration	Durable Power of Attorney for Health Care
Kansas	2	Declaration	Durable Power of Attorney for Health Care Decisions
Kentucky	1	Advance Directive	
Maine	1	Advance Health Care Directive	
Maryland	1	Advance Directive	
Massachusetts	2	Document Directing Health Care	Health Care Proxy
Michigan	2	Document Directing Health Care	Patient Advocate Designation
Minnesota	1	Health Care Directive	
Mississippi	1	Advance Health Care Directive	
Missouri	2	Declaration	Durable Power of Attorney for Health Care
Montana	2	Declaration	Durable Power of Attorney for Health Care
Nebraska	2	Declaration	Durable Power of Attorney for Health Care
Nevada	2	Declaration	Durable Power of Attorney for Health Care Decisions
New Hampshire	1	Advance Directive	
New Jersey	1 or 2	Instruction Directive	Proxy Directive
	If you name a health care agent and leave health care instructions, your wishes will be combined into a single form called a Combined Advance Directive for Health Care.		
New Mexico	1	Advance Health Care Directive	
New York	2	Document Directing Health Care	Health Care Proxy

What Your Documents Are Called (continued)

State	Number of Documents	Living Will	Durable Power of Attorney for Health Care
North Carolina	2	Advance Directive	Health Care Power of Attorney
North Dakota	1	Health Care Directive	
Ohio	2	Declaration	Durable Power of Attorney for Health Care
Oklahoma	1	Advance Directive for Health Care	
Oregon	1	Advance Directive for Health Care	
Pennsylvania	2	Living Will	Durable Health Care Power of Attorney
Rhode Island	2	Declaration	Durable Power of Attorney for Health Care
South Carolina	1 or 2	Declaration	Health Care Power of Attorney
	If you name a health care agent and leave health care instructions, your wishes will be combined into a single Health Care Power of Attorney form.		
South Dakota	2	Living Will Declaration	Durable Power of Attorney for Health Care
Tennessee	1	Advance Health Care Directive	
Texas	2	Directive to Physicians and Family or Surrogates	Medical Power of Attorney
Utah	1	Advance Health Care Directive	
Vermont	1	Advance Directive	
Virginia	1	Advance Medical Directive	
Washington	2	Health Care Directive	Durable Power of Attorney for Health Care
West Virginia	2	Living Will	Medical Power of Attorney
Wisconsin	2	Declaration to Health Care Professionals	Power of Attorney for Health Care
Wyoming	1	Advance Health Care Directive	

Who Can Make Health Care Directives

To make a health care directive, you must be able to understand what the document means, what it contains, and how it works. People with physical disabilities can make valid health care documents; they can direct another to sign for them if they are unable to do so. (See the next section for more information on helping others with documents.)

Age-wise, the general rule is that you must be 18 years old to make a valid document directing your health care. However, there are exceptions:

- In Alabama, you must be 19.
- In Rhode Island and Oklahoma, you must be a resident of that state at the time you sign your document, though these states will honor health care directives made in other states.
- Many states allow people who are younger than age 18 to make health care directives under specific circumstances—for example, they are emancipated, are married, or have children.

Helping Someone Else Make Health Care Directives

If the person you want to help is of sound mind and wants to write down health care wishes, your job should not be difficult. You can use WillMaker to explain the process, answer questions, and help prepare and finalize the right documents.

But if you think someone who needs help will resist your efforts or you're concerned about their mental or physical ability to complete the documents, you need to carefully consider the way you approach the subject.

Explaining why the documents are important. If you're concerned about a loved one who is becoming mentally or physically frail, you might begin by simply talking about the benefits of the documents. Some people might be moved by a request to plan ahead because it will relieve anxiety and pressure for you and other caretakers. Others might be more inclined to make health care documents if they understand that doing so is the best way for them to stay in control and get the kind of medical care they want. (You can emphasize that whomever they name to make decisions for them must follow their instructions in every possible way.)

Helping someone who is becoming forgetful or absentminded. Of course, when you talk with someone who's struggling with increasing mental frailty, you will have to be sensitive to feelings about deteriorating mental abilities. Frustration, shame, or a sense of loss might well make your loved one more resistant to your help. You might want to underscore that planning is a good thing for anybody—including the young and healthy—just in case it's necessary someday.

Ultimately, however, you should never try to force someone to follow a certain course because you think it's best. If you strong-arm someone whose mental abilities are waning and the documents you make are later challenged in court, you could find yourself in a lot of legal trouble.

Assisting someone with intellectual disabilities. An individual with intellectual disabilities can make a legally valid health care directive only if they have the mental capacity to fully understand the document. As with an older person who has become mentally frail, prodding someone with serious intellectual disabilities to sign a health care directive could cause problems down the road. If you have doubts, the best thing to do is to consult a lawyer and consider whether the person needs a court-appointed guardian.

Signing for someone with physical disabilities. You could also get into big trouble if you fake signatures on any legal documents. Even if the person you're helping asks you to sign their name, don't do it.

Someone who is physically unable to sign health care documents can direct you to sign them, but you must carefully follow the instructions in "Making It Legal," at the end of this chapter.

Nevada Offers Specialized Forms

In addition to its standard form, Nevada law provides two health care directives for specific situations. One is for people with intellectual disabilities, and the other is for people with dementia. However, the mental capacity required for signing those documents is every bit as stringent as it is for traditional directives. If you live in Nevada and want to learn more about these specialized directives, talk to a lawyer.

When Your Documents Take Effect

The health care documents you make with WillMaker will take effect only if someday you are so ill or injured that you cannot make and express health care decisions. Generally, this means that:

- you can't understand the nature and consequences of the health care options available to you (including significant benefits, risks, and alternatives), and
- you are unable to communicate your own wishes for care orally, in writing, or through gestures.

If there is some question about your ability to understand your treatment choices or communicate clearly, your doctor (with the input of your health care agent or close relatives) will decide whether it is time for your health care directives to become operative.

Of course, in order for any of this to happen, medical personnel must know about your documents. In most instances, you can ensure that your directives become part of your medical record when you are admitted to a hospital or other care facility. But your need for care could arise unexpectedly or while you are away from home, so it's a good idea to give copies of your documents to several people. (See "Making and Distributing Copies," below.)

SEE AN EXPERT

Making your document effective immediately. In a handful of states, it is possible to give your health care agent the authority to manage your medical care immediately. An immediately effective document would allow your health care agent to step in and act for you at any time, without the need to involve a doctor in the question of whether your health care document should take effect. It won't give your agent the power to override what you want in terms of treatment; you will always be able to direct your own care if you are able to do so. If you like the idea of an immediately effective document, research the law for your state or talk to a lawyer to learn whether this option is available to you. (For tips on doing your own research or finding a lawyer, see Chapter 17.)

What Your Documents Can Cover

Each state can decide what makes a health care document legal. Many states list what you can include in your documents and define specific medical terms—and all states set out rules for having your document witnessed or notarized.

Hospitals Might Have Their Own Rules

While your legal right to direct your own health care is well established, hospitals and other health care institutions (such as nursing homes) have their own policies and practices for providing care at the end of life. Many give great weight to a patient's wishes, but others have strong positions of their own.

For example, Catholic hospitals and care facilities might require that all patients receive artificially administered food and water at the end of life, even if a patient has a valid health care directive saying that's not what the patient wants. In these facilities, patients will have to accept treatment or be transferred to another facility that will respect their wishes.

It might be worthwhile to familiarize yourself with the policies of the facilities you are likely to use. That way, you and your health care representative will know where to go for care in an emergency. And if you're making plans for long-term care, you can do so with your eyes open to the rules of your treatment providers.

If your state law demands a specific form or precise language, the health care documents you produce with WillMaker will contain it. However, in some instances, WillMaker's documents might go beyond what is addressed by your state's law. For example, your state's law might be silent on whether individuals can direct their own health care if they become permanently unconscious, or your state's law might specifically restrict you from removing life support if you are pregnant, or your state's form might not provide a place for you to address your wishes about donating your organs after death. However, if you want to address these issues in your WillMaker health care directive, you can do so.

The U.S. Supreme Court has ruled that the U.S. Constitution guarantees your right to direct your own health care. A state law that restricts your rights contradicts this ruling. The Court also ruled that if an individual has left "clear and convincing evidence" of medical wishes, those wishes should be followed. By far the best way to make your wishes known is to leave detailed written instructions.

If your choices are contrary to what your state law allows, your health care directive will state that your instructions should be respected anyway and followed in keeping with your constitutional right to direct your own health care.

If anyone later challenges your health care directive in a court because it goes beyond your state's law (extremely unlikely), there is an additional legal fail-safe. Your document contains a paragraph that allows the rest of your health care directive to be enforced as written even if any one of the directions you leave is found to be legally invalid.

Entering Your Personal Information

To begin making your health care documents, WillMaker asks you to provide some basic identifying information about yourself. (WillMaker assumes here that you are making documents for yourself. If that is not the case, enter the information for the person you are helping.)

Your State

You are asked to specify the state of your legal residence, sometimes called a domicile. This is the state where you make your home now and for the indefinite future. This information is essential because WillMaker produces health care directives that are geared to the laws of the state you select. (If you travel to another state, your document will be honored in that state as long as it meets the requirements of the state where you live.)

If you divide up the year living in two or more states, you might not be sure which state is your legal residence. To decide, choose the state where you are the most rooted—that is, the state in which you:

- are registered to vote
- register your car
- own valuable property—especially property with a title document, such as a house
- have checking, savings, and investment accounts, or
- maintain a business.

Your Name

Enter your name in the same form that you use on other formal documents, such as your driver's license or bank accounts. If you customarily use more than one name for official purposes, list all of them, separated by a.k.a. ("also known as").

There is room for you to list several names. But use your common sense. For purposes of your health care directive, your name is needed to identify you and to match you with your medical records. Be sure to include any names you have used on other medical documents such as prior hospital or doctor records.

Ability to Conceive

Many states have restrictions or special considerations that can apply if a person's health care directive takes effect while that person is pregnant. If you are or could become pregnant in the future, it might be necessary for you to answer a few more questions to address this possibility. (See "How Pregnancy Might Affect Your Wishes," below.)

Additional Information

A few states ask you to provide more biographical information, such as your address or birth date. If your state does, WillMaker will ask you for the additional information, and your documents will contain it, too.

If You Regularly Spend Time in More Than One State

A health care document made in one state is usually valid in other states, too. Most states accept health care directives from other states as long as the documents are legally valid in the state where they were made. Some states limit reciprocity, however, accepting other states' documents only to the extent that they comply with their own laws. And a few states are silent about whether they will honor documents from other states.

It sounds complicated, but keep in mind that you have a constitutional right to direct your health care; states cannot infringe upon that basic right. This means that your essential health care wishes—such as whether you want to receive life-sustaining treatment when close to death—will most likely be honored from state to state, whether or not your documents exactly comply with state law.

Rarely would you want to make a set of health care documents for more than one state. If your health care instructions for each state weren't absolutely identical, signing one document could simply revoke the other—whichever document was signed later would have control. To make it even trickier, differences in state forms can make it almost impossible to prepare two sets of documents with identical directions.

If you spend a good deal of time in more than one state, do what you can to find out whether your home state's health care documents fully protect you in the second state. You might be able to get the information you need by speaking to a patient representative at a hospital in the second state—explain your situation and ask what they recommend. At minimum, you should be sure your home state's signature requirements—witnessing and notarization—cover the requirements for the second state, too. (See "State Witnessing and Notarizing Requirements," near the end of this chapter.) If they don't, ask an extra witness to sign, or get your documents notarized so they are fully compliant with the requirements of both states.

If you don't feel confident that your health care wishes will be honored in both states where you spend time, ask an experienced estate planning lawyer for guidance.

Naming Your Primary Physician

Next, you can name a health care professional to serve as your primary physician. This is the person who will:

- oversee your medical care, and
- make legally significant determinations regarding your mental capacity and the state of your health, if necessary.

You will probably want to name a primary physician if you already have an established relationship with a health care provider you trust and with whom you have discussed—or will discuss—your health care wishes. (See "Talking to Your Physician," below.)

As a default, people usually name a medical doctor (M.D.) as their primary physician. However, many states allow you to name other types of health care providers. See the chart below. If you live in a state that is not on that list and the person who knows most about your health care is not a medical doctor, you can either name a doctor that knows less about you, or don't name anyone. In any case, you can use the "Other Wishes" section of your health care directive to describe your primary care provider that knows you best.

If you don't list a health care provider here, you can skip to the next section.

What Your Primary Physician Does

Your primary physician might be required to make important decisions about your mental state and your overall health. For example, your health care documents will take effect if you ever lack the capacity to make health care decisions for yourself, and somebody might need to decide whether that time has come. The provider you name will be responsible for making the determination.

In addition, your health care documents can set out instructions for end-of-life care in very specific situations—for instance, you might leave one set of instructions to take effect if you are permanently unconscious and another to govern your care if you are terminally ill. (You'll learn more about this in "Specifying Your Health Care Wishes," below.) Your primary physician will diagnose these conditions, putting your specific instructions into effect.

Naming Non-Physician Primary Care Providers

In an increasing number of states, the person who helps decide when your agent should make decisions on your behalf doesn't have to be a doctor. For example, some states allow you to name an advanced practice nurse (APN)* or a physician's assistant (PA) to do this job. See the chart below. Other states are sure to follow this trend of recognizing that sometimes the provider who knows most about a person's condition is not a doctor.

State	Instead of a physician, you can name
Alaska	APN or PA
Arkansas	"authorized independent health care provider"
Colorado	APRN
Connecticut	APN
Delaware	"health care professional"
Idaho	"licensed independent provider"
Indiana	"health care provider"
Iowa	"attending physician assistant"
Minnesota	APN or PA
Montana	APN
Nevada	APN
New Hampshire	"attending practitioner"
New Mexico	APN or PA
New York	APN or PA
Oregon	"health care provider"
Utah	APRN or PA
Vermont	APN or PA
Virginia	APN
West Virginia	APN
Wisconsin	APN or PA
Wyoming	APN or PA

* Instead of APN, some states use APRN (advanced practice registered nurse), which has the same meaning.

Choosing Your Primary Physician

If you have more than one primary health care provider and you're not sure which one to pick, think about who would do the best job of supervising your overall care. This might be your family doctor or general practitioner, rather than a specialist. If you're really on the fence, you can talk to each health care provider you're considering. You might find that one of them seems more comfortable taking on the responsibility of managing your care or you might just get a better sense of whom to pick.

Another possibility is to name one provider as your first choice and another as an alternate.

Choosing an Alternate

WillMaker also asks you to name an alternate physician. Choose your alternate with the same care you use for your first pick. Keep in mind that this health care provider might be responsible for making critical decisions about your care. If there isn't a second provider you know and trust, skip this question.

Talking to Your Physician

It's wise to talk to your primary health care provider about your treatment preferences before you finalize your health care documents. Talking with your primary physician (and alternate, if any) is especially important because your primary physician will be in charge of other caregivers. Make sure your provider understands your health care wishes and is willing to follow them. If you have questions or concerns about specific treatments, your primary physician should be able to answer them. If you have other, more subjective concerns about a particular medical condition, such as the effects of certain treatments or how the condition is likely to affect you, discuss those, too.

Let your primary physician know that you are completing a health care directive. If you will name an agent, be sure your physician knows how to contact that person in an emergency. Better still, introduce your agent to your primary health care provider if you have not already done so.

Naming Your Health Care Agent

This is one of the most important parts of making a health care directive. It's where you name the person who will work with your health care providers to direct your health care and make treatment decisions for you if you are unable to do so. This person is usually called your "health care agent," though some states use a term such as "representative," "proxy," or "surrogate." Your health care documents will use the correct term for your state.

You should appoint a health care agent—and at least one alternate—if you know someone you trust enough to take the job. The chances that your health care wishes will be enforced increase greatly if you name someone to supervise your care and speak for you if necessary.

Also, because life is unpredictable, there is no way your health care instructions can cover every possible health-related situation that might arise. Rapidly developing technology and new medical treatments underscore the need for flexible decision making. The best approach is to choose a trusted person who fully understands your feelings, beliefs, and wishes.

If you absolutely cannot think of anyone you trust to oversee your medical care, you can skip this section. It is better not to name anyone than to name someone who is not likely to strongly assert your wishes.

It's still a good idea to put your wishes for final health care in writing. Medical personnel are legally bound to follow your written wishes—or to find someone who will. If you do not name a health care agent, make an extra effort to discuss your wishes for medical care with a doctor or patient representative likely to be involved in providing that care.

What a Health Care Agent Does

If you become unable to direct your own health care, your agent will:

- supervise any treatment instructions you set out in your health care documents, and
- make decisions about any health care matters your documents do not cover.

Mental Health Care Decisions

Most states define health care to include mental health. To leave no confusion on the matter, our health care documents explicitly give your agent the power to make mental health decisions for you. This can include the power to discuss mental health treatments with your health care providers, to request or change medications, or even to admit you to a mental health care facility if necessary. However, some states require special documents or authorization before they will allow a health care agent to authorize extreme treatments, such as shock therapy, or to commit someone under their care to a psychiatric facility. Because of these state restrictions, a mental health care directive can be quite useful for individuals with serious mental illness, including those in the early stages of Alzheimer's disease or who have Alzheimer's in their families.

If you have particular concerns about your mental health treatment, you can fill out a special medical health care directive, giving your agent the maximum authority allowed by your state's laws. About half the states offer forms specifically designed to cover mental health issues in detail. In other states, you must modify a standard advance directive form to include mental health treatment instructions. Those instructions can cover matters such as:

- medication preferences
- electroconvulsive therapy, and
- involuntary commitment to a mental health facility.

You can find detailed information for your state by visiting the website of the National Resource Center on Psychiatric Advance Directives (NRC-PAD) at https://nrc-pad.org and clicking "State by State Info."

If you make a separate health care document, take care not to prepare overlapping directives—that is, two directives covering the same issues. The risk of confusion would be too great.

Start your research at NRC-PAD and consult a trusted health care professional if you're not sure which documents are best for you.

Your health care power of attorney can give your agent very broad authority to direct your medical care. Or you can fine-tune your document by answering some questions about your agent's specific powers, discussed below.

To carry out your wishes and make decisions for you, your agent will always be allowed to:

- review your medical records
- grant releases to medical personnel so that they can perform necessary treatments
- go to court, if necessary, to ensure your wishes are followed
- hire and fire medical personnel, and
- visit you in a hospital or other health care facility.

This should allow your agent to do everything needed to make sure your health care wishes are carried out—and if they are not, to get you transferred to another facility or to the care of another doctor who will enforce them.

Your Agent's Responsibility to You

You might be concerned that by naming a health care agent, you are giving up control of your own medical treatment, but you needn't worry. Your agent is legally required to follow your known wishes and to act in your best interest. If you leave written health care instructions, your agent is required to follow them, as are your health care providers. On the other hand, if you want to leave certain treatment decisions entirely in the hands of your agent, you can do so.

The decisions your agent makes for you must always agree with what you direct in your health care documents and any other wishes you make known to your agent. If a situation arises in which your agent does not know your specific wishes, your agent must make the decision that your agent believes you would make if you were capable of doing so. (For possible state-specific exceptions, see "State-Specific Powers," later in this chapter.)

The Health Insurance Portability and Accountability Act (HIPAA)

As you probably know from visits to the doctor, there's a law that requires patients to sign forms regarding medical privacy and the release of medical information. This federal law is called HIPAA, the Health Insurance Portability and Accountability Act. Some folks have worried that HIPAA requirements apply to your agent's powers under your health care documents and that you must prepare special HIPAA release forms to give your agent the authority to take over your health care decisions for you. In fact, this is not the case. An agent is authorized to obtain the medical information necessary to put your document into effect and carry out your wishes.

The health care power of attorney you make with WillMaker contains an explicit statement that your agent is allowed to act as your personal representative under HIPAA, authorized to receive full medical information about you. WillMaker took this extra step to avert any hassles for your agent.

To ensure you get the care you want, one of the most important things to do is talk with your agent (and other loved ones) about your wishes. (For tips on having this important conversation, see "Talking to Your Agent," below.)

You might wonder what happens if your health care agent lets you down. If someone goes to court and proves that your agent is harming you by acting in ways that you would not want, a court could revoke your agent's authority. In this case, the first person to take over would be an alternate agent you've named in your power of attorney for health care. If you haven't named an alternate or if your alternate is not available, the court will appoint a guardian or conservator to make your health and personal care decisions. (See "Nominating a Guardian," below.)

Choosing Your Agent

The person you name as your health care agent should be someone you trust and someone with whom you feel confident discussing your wishes. Choose someone who respects your right to get the kind of medical care you want, even if that person doesn't completely agree with your wishes.

CAUTION

How marriage or divorce can affect your document. The health care directive you create with WillMaker revokes the appointment of your spouse or registered partner if you file for divorce or legally separate. If this happens, you should prepare a new document or know that an alternate agent will step in to serve.

It's also a good idea to prepare a new health care document if you get married, unless your new spouse is already named as your health care agent. You are never required to name your spouse as your health care agent, but if you want to name someone else, be sure you do it in a document created after the date of your marriage. If you have an old document naming someone other than your spouse as your agent, some states will consider it automatically revoked when you marry.

You can choose your spouse or partner, a relative, or a close friend. Keep in mind that your agent might have to assert your wishes in the face of medical personnel and family members who might be driven by their own beliefs and interests, rather than yours. If you foresee the possibility of conflict in enforcing your wishes, try to choose someone who is strong-willed and assertive.

Naming More Than One Agent: A Bad Idea

WillMaker's health care directive allows you to name just one person at a time to serve as your agent. It's usually unwise to name two people to serve together, even if you know two people who are willing to take the job. There might be problems, brought on by passing time and human nature, with naming coagents. In the critical time during which your representatives will be overseeing your wishes, they could disagree or suffer a change of heart, rendering them ineffective as lobbyists on your behalf while they argue with each other.

If you know of two people you would like to name as your agents, choose one to serve first and name the other as your alternate.

While you need not name someone who lives in the same state as you do, proximity is one factor to consider. If you have a protracted illness, the person you name might be called upon to spend weeks or months near your bedside, making sure health care providers abide by your wishes for treatment.

Finally, if you have made—or are planning to make—a durable power of attorney for finances (see Chapter 14), you should think strongly about naming the same person to oversee both your finances and your health care. If you decide not to name the same person—perhaps because one has a much better head for business and the other is likely to be better at your bedside—keep in mind that your health care agent and your agent for finances might have to work very closely at times. (For example, your agent for finances will be responsible for paying your medical and insurance bills at your health care agent's direction.)

State Restrictions on Who Can Serve as Your Agent

A number of states have rules about who can serve as your agent. Attending physicians and other health care providers are commonly prohibited from serving. Some states presume that the motivations of such people might be clouded by self-interest. For example, a doctor might be motivated to provide every medical procedure available—to try every heroic or experimental treatment—even if that goes against a patient's wishes. On the other side, treatments might sometimes be withheld because of concerns about time or cost.

Before you select an agent, consult the list below for the specifics of your state's agent requirements and restrictions.

Choosing Alternate Agents

You can name one or two alternate agents. Your first alternate will serve only if your first choice becomes unavailable. Your second alternate will step in only if your primary agent and first alternate are unable or unwilling to act or cannot quickly be located.

Use the same principles to choose your alternates as you did when making your first pick: trustworthiness, dependability, assertiveness, and availability.

Do not choose as an alternate someone who is disqualified by state law from serving in your state. (See the list below.)

Granting Specific Powers to Your Agent

After you name your agent, WillMaker will ask you some questions about granting specific powers to your agent. This section explains each of these powers.

Withdrawing Life-Prolonging Procedures

It is important to specify whether your agent can direct health care providers to withhold or withdraw life-prolonging procedures when you are close to death.

A life-prolonging procedure or treatment is one that would only prolong the process of dying or sustain a condition of permanent unconsciousness. In other words, the patient would die soon—or die without regaining meaningful consciousness—whether or not the treatment was administered.

It is generally agreed that cardiopulmonary resuscitation (CPR), dialysis, artificial respiration, and complicated invasive surgery are life-prolonging procedures when performed on a terminally ill or permanently comatose patient. (For more information, see below.)

In most states, agents automatically have the power to withdraw life-prolonging procedures. In other states, if you wish to grant the power it must be specifically spelled out in your health care document.

To avoid any confusion, the health care directive you make with WillMaker clearly states whether your agent has the power to withdraw life-prolonging procedures, knowing that to do so might result in your death. You will be instructed to sign or initial this specific clause to underscore that you knowingly granted or denied this power to your agent. Doing this ensures that your wishes will be honored in any state.

State Law Restrictions on Agents

Alabama

Your health care proxy may not be:

- your treating health care provider
- an employee of your treating health care provider, unless the employee is related to you, or
- under the age of 19.

Alaska

Your health care agent may not be an owner, operator, or employee of the health care institution at which you are receiving care, unless related to you by blood, marriage, or adoption.

Arizona

Your health care agent must be at least 18 years old.

Arkansas

Your health care agent must be at least 18 years old.

California

Your health care agent may not be:

- your treating health care provider or an employee of your treating health care provider, unless the individual is your registered domestic partner or is related to you, or you and the employee both work for your treating health care provider
- an operator or employee of a community care facility, unless the individual is your registered domestic partner or is related to you, or you and the employee both work at the community care facility, or
- an operator or employee of a residential care facility for the elderly, unless the individual is your registered domestic partner or is related to you, or you and the employee both work at the residential care facility.

Colorado

No restrictions on who may serve as your health care agent.

State Law Restrictions on Agents (continued)

Connecticut

If, when you appoint your health care agent and attorney-in-fact for health care decisions, you are a patient or a resident of, or have applied for admission to, a hospital, residential care home, rest home with nursing supervision, or chronic and convalescent nursing home, your health care agent and attorney-in-fact for health care decisions may not be:

- an operator, unless the operator is related to you by blood, marriage, or adoption
- an administrator, unless the administrator is related to you by blood, marriage, or adoption, or
- an employee, unless the employee is related to you by blood, marriage, or adoption.

In any case, your health care agent and attorney-in-fact for health care decisions may not be:

- your attending physician or advanced practice registered nurse, or
- an employee of a government agency that is financially responsible for your medical care—unless that person is related to you by blood, marriage, or adoption.

Delaware

A person may not be your agent if:

- the person is an owner, operator, employee, or contractor of a long-term health care institution where you are receiving care, unless that person is a family member, lives with you, or is the offspring of someone who lives with you
- the person is the subject of a civil or criminal order that limits contact with you
- you have a protection from abuse order (or petition) against that person, or
- a court finds that the person poses a threat to your well-being, even if there is no protection from abuse order or petition.

District of Columbia

Your health care attorney-in-fact may not be your health care provider.

State Law Restrictions on Agents (continued)

Florida

No restrictions on who may serve as your health care representative.

Georgia

Your health care agent may not be a physician or health care provider who is directly involved in your health care.

Hawaii

Your health care agent may not be an owner, operator, or employee of your treating health care provider, unless the person is related to you by blood, marriage, or adoption.

Idaho

Your health care representative must be at least 18 years old.

Illinois

Your health care agent may not be:

- your attending physician
- your health care provider, or
- any other health care professional directly involved in your care.

Indiana

Your health care representative must be at least 18 years old.

Iowa

Your health care agent may not be:

- your health care provider, or
- an employee of your health care provider, unless these individuals are related to you by blood, marriage, or adoption—limited to parents, children, siblings, grandchildren, grandparents, uncles, aunts, nephews, nieces, and great-grandchildren.

Kansas

Your health care agent may not be:

- your treating health care provider
- an employee of your treating health care provider, or
- an employee, an owner, a director, or an officer of a health care facility.

State Law Restrictions on Agents (continued)

These restrictions do not apply, however, if your agent is:

- related to you by blood, marriage, or adoption, or
- a member of the same community of people to which you belong who have vowed to lead a religious life and who conduct or assist in conducting religious services and actually and regularly engage in religious, charitable, or educational activities or the performance of health care services.

Kentucky

Your health care surrogate may not be an employee, an owner, a director, or an officer of a health care facility where you are a resident or patient, unless they are:

- related to you more closely than first cousins, once removed, or
- a member of the same religious or fraternal order.

Maine

Your health care agent may not be an owner, operator, or employee of a residential long-term health care institution in which you are receiving care, unless related to you by blood, marriage, or adoption.

Maryland

Your health care agent may not be:

- an owner, operator, or employee—or the spouse, parent, child, or sibling of an owner, operator, or employee—of a health care facility where you are receiving treatment unless they would qualify as your surrogate decision maker under Maryland law or are appointed before you receive, or contract to receive, health care from the facility
- a person subject to a protective order (restraining order) that protects you from that person, or
- your spouse, if either of you have filed for divorce or together you have executed a separation agreement, unless after the date of filing or execution you indicate that you want that person to be your agent.

Massachusetts

Your health care agent may not be an operator, administrator, or employee of a facility where you are a patient or resident or have applied for admission, unless the operator, administrator, or employee is related to you by blood, marriage, or adoption.

State Law Restrictions on Agents (continued)

Michigan

Your patient advocate must be at least 18 years old.

Minnesota

Your health care agent may not be your treating health care provider or an employee of your treating health care provider, unless related to you by blood, marriage, registered domestic partnership, or adoption.

Mississippi

Your health care agent may not be an owner, operator, or employee of a residential long-term care facility where you are receiving treatment, unless related to you by blood, marriage, or adoption.

Missouri

Your health care attorney-in-fact may not be:

- your attending physician
- an employee of your attending physician, or
- an owner, operator, or employee of the health care facility where you live, unless:
  - you and your attorney-in-fact are related as parents, children, siblings, grandparents, or grandchildren, or
  - you and your attorney-in-fact are members of the same community of people who have vowed to lead a religious life and who conduct or assist in conducting religious services and actually and regularly engage in religious, charitable, or educational activities or the performance of health care services.

Montana

Your health care agent must be at least 18 years old.

Nebraska

Your health care attorney-in-fact may not be:

- under the age of 18
- your attending physician or a member of your mental health treatment team

State Law Restrictions on Agents (continued)

- an employee of your attending physician or a member of your mental health treatment team, unless the employee is related to you by blood, marriage, or adoption
- a person unrelated to you by blood, marriage, or adoption who is an owner, operator, or employee of a health care provider of which you are a patient or resident, or
- a person unrelated to you by blood, marriage, or adoption who is presently serving as a health care attorney-in-fact for 10 or more people.

Nevada

Unless the person you name is your spouse, legal guardian, or next of kin, your health agent may not be:

- your health care provider
- an employee of your health care provider
- an owner or operator of a health care facility, or
- an employee of a health care facility.

Additionally, if you reside or are about to reside in a hospital, an assisted living facility, or a facility for skilled nursing, the agent cannot be:

- an owner, operator, or employee of the hospital or facility, or
- the hospital or facility itself.

These restrictions do not apply if the person you name is your spouse, legal guardian, or next of kin. Also, in some situations, you can name the hospital or facility itself if you're doing so to establish eligibility for Medicaid.

New Hampshire

Your health care agent may not be:

- your attending practitioner
- an employee of your attending practitioner, unless the employee is related to you
- your residential care provider, or
- an employee of your residential care provider, unless the employee is related to you.

State Law Restrictions on Agents (continued)

New Jersey

Your health care representative may not be:

- under the age of 18, or
- an operator, administrator, or employee of a health care institution in which you are a patient or resident, unless the operator, administrator, or employee is related to you by blood, marriage, domestic partnership, civil union, or adoption or, in the case of a physician, is not your attending physician.

New Mexico

Your health care agent may not be an owner, operator, or employee of a health care facility at which you are receiving care—unless related to you by blood, marriage, or adoption.

New York

Your health care agent may not be:

- under the age of 18, unless they are a parent or married
- your attending physician, nurse practitioner, or physician's assistant
- presently appointed agent for 10 or more other people, unless they are also your spouse, child, parent, brother, sister, or grandparent
- an operator, administrator, or employee of a hospital if, at the time of the appointment, you are a patient or resident of, or have applied for admission to, such hospital. This restriction shall not apply to:
  - an operator, administrator, or employee of a hospital who is related to you by blood, marriage, or adoption, or
  - a physician who is not your attending physician, except that no physician affiliated with a mental hygiene facility or a psychiatric unit of a general hospital may serve as agent for you if you are living in or being treated by such facility or unit unless the physician is related to you by blood, marriage, or adoption.

North Carolina

Your health care agent must be at least 18 years old and may not be providing health care to you for pay.

State Law Restrictions on Agents (continued)

North Dakota

Your health care agent may not be:

- your treating health care provider
- an employee of your treating health care provider, unless the employee is related to you
- an operator of a long-term care facility, or
- an employee of an operator of a long-term care facility, unless the employee is related to you.

Ohio

Your health care attorney-in-fact may not be:

- under the age of 18
- your attending physician
- an administrator of any nursing home in which you are receiving care
- an employee or agent of your attending physician, or
- an employee or agent of any health care facility in which you are being treated.

These restrictions do not apply, however, if your attorney-in-fact is 18 years of age or older and a member of the same religious order as you, or is related to you by blood, marriage, or adoption.

Oklahoma

Your health care proxy must be at least 18 years old.

Oregon

Your health care representative may not be:

- under the age of 18, unless emancipated or married
- your attending physician or attending health care provider—or an employee of your attending physician or attending health care provider—unless the physician, health care provider, or employee is related to you by blood, marriage, or adoption
- an owner, operator, or employee of a health care facility in which you are a patient or resident, unless related to you by blood, marriage, or adoption—or appointed before you were admitted to the facility, or

State Law Restrictions on Agents (continued)

- your parent or former guardian, if you were ever permanently removed from that person's care by court order. (If you have questions about this restriction, consult a lawyer.)

Pennsylvania

Your health care agent may not be:

- your attending physician or other health care provider, unless related to you by blood, marriage, or adoption, or
- an owner, operator, or employee of a health care provider from which you are receiving care, unless related to you by blood, marriage, or adoption.

Rhode Island

Your health care agent may not be:

- your treating health care provider
- an employee of your treating health care provider, unless the employee is related to you
- an operator of a community care facility, or
- an employee of an operator of a community care facility, unless the employee is related to you.

South Carolina

Your health care agent may not be:

- under the age of 18
- your health care provider at the time you execute your health care power of attorney, unless related to you
- a spouse or an employee of your health care provider, unless related to you, or
- an employee of the nursing care facility where you live, unless related to you.

South Dakota

No restrictions on who may serve as your health care agent.

State Law Restrictions on Agents (continued)

Tennessee

Your health care agent may not be:

- your treating health care provider
- an employee of your treating health care provider, unless related to you by blood, marriage, or adoption
- an operator of a health care institution
- an employee of an operator of a health care institution, unless related to you by blood, marriage, or adoption, or
- your conservator, unless you are represented by an attorney who signs a specific statement—required by Tennessee Code § 34-6-203(c).

Texas

Your health care agent may not be:

- your health care provider
- an employee of your health care provider, unless the employee is related to you
- your residential care provider, or
- an employee of your residential care provider, unless the employee is related to you.

Utah

Your health care agent may not be:

- a person who poses a danger to your well-being, or
- an owner, operator, employee, or contractor of a nursing home or assisted living facility in which you reside or receive care (unless the owner, operator, employee, or contractor is your family member, your cohabitant (someone you live with as a couple), or a descendant of your cohabitant).

Vermont

Your health care agent may not be:

- your health care provider, or
- an owner, operator, employee, agent, or contractor of a residential care facility, health care facility, or correctional facility in which you reside, unless related to you by blood, marriage, civil union, or adoption.

State Law Restrictions on Agents (continued)

Virginia

Your health care agent must be at least 18 years old.

Washington

Your health care agent may not be:

- your physician
- your physician's employee, or
- an owner, administrator, or employee of the health care facility where you live or receive care.

These restrictions do not apply, however, if your agent is your spouse, state-registered domestic partner, parent, adult child, or sibling.

West Virginia

Your health care representative may not be:

- your treating health care provider
- an employee of your treating health care provider unless related to you
- an operator of a health care facility serving you, or
- an employee of an operator of a health care facility serving you, unless the employee is related to you.

Wisconsin

Your health care agent may not be:

- your health care provider or the spouse or employee of your health care provider unless related to you, or
- an employee or the spouse of an employee of the health care facility in which you live or are a patient, unless that person is related to you.

Wyoming

Your health care agent may not be an owner, operator, or employee of a residential or community care facility where you are receiving care, unless related to you by blood, marriage, or adoption.

Note that giving your agent the power to make this decision is not the same as telling your agent what decision to make. Later in the interview, you can leave specific instructions about whether you want to receive life-prolonging procedures—and when. Your agent is legally bound to follow your wishes. Here, you are just giving your agent power to direct your care on this matter. You should grant your agent this power if you know that you do not want some or all life-prolonging procedures when you are close to death.

Withdrawing Food and Water

If you are close to death and cannot communicate your wishes for health care, it is also likely that you will not be able to eat or drink normally. The medical solution to this is to provide you with food and water—as a mix of nutrients and fluids—through tubes inserted in a vein or into your stomach, depending on your condition. This is typically called "artificially administered nutrition and hydration," though your state might use a slightly different term.

Even though artificially administered food and water is often considered a life-prolonging procedure, it is wise to state your wishes about this issue separately from other life-prolonging procedures. Many states require you to give explicit instructions about artificially administered food and water. WillMaker's health care directive requires it no matter where you live. The withdrawal of food and water from terminally ill or permanently unconscious patients has proven to be a bitterly contested personal and political issue. Your document will explicitly state your wishes on this matter so there is no chance of confusion about what you want. You should grant your agent this power if there are any circumstances under which you would not want to receive artificially administered food and water.

Authorizing Organ, Tissue, or Body Donation

With WillMaker's health care directive, you can give your agent the authority to carry out your wishes for organ, tissue, or body donation after your death—or specify that your agent should not have this power.

In almost all cases, it's wise to give your agent the power to assert your wishes about anatomical gifts. If you want to be a donor, giving your agent clear authority to approve your donation will help to expedite the procedure. (Donations must be carried out quickly in order to succeed.) If you don't want to donate, your agent can ensure your wishes are carried out by speaking firmly on your behalf, even in the face of others who might disagree with your choice. And if you're not sure what you want, you can be assured that someone you trust will have the authority to make a decision based on the circumstances when the time comes.

If you give your agent this authority, you will have the opportunity to provide further instructions about anatomical gifts—or to assert that you do not want to be an organ donor, if that is your wish. (See "Stating Your Wishes for Organ Donation," below.) Your agent must try to follow any wishes you express.

If you don't grant your agent this authority and the question of whether to donate your organs arises after your death, your doctors will ask your next of kin to make the decision.

Authorizing an Autopsy

In some circumstances, such as a sudden or suspicious death, state law might require an autopsy. In these cases, a medical examiner does not need to get permission before proceeding.

In other situations, your loved ones or family members might request an autopsy—for example, if they have questions about the cause of your death or wish to advance society's medical knowledge about a little-understood disease, such as Alzheimer's. You can give or refuse consent to this type of autopsy, or you can give your agent the power to make the decision for you. Here is a little information about each choice.

Advantages of authorizing an autopsy. Your first option is to state that you authorize an autopsy after your death. This doesn't mean there will be an autopsy; it just allows your loved ones to get more information about your death if they feel they need it.

This type of information can provide comfort to grieving family members, but there is a practical reason for it as well: An autopsy might reveal conditions that could be inherited by other members of your family, giving them opportunities for early diagnosis and treatment.

When you might not want to authorize an autopsy. Your second option is to refuse consent to an autopsy after your death. You might want to avoid an autopsy for personal or practical reasons. For example, some people have religious concerns about the procedure. If that's true for you, you might want to discuss the issue with a clergy member or other spiritual adviser before making your decision.

The most common practical reason for refusing an autopsy is the cost. A complete autopsy can cost several thousand dollars and is usually not covered by insurance. Before you consent to an autopsy, you might want to investigate the costs and be sure your estate has money on hand to cover them.

In rare cases, grants are available to cover the cost of an autopsy. For example, in cases of Alzheimer's or dementia, the National Institutes of Health provides some autopsy services without charge to the family. In order to receive these benefits, however, you must be enrolled in a research program before your death.

Letting your agent decide. When you consider the pros and cons of consenting to an autopsy, you might find that the third option is best. It allows you to leave the matter in your agent's hands.

Whether an autopsy is helpful or prudent will depend on the circumstances of your death—many of which are unpredictable ahead of time. If you talk to your agent about your general feelings and wishes, your agent can make a decision when the time comes, taking into account all the circumstances.

Authorizing Disposition of Your Remains

Unless you specify otherwise, your closest family members will decide whether your body will be buried or cremated. WillMaker's health care directive offers three ways to express your wishes about this decision.

Directing your agent to follow existing wishes. If you want to write down your preferences for final arrangements, including burial or cremation, you can use our "final arrangements" letter for this purpose. It allows you to prepare a detailed document stating your preferences about burial, cremation, and funeral or memorial services. (See Chapter 16.) After you have done this—or prepared a similar document—you can select the option that states you have already made arrangements that your agent should follow. You will then have the opportunity to describe the document or arrangements you've made, so that your agent and others can locate your papers and carry out your wishes when the time comes.

Letting your agent decide. If you choose this option, your agent will have the power to decide how your body should be handled after you die. You can either leave these matters entirely in the hands of your agent or, better for everyone involved, discuss your wishes with your agent and other loved ones.

Letting family decide. If there is some reason why you do not want to give your agent the authority to make decisions about burial or cremation, you can select the third option, which denies your agent this power. The practical result is that your closest family members will make decisions about your remains, following any wishes that you might have expressed.

If You Give Your Agent This Power: Special Signing Requirements

In some states, giving your agent the authority to make decisions about your burial or cremation changes the execution requirements for your document.

For example, in Nevada, to make your durable power of attorney for health care decisions legal, you can either have it signed by two witnesses or have it notarized. Usually, the choice is yours. However, if you grant your agent the power to direct your final arrangements, you do not have a choice; you must have the document notarized—and witnesses are not necessary.

WillMaker provides the correct finalization instructions for your state, depending on the choices you make when you prepare your document. To learn whether your state has special requirements, see "State Witnessing and Notarizing Requirements," below.

CAUTION

If you live in Kentucky, New Jersey, or New Mexico, WillMaker will not ask you about authorizing the disposition of your remains. Each of these states requires that you use a document other than your health care directive to make this authorization:

- In Kentucky, to direct the disposition of your remains you must use a state-authorized "funeral planning declaration." (Ky. Rev. Stat. § 367.93103 and Ky. Rev. Stat. § 367.93117.)
- In New Jersey, to name a "funeral agent," you must use either a will or a state-approved form. (N.J. Stat. § 3B: 10-21.1 and N.J. Stat. § 45: 27-22.)
- In New Mexico, to designate someone who is legally authorized to carry out your final arrangements you must use a will. (N.M. Stat. § 45-3-701.)

For more information about leaving instructions for burial, cremation, and other final arrangements, see Chapter 16.

State-Specific Powers

A handful of states ask you to make decisions about very specific powers you can grant to your agent. If you live in one of the states below, WillMaker guides you step by step through your choices. The next section provides a brief overview of each power.

New Hampshire. WillMaker asks whether, under certain circumstances, your agent may override your objections to treatment. New Hampshire, like most other states, requires your agent and medical practitioners to make an effort to inform you of any proposed medical treatments or of any proposal to withdraw or withhold treatment from you. Usually, your caretakers may not provide or withhold treatments if you object, even if you are determined to be incapacitated and incapable of making informed health care choices.

In New Hampshire, however, you can state that your agent should carry out your treatment wishes when your health care practitioners have determined that you are no longer capable of making informed decisions—even if you verbally object to those treatments when the time comes. (N.H. Rev. Stat. § 137-J: 5(IV).) When you make your health care document, WillMaker asks you whether you want to give your agent this power.

You might want to grant this authority if you are concerned about being diagnosed with Alzheimer's disease or another form of severe dementia. Dementia might cause you to become argumentative and resist the reasoned treatment decisions that you made before you became ill.

This power can make it much easier for your agent to carry out your wishes if you ever become incapable of making rational decisions. But do think carefully before you add it to your document. It places an enormous amount of authority in your agent's hands. Before granting the power, be certain your agent is someone you completely trust to treat you well and that your agent fully understands your wishes for care.

Utah. WillMaker will ask you whether your agent can admit you to a nursing home. In most states, a health care agent automatically has the power to decide whether to admit you to a nursing home—whether for a short stay or a long one. In Utah, however, if you want your agent to have the power to admit you to a nursing home for more than 100 days, you must authorize that power specifically in your health care directive. (Utah Code § 75A-9-117.) WillMaker asks you to express your wishes on this matter.

Granting this authority to your health care agent does not mean that you want or prefer to be admitted to a nursing home. As with other matters, your agent must follow your specific wishes. For example, if you would consent to be admitted to a nursing home only as a last resort, you can give your agent the power to admit you, but make sure your agent understands your feelings and preferences.

Keep in mind that if you do not grant this authority and your situation changes or deteriorates to the extent that your health care providers and agent agree that admitting you to a nursing home is best for you, your agent might be required to initiate court proceedings in order to get you the care you need.

Ultimately, the choice is deeply personal. The best you can do is make the choice that feels right to you now—and be sure to talk with your agent about your wishes.

Virginia. WillMaker asks you about four special powers:

- **Authorizing mental health treatment.** If you grant this power, your agent will be able to admit you to a health care facility for mental health treatment after a physician examines you and certifies that you need such care. Without this power, your agent will be required to ask a judge for permission to admit you. If you don't think you'll need mental health treatment, or if you'd rather have a court oversee your mental health care, you might not want to grant this power. But if you are concerned that you might require mental health treatment and you fully trust your agent to decide for you, granting this power could avoid a lot of time, expense, and trouble.
- **Authorizing treatment over your objections.** This power is very similar to the power for New Hampshire agents described above. See that description for more information.
- **Continuing to serve over your objection.** This power states that, if you are incapable of making informed health care decisions, your agent may continue to represent you even if you protest your agent's authority at the time. If you don't grant this power, your agent's authority will be revoked upon your objection and your alternate agent will step in. If you haven't appointed an alternate or none of your alternates are available, Virginia law will determine who makes medical decisions for you.
- **Enrolling you in health care studies.** If you grant this power, your agent will have permission to enroll you in qualified health care studies. You can limit your participation to studies that might personally benefit you, or you can allow studies that might not help you personally, but might contribute to greater scientific knowledge and advances for patients in the future. As with any other health care choice, your agent will be required by law to act in your best interests and avoid any decisions that conflict with your known beliefs and values.

Wisconsin. You will be asked to decide whether your agent can admit you to a nursing home. For more information, see the note for Utah, above.

Note for Vermont Readers

Similar to New Hampshire and Virginia, discussed above, Vermont law also allows you to state in an advance directive that your agent may authorize medical treatment over your objections. Such a provision would take effect only if you lack the mental capacity to make your own decisions. However, to protect your right to direct your own health care, Vermont has created very detailed requirements you must meet to give your agent this power. For example, your advance directive must be specific about the treatments your agent can authorize under these circumstances, and the provision must be signed by three people in addition to you: your agent, your health care provider, and another official such as a lawyer, hospital ombudsman, or probate court official. (You can find the law that describes this power in Title 18, § 9707(h), of the Vermont Statutes.)

If you live in Vermont and want to give your agent the power to override your objections, consult a lawyer. A qualified estate planning lawyer can ensure your document will work as you intend.

Talking to Your Agent

It might not be an easy conversation to start, but those who make the effort to discuss the hard topic of what kind of medical care they want at the end of life usually find the effort worth the price. You'll probably want to begin by talking with your agent; then, if you can, discuss your feelings with close family members and friends as well. If the topic seems too difficult to broach, consider using a relevant news item, television show, or film as a catalyst for discussion.

There are three basic goals when talking with your agent:

- making sure the person you've picked is willing to take on the responsibility of acting on your behalf
- sharing your written directions and other wishes, and
- allowing your agent to ask questions so you are both clear on what you want.

During your discussion, your agent might ask about issues you haven't considered. This is a great opportunity for each of you to clarify the understanding between you so that you both can feel confident that your agent will know what to do if you cannot speak for yourself.

If you have a primary care provider, you might want to encourage your doctor and your agent to meet. If you are already a patient in a medical facility, your agent will also want to get to know the social worker or patient representative of the facility.

Why are these discussions so important? First, having them gives you the opportunity to let people know that you are preparing health care documents and why you feel strongly about doing so.

Second, it is impossible to foresee all of the circumstances or illnesses that might arise and address them in your documents. Giving people a clear understanding of your personal views and values can avoid future disagreements as to how your written desires should be applied to specific circumstances.

In discussing your values, you might want to cover some or all of the following:

- your overall attitude toward life, including what gives you feelings of purpose and meaning and how you feel about your independence
- fears you might have about no longer being able to speak for yourself or make your own decisions
- any strong feelings you have about medical treatments that you do or do not wish to receive at the end of your life, including life support and feeding tubes
- where you would prefer to be at the end of your life (for example, many people feel that they would rather die at home or in a hospice facility than in a hospital)
- what a phrase such as "death with dignity" or "no heroic measures" actually means to you
- anything you want others to know about the spiritual or religious part of your life and how it affects your feelings about serious illness and death

- what you might want for comfort and support when you are close to death (for example, to have certain people present, to be read to, or to have music playing)
- your feelings about doctors and caregivers in general, as well as any opinions about specific caregivers, and
- what you want after your death, including feelings about organ donation, an autopsy, and final arrangements (for example, burial, cremation, or memorial ceremonies).

Obviously, these conversations are not always easy to initiate or carry out, but they present all involved with an opportunity for greater peace of mind. Your loved ones will know your true wishes, and you might find that this is a chance to gain clarity, understanding, and a bridge to closer relationships.

Nominating a Guardian

In most cases, your health care agent will be able to make all necessary health care and personal decisions for you, perhaps working with a financial agent you've named under a durable power of attorney for finances (this document is discussed in Chapter 14). However, although it's unlikely, there might come a time when a court must name someone to make personal decisions for you that go beyond the authority granted in your health care documents. If you need a great deal of help, this person, usually called a "guardian of the person" or "conservator of the person," may be granted the power to decide where you live, what you eat, the clothes you wear, or what your daily activities will be.

You can use the WillMaker health care directive to nominate your agent to serve as guardian if it's ever necessary. Doing so strengthens your statement that you want your agent to speak for you in all matters relating to both your health and your personal care.

In almost all cases, a court will appoint the person you nominate to be your conservator or guardian. The only time a court will override your nomination is if someone proves to the court that your choice is unlikely to act in your best interests. These types of disputes are very rare.

If your agent is unavailable. If you nominate your agent as your guardian or conservator and your agent is not willing or able to take the job if called on, your document will automatically nominate any alternate agents you have named, in the order designated.

If you don't nominate your agent. If you don't nominate your agent as guardian or conservator and a court must later appoint one, who gets the job depends on where you live. In some states, your health care agent is automatically nominated for the position. In others, priority is given to your spouse—or registered partner in a few states—followed by close relatives in an order established by state law.

Nominating a guardian or conservator of your estate. While a guardian or conservator of your person is responsible for your personal comfort and care, a guardian or conservator of your estate is responsible for your finances. If you make a durable power of attorney for finances, you can nominate your financial agent to serve as the guardian or conservator of your estate if that ever becomes necessary. (See Chapter 14 for more information.)

Specifying Your Health Care Wishes

After you have named (or declined to name) a health care agent, you have the opportunity to express your wishes and feelings about medical treatment in as much detail as you choose. You have four basic options:

- leave all health care decisions in the hands of your agent, if you have named one
- make a general statement that you do not wish to receive life support when death is imminent
- make a general statement that you wish to be kept alive as long as possible, or
- specify different treatment wishes for different situations.

In this section, you will also have a chance to express any additional general wishes about end-of-life health care.

Types of Medical Care: What You Should Know

This section briefly describes some medical procedures that you should be familiar with before you provide directions about your care. Dry or off-putting as it might seem, it's a good idea to at least read quickly through the sections below to gain a basic understanding of:

- what the term "life-prolonging" means from a medical perspective
- what "artificially provided food and water" is and when it might be necessary, and
- what constitutes comfort or "palliative" care.

However, you will not need to deal with these definitions if you are already certain of any of the following:

- You want your agent to make all decisions for you.
- You want all procedures to be withheld.
- You want all procedures to be provided.

If any of these apply to you, you can skip directly to "If Your Wishes Are Simple," below.

Life-Prolonging Medical Care

When completing your health care instructions, WillMaker asks for your preferences about life-prolonging treatments or procedures. Many people need a little more information before answering these questions.

A life-prolonging procedure or treatment is one that would only prolong the process of dying or sustain a condition of permanent unconsciousness. In other words, the patient would die soon—or die without regaining meaningful consciousness—whether or not the treatment was administered. This section describes the most common life-prolonging treatments—a respirator, cardiopulmonary resuscitation (CPR), surgery, and so on—in some detail.

Bear in mind that the types of medical procedures that are available will change over time. Technological advances mean that currently unfathomable procedures and treatments will become available and treatments that are now common will become obsolete. Also, the treatments that are available vary drastically depending on the sophistication of medical facilities.

Blood and blood products. Partial or full blood transfusions might be recommended to combat diseases that impair the blood system, to foster healing after a blood loss, or to replenish blood lost through surgery, disease, or injury.

Cardiopulmonary resuscitation. CPR is used when a person's heart or breathing has stopped. CPR includes applying physical pressure and using mouth-to-mouth resuscitation. Electrical shocks are also used if available. CPR is often accompanied by intravenous drugs used to normalize body systems. A final step in CPR is often attaching the patient to a respirator.

Diagnostic tests. Diagnostic tests are commonly used to evaluate urine, blood, and other body fluids and to check on all bodily functions. Diagnostic tests can include X-rays and more sophisticated tests of brainwaves or other body systems. Some tests—including surgery—can be expensive, painful, and invasive.

Dialysis. A dialysis machine is used to clean and add essential substances to the blood—through tubes placed in blood vessels or into the abdomen—when kidneys do not function properly. The entire cleansing process takes three or more hours and is performed on most dialysis patients two or three times a week. With portable dialysis machines, it is possible for some patients to have the procedure performed at home rather than in a hospital or other advanced care facility.

Drugs. The most common and most controversial drugs given to seriously ill or comatose patients are antibiotics—administered by mouth, through a feeding tube, or by injection. Antibiotics are used to arrest and squelch infectious diseases. Patients in very weakened conditions might not respond even to massive doses of antibiotics.

Many health care providers argue that infectious diseases can actually be a benefit to those in advanced stages of an illness, because they can render a patient unconscious, and presumably not in pain, or help to speed up the dying process. Others contend that if an antibiotic can eliminate symptoms of an illness, it is almost always the proper medical treatment.

Drugs may also be used for pain. If, within your health care directive, you state that you do not want drugs to prolong your life, they will still be administered for pain control unless you specifically indicate that you do not want them.

Respirator. A mechanical respirator or ventilator assists or takes over breathing for a patient by pumping air into and out of the lungs. Patients are connected to respirators by a tube that either goes through the mouth and throat into the lung or attaches directly to the lung surgically.

Respirators are often used to stabilize patients who are suffering from an acute trauma or breathing crisis, and they are removed as soon as they are no longer needed. If a respirator has been attached to a person who is terminally ill or in a permanent coma, however, most doctors will resist removing the machinery unless there is clear written direction that this is what the patient would want.

You Control Your Health Care If You Are Able

Most people know it is a good idea to write down their health care wishes. But some run smack into a psychological roadblock. They are worried that they might experience a change of heart or mind later—and that they will receive more or less medical care than they would want in a particular situation.

If this concerns you, it might help to keep the following in mind. First, the directions set out in your health care documents will be followed only if you someday become unable to communicate your wishes about your treatment. If, for example, you indicate in a health care directive that you do not wish to have water provided, health care providers will not deny you a glass of water as long as you are able to swallow and can communicate your wishes for one—even through gestures.

Second, you can change or revoke your written health care wishes at any time. If you find that your document no longer accurately expresses your wishes for your medical care, you can easily create a new one to meet your needs. (See "Revoking Your Documents," below.)

Surgery. Surgical procedures, such as amputation, are often used to stem the spread of life-threatening infections or to keep vital organs functioning. Major surgery such as a heart bypass is also typically performed on patients who are terminally ill or comatose. You might want to consider the cost, time spent recovering from the invasive surgery, and inevitability of death when deciding whether to include surgery in your final medical treatment.

Artificially Administered Food and Water

If you are permanently comatose or close to death from a serious illness, you might not be able to survive without the administration of food and water. Unless you indicate that treatment should be withheld, doctors will provide you with a mix of nutrients and fluids through tubes inserted in a vein, into your stomach through your nose, or directly into your stomach through a surgical incision, depending on your condition.

Intravenous (IV) feeding, where fluids are introduced through a vein in an arm or a leg, is a short-term procedure. Tube feeding, however, can be carried on indefinitely.

Permanently unconscious patients can sometimes live for years with artificial feeding and hydration without regaining consciousness. If food and water are removed, death will occur in a relatively short time due to dehydration, rather than starvation. Such a course of action generally includes a plan of medication to keep the patient comfortable.

When you make your health care documents, you can choose whether you want artificially administered food and water withheld or provided. This decision is difficult for many people. Keep in mind that as long as you are able to communicate your wishes by whatever means, you will not be denied food and water if you want it.

Voluntarily Stopping Eating and Drinking (VSED)

When close to death or in a state of extreme suffering, some people want the option to hasten death by voluntarily stopping eating and drinking (also known as VSED). And when lacking the capacity to make their own health care decisions—for example, due to a disease such as Alzheimer's—those same people might want their health care agents to enforce those wishes by telling health care providers to stop feeding them.

Though there is much evidence that voluntarily stopping eating and drinking can lead to a natural, pain-free death, the practice is not yet widely understood or accepted. Many health care providers hesitate or refuse to accept requests for VSED from patients or their health care agents. Some states even explicitly forbid health care agents from authorizing the withholding of food or drink that you could ingest normally (without a feeding tube).

If you want your agent to be able to tell health care providers to stop feeding you or giving you liquids to drink by mouth, when WillMaker asks you whether you want to write down other wishes for your care (see "Expressing Additional Wishes for Your Care," below), be clear that you want to be allowed to stop eating and drinking. Here's how one man expressed his wish:

"If I ever suffer irreversible central nervous system damage to the point that I do not recognize my family, I believe that it would be best for me to die. ... [D]o not place food or water in my mouth. Instead, place it on my bed table. If I feed myself, I live another day; if I do not, I will die and that is fine." (William A. Hensel, *My Living Will*, 275 JAMA 588 (1996).)

You can also state that you want your health care agent to be able to enforce this wish for you if you lack the capacity to make decisions for yourself. Be aware, however, that your wishes might not be honored in some medical facilities or even in some states. The best you can do is make your desires clearly known.

If this is an issue of special concern for you, consult an experienced estate planning attorney or elder law specialist to ensure that your document is drafted to maximize the chance that your wish to forgo eating and drinking will be honored.

Palliative Care

If you want death to occur naturally—without life-prolonging intervention—it does not mean you must forgo treatment to alleviate pain or keep you comfortable. In fact, WillMaker's health care directive will state that you wish to receive any care that is necessary to keep you pain free, unless you specifically state otherwise.

This type of care, sometimes known as "comfort care," is now more commonly called "palliative care." Rather than focusing on a cure or prolonging life, palliative care emphasizes quality of life and dignity by helping a patient to remain comfortable and free from pain until life ends naturally.

Studies have shown that palliative care services are greatly appreciated by the family and friends of dying patients. Numerous organizations promote public awareness of palliative care options, and information about treatment options is widely available online. See "More information about palliative care," below. However, despite the wide recognition of the benefits of palliative care, it still does not get the attention it deserves. Most hospitals do not have integrated palliative care plans among their treatment options. Very few doctors understand it well, and it is still not emphasized in medical training. As a result many people die in hospital intensive care units, sometimes in severe pain, not knowing their suffering could have been greatly eased. You might wish to spend some time educating yourself about palliative care so that you can discuss your wishes with your health care agent and your treatment providers. Your WillMaker health care directive gives you the opportunity to express any particular wishes you have about palliative care.

RESOURCE

More information about palliative care. There are many resources to help you understand your options for palliative care. To learn more, you might want to start with Get Palliative Care (https://getpalliativecare.org), a comprehensive website developed and maintained by the Center to Advance Palliative Care (CAPC). The following books might also be useful:

- *Care at the Close of Life: Evidence and Experience,* by Stephen J. McPhee, Margaret A. Winker, Michael W. Rabow, Steven Z. Pantilat, and Amy J. Markowitz (McGraw-Hill Publishing)
- *Final Gifts: Understanding the Special Awareness, Needs, and Communications of the Dying,* by Maggie Callanan and Patricia Kelley (Simon & Schuster)
- *The Needs of the Dying: A Guide for Bringing Hope, Comfort, and Love to Life's Final Chapter,* by David Kessler (HarperCollins Publishers), and
- *Living Well with a Serious Illness: A Guide to Palliative Care for Mind, Body, and Spirit,* by Robin Bennett Kanarek (Johns Hopkins University Press).

If Your Wishes Are Simple

After you've familiarized yourself with the types of medical treatment that are typically administered at the end of life, it is time to express your own wishes. To begin, WillMaker's health care directive offers several ways for you to indicate your preferences if you don't want to delve into the specifics of different types of treatments. These are:

- leaving all decisions in the hands of your health care agent, if you've named one
- making a general statement that you do not want your life prolonged when you are close to death, or
- making a general statement that you want your life to be prolonged as long as possible, no matter what your condition.

Letting your agent make all treatment decisions. The first question you will be asked is whether you want to express specific wishes for medical treatment or whether you want your agent to make all decisions for you. If you specify your wishes for treatment, your agent will make decisions for you only on matters you do not specifically address.

Of course, the best way to be sure you'll get the medical care you want if you are someday unable to speak for yourself is to clearly state any preferences that you have. This is especially true if your choices could be considered in any way controversial. For instance, the withholding of artificially administered food and water (feeding tubes) has proved to be culturally and politically contentious. If you know that you do not want to receive artificially administered food and water (feeding tubes) when you are close to death, it's wise to continue so you can make that wish explicit.

However, if illness or exhaustion has left you feeling that it is too much to formulate and express specific wishes—or if the most important thing to you is simply to name a trusted agent who can act for you—you can leave all decision-making authority in the hands of your agent. If you do, WillMaker won't ask for more information about your treatment wishes, and you can quickly finish up your documents.

On the other hand, if you indicate that you want to specify your wishes for medical treatment, you will first be given the opportunity to make one of the two simple statements below about your wishes.

Asking that your life not be prolonged when you are close to death. If you choose this option, your document will specify that you do not want to receive life-prolonging treatments when you are close to death from any of the conditions defined by your state's law. Usually, this means that your life will not be artificially prolonged if you are close to death from a terminal condition or are diagnosed as being permanently unconscious. (If you want more information about these specific medical conditions, see the next section.)

You will also be asked to specifically state whether you want to receive artificially administered food and water if you are in any of these conditions.

If you make this choice, you will still receive palliative care—that is, treatment to keep you comfortable—unless you specifically state that you do not want it.

Asking for all life-prolonging measures. This option is the opposite of the one just above. If you choose it, your document will state that you want your life to be prolonged for as long as possible within the limits of generally accepted health care standards. This includes receiving artificially administered food and water when you are close to death from a terminal condition or permanently unconscious.

If You Want to Specify Care for Different Situations

Despite rapid technological advances in medicine, much about the end of life remains uncharted. For example, medical experts disagree over whether comatose patients can feel pain and over whether some treatments are universally effective.

People who have strong feelings about what medical care they want to receive are usually guided by personal experience rather than extensive medical knowledge. For example, if you have watched a parent suffer a prolonged death while attached to a respirator, you might opt not to have a respirator as part of your medical care. If a friend who was diagnosed as terminally ill was much improved by a newly developed antibiotic, you might demand that drugs be administered to you, no matter what the medical prognosis.

To accommodate such wishes, while balancing the unknowns of medicine, some flexibility is built into health care documents. You can specify that you should receive different kinds of medical care under certain conditions defined by your state's law. In most states, this means you can leave specific instructions for the care you want when you are permanently unconscious and when you are diagnosed to be close to death from a terminal condition. In a few states, other conditions are covered as well.

For example, medical personnel usually give those diagnosed to be terminally ill a short time to live—less than six months or so. Some people feel that the best medical care under such a prognosis would be to have as much pain and suffering alleviated as possible through drugs and IVs, without any heroic medical maneuvers, such as invasive surgery or painful diagnostic tests.

However, patients often prove doctors wrong. Some people who are expected to die of a terminal illness within a few months stabilize or improve and live on for many years. If you opt to direct that no life-prolonging treatments be provided, you gamble that your condition will not improve—a gamble you must weigh against the chances you will beat the odds.

Permanently unconscious patients can be kept alive for many years with some mechanical assistance to keep breathing, circulation, and other vital bodily functions operating. While chances are statistically miniscule that these patients will ever regain consciousness in these cases, there is a chance that the diagnoses were incorrect in the first place.

There is no general rule to offer on this topic. You must be guided by your own very personal definitions of quality of life. Some people direct that all possible medical treatments be administered to them if they become permanently unconscious, just in case a medical cure becomes available. Others feel strongly that life without consciousness would completely lack meaning—and direct that all medical procedures, including food and water, be discontinued. Still others walk the middle ground, opting to be kept alive by feeding tubes, but not by other life-sustaining measures.

If you are having a difficult time making this choice, you might get good guidance by discussing the matter with a doctor or other experienced health care worker you trust. Internet resources also discuss the medical, spiritual, and philosophical aspects of this decision.

If you want to direct that you receive different types of treatment in different situations, the following information will help you understand and evaluate the various conditions for which you can leave directions.

Close to Death From a Terminal Condition

Generally, a terminal condition is any disease or injury from which doctors believe there is no chance of recovery and from which death is likely to occur within a short time—such as the final stages of cancer.

State laws on health care directives define terminal condition slightly differently, but commonly refer to it as "incurable" or "hopeless." Many state laws explain in addition that a patient who is terminally ill will die unless artificially supported through life-sustaining procedures.

Most states require that one or two physicians verify that the patient has a terminal condition before health care instructions will go into effect. In some states, this verification must be in writing.

Permanently Unconscious

Permanent unconsciousness can be caused by various medical conditions, head traumas, or other body injuries. Sometimes, permanent unconsciousness is referred to as a persistent vegetative state (PVS).

While permanently unconscious people appear to go through sleep cycles and to respond to some noises and physical stimulation, medical experts disagree about whether a permanently unconscious person is capable of experiencing pain or discomfort. Most permanently unconscious people do not require mechanical assistance with breathing or circulation but must be provided food and water—usually through tubes inserted in the veins or stomach—if the condition persists.

Generally, people who lose consciousness either recover it within a short time (often a matter of hours, days, or sometimes weeks) or enter a permanent coma or a persistent vegetative state in which it is extremely unlikely that they will ever regain consciousness. Medical personnel usually declare that a person who remains in a persistent vegetative state for many months without change has passed into a terminal condition.

Once unconsciousness is diagnosed as permanent, the chances of recovery are statistically extremely low. But medical technology (respirators and tube feeding and hydration) can typically keep an unconscious person alive indefinitely—48 years in one case. Consequently, the only way to allow a permanently unconscious person to die naturally might be to discontinue tube feeding and hydration.

To complicate matters, the external symptoms of permanent unconsciousness are somewhat subjective and can be misdiagnosed or the subject of dispute. The highly publicized case of Terri Schiavo involved a Florida woman kept alive by feeding tubes for more than 10 years. While most medical experts declared her to be unconscious of her surroundings, at least one doctor offered the opinion that her responses to stimuli were not just reflexive, but were, in fact, evidence that she was conscious of her environment. (After her death in 2005, an autopsy showed that she had massive and irreversible brain damage and was indeed in a persistent vegetative state.)

Special Conditions: State by State

If you live in one of the following states, WillMaker asks you about the additional condition or conditions listed here. As you prepare your document, WillMaker defines these conditions to help you make your decisions about care.

Florida	End-Stage Condition
Illinois	Incurable or Irreversible Condition
Maryland	End-Stage Condition
New Hampshire	Advanced Life-Limiting, Incurable, and Progressive Condition
North Carolina	Advanced Dementia
Oklahoma	End-Stage Condition
Oregon	Advanced Progressive Illness
Pennsylvania	End-Stage Medical Condition
Tennessee	End-Stage Illness
Texas	Irreversible Condition

Other factors, such as overmedication, can cause an unresponsive, unconscious condition that might abate once the treatment is halted or changed. To guard against misdiagnosis, many states require two physicians, at least one of whom is an expert on such conditions, to declare a patient permanently unconscious before any stated wishes are carried out.

In cases such as these, the person you appoint as your health care agent can play a crucial role, making sure that diagnoses are not made in haste or that second opinions can be sought if there is reason to doubt the initial diagnosis.

Other Medical Conditions

A few states define a condition where death might not be imminent but the medical condition is nonetheless irreversible. If your state's official form addresses a condition like this, WillMaker allows you to choose the kind of treatment you want.

If the Burdens of Treatments Outweigh the Benefits

In addition to addressing your care in the specific conditions outlined above, you will have the opportunity to give your agent or other surrogate decision maker the power to withhold or withdraw medical treatments that are not in your best interest. (This option is not allowed in Oregon, which requires a health care form that covers only certain conditions.)

This broad, catchall instruction will be offered to you only if you have stated that you do not wish to receive life-prolonging treatment or artificially administered food and water in all other conditions. It lets your decision maker evaluate your situation and direct that treatments be withheld in situations that might go beyond those conditions defined by your state's law. One good example of this is late-stage Alzheimer's disease, which can fall outside the definitions of both "terminal condition" and "permanent unconsciousness."

If you grant this power, a clause like the following will appear in your document:

> If I have expressed, in this document or in any other manner, a clear wish regarding a specific treatment or condition, I want that wish to be followed. In all other situations, I direct that my life not be prolonged and that life-prolonging procedures not be provided or continued, in accordance with what my agent determines to be my best interest. In determining my best interest, my agent shall weigh the burdens of treatment against the expected benefits, considering my personal values to the extent known to my agent.

Your known wishes carry much weight in determining what is in your "best interest." In some states, they are conclusive—that is, the law says that a patient's wish is, by definition, the patient's "best interest." In other states, your doctor has some say in determining your best interest when it comes to medical decisions. Regardless of the law in your state, including this provision in your document should shorten the debate by putting clear authority in the hands of your appointed decision maker.

Who Makes the Decision?

If you appoint a health care agent, your agent will be making the determination of whether a particular treatment is in your best interest. If you do not appoint a health care agent, you can still include this power in your document. The decision will be placed in the hands of whomever the law appoints as your surrogate decision maker—usually a spouse or other close family member.

Do understand that if you grant this power, you are giving your decision maker considerable authority to decide what's best for you. Be sure to talk with your agent, if you have named one, and other loved ones about any specific benefits or burdens that matter to you. For example, would the burden of having to leave your home and spend the rest of your days in a hospital be so significant that you would not wish to receive life-prolonging treatment?

In the next section, when you are asked to provide additional instructions or wishes for your health care, you can include any strong feelings or preferences for your treatment.

Expressing Additional Wishes for Your Care

For some people, health care directives—no matter how detailed about things like respirators and surgery—do not reach the heart of their concerns: spiritual matters, money available for care, dying with dignity, quality of life, or the well-being of those who care for them.

If you have such concerns, you should discuss them with your health care agent if you have named one—but you can also include them in your written health care instructions. WillMaker asks you whether you would like to describe, in your own words, your feelings on any of the following topics:

- the location of your care
- palliative care
- limits or exceptions for pain relief
- personal or religious values, and
- any additional wishes.

This section provides you with a little more information about each option.

CAUTION

State your wishes carefully to avoid confusion. You don't want your health care instructions to be confusing to those charged with carrying them out. Be sure that any wishes you specify here do not conflict with other directions you have given.

Location of Care

If where you receive care in the final months, weeks, or days of your life is very important to you, you have many ways to set out your wishes. You can state a specific location that you would prefer, such as at home or at a particular hospital or hospice facility. Or, you might want to make a more general statement of your preferences, such as any location that lets you be with loved ones at all times.

On the other hand, you might wish to make clear that the location of your care is not as important as getting the treatment you desire. Perhaps you feel that if getting the care you want means being in the intensive care unit of a hospital, you would want to be there. You can state that whatever it takes to prolong your life is more important than where your care is administered.

Location of care might also arise as an issue surrounding diseases such as Alzheimer's or other types of severe dementia. If you have preferences regarding nursing homes or other long-term care options, you can say so.

When specifying wishes for the location of your care, be mindful of creating possible inconsistencies with other health care instructions you have given. For example, if you've expressed a wish for continuation of life-prolonging treatments during a terminal illness, and you've also expressed a preference to receive care at home, make clear which factor is more important. That is, are you willing to forgo some care in order to remain at home, or does the availability of life-sustaining treatment trump your concern about location?

Most important, don't forget to discuss your feelings and wishes with your primary care physician, your health care agent (if you have named one), and other loved ones.

Palliative Care

Whether or not you want to forgo treatments designed to prolong your life, your health care directive will state that you wish to receive treatment to keep you comfortable and alleviate pain. As discussed above, this type of care is commonly called comfort care or palliative care. Such care not only attempts to provide physical comfort, but also tends to emotional and spiritual needs.

If you wish, you can use your document to express any additional or specific wishes you have regarding the way comfort care should be administered. For example, if you prefer a particular course of treatment for pain, including specific medications, you can describe that here.

In addition, you can use this section to describe any wishes or arrangements you have made for hospice or other end-of-life comfort care, and you can set out specific feelings about what would help you remain comfortable at the end of your life. Perhaps you'd like some particular music played or to have favorite stories, poems, or passages read aloud during your final days, when you might be too weak to speak for yourself. This kind of wish is appropriate for this section as well as for a discussion with your doctor and loved ones.

Pain Relief Exceptions

Unless you specify otherwise, your health care document authorizes your doctors to provide you with as much medication as they deem necessary to keep you pain free. If for any reason you do not want this, you can state your wishes in this section.

Non-Opioid Directives

To combat opioid addiction, an increasing number of states are creating voluntary "non-opioid directives." In these states, you can prepare this specific directive to make it clear to health care providers that you do not want opioids prescribed or administered.

If you make your wishes clear in your WillMaker health care directive—and you believe that your agent understands what you want—there is no need to make a separate directive to address your concerns about opioids. However, if you have strong concerns about this issue, ask your doctor if your state has a non-opioid directive, and if not, how else you can make your wishes known. You can create a non-opioid directive in addition to your main health care directive. But if you do, make sure that your wishes are consistent between the two documents.

For example, if you have concerns about potential opioid addiction or if you are allergic to certain painkillers, you might wish to specify that you do not want those types of pain drugs. Or, you might state that you do not want so much pain medication that it compromises your ability to remain alert and aware of your loved ones.

Of course, your doctor might have access to things like bad reactions or addictions through your medical records. But including these preferences in your health care directive puts this information in the hands of your agent, so that your agent can make sure you get the treatment you want.

Personal or Religious Values

At the end of life, health care issues inevitably arise that are not covered by specific directions. When that happens, a statement of your overall philosophy or religious beliefs on matters of medical treatment and dying can help your care providers make decisions on your behalf.

This can be a difficult subject to address, but you might want to consider topics such as:

- your overall goals for your health care
- any fears that you have
- your spiritual or religious beliefs or traditions
- your beliefs about when life would no longer be worth living, and
- your thoughts about how your medical condition might affect your family—personally, practically, financially, or otherwise.

Certainly, you should not feel obligated to write a treatise on these matters in your health care directive. If you have any particularly strong feelings, however, they are worth noting. You should also make a particular point to discuss these issues with your health care agent, if you have named one, and other loved ones.

Any Additional Wishes or Statements

Finally, WillMaker provides a place where you can write out any other feelings or preferences for your health care. You can use this section to write whatever you like, being careful not to create conflicts with any instructions you've already given. In addition, you will want to be sure you've thoroughly discussed your other wishes with your health care agent or other caretakers.

Where to Get More Information

If you are not sure what kind of care you would want if you could not speak for yourself, consider talking with your primary care physician, a health care professional at a senior center, or a patient representative at a local hospital.

You can also do some additional research on your own. For example, here are a few good books that provide practical information as well as insights that might help you sort out the concerns that naturally arise when contemplating illness and death:

- *Hard Choices for Loving People: CPR, Feeding Tubes, Palliative Care, Comfort Measures, and the Patient with a Serious Illness,* by Hank Dunn (Quality of Life Publishing Co.)
- *A Beginner's Guide to the End: Practical Advice for Living Life and Facing Death,* by BJ Miller and Shoshana Berger (Simon & Schuster)
- *Own Your Care: A Family Guide to Navigating Complex Illness, Changing Health, or Unexpected Prognosis,* by Jeanne Lee (Real Palliative Care), and
- *The Good Death: A Guide for Supporting Your Loved One Through the End of Life,* by Suzanne O'Brien (Little, Brown Spark).

In an Emergency: DNR Orders and POLST Forms

In addition to the health care documents WillMaker produces, some people might want to make a Do Not Resuscitate, or DNR, order. Some states are supplementing or replacing DNR orders with a similar form, often known as a POLST form.

DNR Orders

A DNR order tells emergency medical personnel that you do not wish to be administered CPR. DNR orders are used both in hospitals and in situations where a person might require emergency care outside of the hospital. In some states, DNR orders go by a different name, such as

"Comfort One." In other states, if you are using the document outside of a hospital or other health care facility, the document might be simply called a "DNR form" or "DNR directive." This discussion uses "DNR order" because that is the most common name for the document.

You might want to consider a DNR order if you:

- have a terminal illness
- are at significant risk for cardiac or respiratory arrest, or
- have strong feelings against the use of CPR under any circumstances.

In most states, any adult can secure a DNR order.

Because emergency response teams must act quickly in a medical crisis, they often do not have the time to determine whether you have a valid health care directive explaining treatments you want provided or withheld. If they do not know your wishes, they must provide you with all possible lifesaving measures. But if emergency care providers see that you have a valid DNR order—which is often made apparent by an easily identifiable bracelet, anklet, or necklace—they will not administer CPR.

If you ask to have CPR withheld, you will not be given:

- chest compression
- electric shock treatments to the chest
- tubes placed in the airway to assist breathing
- artificial ventilation, or
- cardiac drugs.

If you want a DNR order, or if you would like to find out more about DNR orders, talk with a doctor. In most states, a doctor's signature is required to make the DNR valid and your doctor might need to obtain and complete the necessary paperwork. If the doctor does not have the form or other information you need, call the Health Department for your state and ask to speak with someone in the Division of Emergency Medical Services.

POLST Forms

Most U.S. states use a form that is similar to a DNR order, but differs in a few important ways. The form is most often called Physician Orders for Life Sustaining Treatment (POLST), though some states use other terms, such as Clinician Orders for Life Sustaining Treatment (COLST) or

Medical Orders for Scope of Treatment (MOST). A POLST form can be used in addition to—or instead of—a DNR order.

A POLST is often prepared to ensure that different health care facilities and service providers (including EMS personnel) understand a patient's wishes. In most states, a POLST form is printed on bright paper so it will easily stand out in a patient's medical records. To be valid, the form must be signed by a doctor or other approved health care professional.

Unlike a DNR order, a POLST form includes directions about life-sustaining measures—such as intubation, antibiotic use, and feeding tubes—in addition to CPR. The POLST form helps to ensure that medical providers will understand your wishes at a glance, but it is not a substitute for a thorough and properly prepared advance directive.

When you enter a hospital, hospice, or another health care facility, a member of the staff might ask whether you want to complete a POLST form. If they don't ask, you can ask for one.

RESOURCE

Learn more. You can read more about POLST forms, including information about POLST forms in your state, at www.nolo.com/legal-encyclopedia/about-physician-orders-life-sustaining-treatment-polst-forms.html.

Letting People Know About Your Wishes

If you obtain a DNR order or make a POLST form, discuss your decision with your family or other caretaker. If you are keeping a DNR form at home, be sure that your loved ones or caretakers know where it is. Even if you are wearing identification, such as a bracelet or necklace, keep your form in an obvious place. You might consider keeping it by your bedside, on the front of your refrigerator, in your wallet, or in your suitcase if you are traveling. If your form is not apparent and immediately available, or if it has been altered in any way, CPR will most likely be performed.

How Pregnancy Might Affect Your Wishes

There is one limited situation in which your specific directions about health care might be challenged or ignored: if you are pregnant. Some states' laws say that medical providers may not withdraw or withhold life support from a pregnant person—or that such treatment may not be withheld if the fetus can be brought to viability (live birth).

These state restrictions rankle supporters of women's rights, and for many years these restrictions were legally suspect under U.S. Supreme Court rulings that the Constitution protects a person's right to choose whether to bear children. The Supreme Court's recent undoing of the national "right to choose" has only increased tension around whether life support must be provided to pregnant people, even against their wishes.

Because this is a contentious issue, and because other players (like the hospital or your family) might have their own strong opinions, it's important for you to be clear about your wishes. For this reason, if you are a person who could become pregnant, WillMaker asks you to decide whether you want your health care directions to be:

- given no effect if you are pregnant, or
- carried out as written.

If you specify that your health care directives be given no effect, your health care providers will have the discretion to decide what care is appropriate. They are most likely to administer whatever life-prolonging procedures are available—particularly if the fetus is at least four or five months old and potentially viable and unharmed.

If you choose that your health care directions be carried out as written if you are pregnant, beware that you might meet some resistance from the medical establishment. This is particularly true if you have directed that life-prolonging treatment, food and water, or palliative care should be withheld. And you are more apt to run into resistance the more advanced your pregnancy becomes. If you are into the second trimester—fourth through sixth months—doctors are likely to administer all medical care they deem necessary to keep you and the fetus alive.

By the third trimester, it might be practically impossible to overcome a state's proscription against withholding life-prolonging medical care.

If you have strong feelings about overcoming your state's strictures—that is, you live in a state that renders your directive completely ineffective if you are pregnant, but you wish to have it enforced—it is important for you to discuss your wishes and alert your health care agent to lobby on your behalf. It would also be wise to write a brief explanation of your thoughts on this specific issue in the "Other Wishes" section of your health care directive. (See "Expressing Additional Wishes for Your Care," above.)

Stating Your Wishes for Organ Donation

Before finalizing your health care documents, you can express your wishes on one more matter: donating your organs, tissues, or body after death.

If you already know whether you want to be an organ donor—or have already made arrangements to donate your organs or body—simply follow the instructions on the screen to indicate your wishes or plans. (Skip to "Making Your Wishes Known," below, for help.) If you are not yet certain whether you want to be a donor, the following information might help you make your decision.

The Need for Donated Organs

Although the number of organ donations has been steadily and slowly rising, the need for organs still far exceeds the number of organs donated. More than 100,000 people are currently waiting for lifesaving organ transplant surgery. Based on current rates of donation, 13 people will die each day waiting for an organ. In some cases, a single organ donor can save as many as eight lives. (For the latest statistics, visit www.organdonor.gov.)

State Laws on Pregnancy and Health Care Directives

No Effect: The law in your state does not allow your document directing health care to take effect when you are pregnant.

To Term: The law in your state will not allow your document directing health care to take effect if you are pregnant and your doctors believe the fetus could be brought to term while you are receiving life-sustaining treatment.

No Statute: Your state does not have any law about prohibiting withdrawal of life support if you are pregnant.

Alabama	No Effect
Alaska	To Term
Arizona	You may state whether you want your health care directions to be carried out if you are pregnant and it is possible for the fetus to develop to the point of live birth.
Arkansas	To Term
California	No Statute
Colorado	No Statute
Connecticut	You may indicate whether you want your health care directions to be carried out in the event of your pregnancy.
Delaware	No Statute
District of Columbia	No Statute
Florida	Life-prolonging procedures will be provided unless you have expressly stated that your health care surrogate may authorize that life-prolonging procedures may be withheld if you are pregnant, or if your health care surrogate obtains court approval for withholding life-prolonging procedures.
Georgia	Life-sustaining procedures will be provided unless the fetus could not develop to the point of live birth and you expressly state that you want your health care instructions carried out.
Hawaii	No Statute
Idaho	No Statute
Illinois	To Term

State Laws on Pregnancy and Health Care Directives (continued)	
Indiana	No Effect
Iowa	To Term
Kansas	No Effect
Kentucky	No Effect
Maine	No Statute
Maryland	You may indicate whether you want your health care directions carried out in the event of your pregnancy.
Massachusetts	No Statute
Michigan	If you are pregnant, your health care representative cannot make any medical decision to withhold or withdraw treatment that would result in your death.
Minnesota	You may indicate whether you want your health care directives to be carried out in the event of your pregnancy.
Mississippi	No Statute
Missouri	No Effect
Montana	To Term
Nebraska	To Term
Nevada	To Term
New Hampshire	Life-sustaining treatment will be provided unless your health care providers conclude that such treatment will not permit the fetus to develop to the point of live birth, or that such treatment will cause you physical harm or prolong severe pain that cannot be alleviated by medication.
New Jersey	You may indicate whether you want your health care directions to be carried out in the event of pregnancy.
New Mexico	No Statute
New York	No Statute
North Carolina	No Statute

State Laws on Pregnancy and Health Care Directives (continued)	
North Dakota	Life-sustaining procedures will be provided unless those procedures will not permit the fetus to develop to the point of live birth, or your doctor concludes that prolonging your life would cause you physical harm or severe pain or would prolong severe pain that cannot be alleviated by medication.
Ohio	To Term
Oklahoma	You may indicate whether you want your health care directions carried out in the event of pregnancy.
Oregon	No Statute
Pennsylvania	Life-sustaining procedures will be provided unless your doctors conclude that the fetus could not develop to the point of live birth with continued application of those life-sustaining procedures, or prolonging your life would be physically harmful to you or cause you pain that could not be alleviated by medication.
Rhode Island	To Term
South Carolina	No Effect
South Dakota	Life-sustaining procedures will be provided unless your doctors conclude that the fetus could not develop to the point of live birth with continued application of those life-sustaining procedures, or that prolonging your life would cause you physical harm or prolong severe pain that cannot be alleviated by medication.
Tennessee	No Statute
Texas	No Effect
Utah	No Statute
Vermont	You may indicate whether you want your health care directions carried out in the event of pregnancy.
Virginia	You may provide additional or modified health care instructions that will apply only if you are pregnant when your document takes effect.
Washington	No Statute
West Virginia	No Statute
Wisconsin	No Effect
Wyoming	No Statute

Religious Views and Concerns

Most major religions support organ donation. Reverence for life is the basis for almost all religious traditions, and organ donation is viewed as a lifesaving act of compassion and generosity. Donated organs must be removed immediately after death, however, and some religions strongly believe that a deceased person's body should remain undisturbed for a number of days. For the practitioner of a religion that holds both of these views—such as many types of Buddhism—a dilemma might arise. On one hand, it is beneficial and compassionate to donate organs, while on the other, it might violate the body. If you are uncertain about the right choice for you, it might be helpful to discuss the issue with your religious or spiritual adviser.

Costs of Organ Donation

It will not cost your family anything if you want to donate your organs. The recipient pays the expenses, usually through insurance.

Ohio Residents: Your Choice Here Might Not Be Enough

In Ohio, if you want to be an organ donor, sign up on Ohio's Bureau of Motor Vehicles Organ Donor Registry (www.bmv.ohio.gov). Under Ohio law, stating your wish to be an organ donor in your declaration (living will) might not be enough to authorize your anatomical gift.

To maximize the chances of having your wish followed, sign up on the BMV registry and then use your health care directive to:

- appoint an agent
- give that agent power over organ donation, and
- describe your wishes or plans.

The Ohio BMV does more to make your wishes known by allowing you to indicate on your driver's license that you have a health care power of attorney and/or living will. Get more information about this on the website of the Ohio BMV (www.bmv.ohio.gov).

The Organ Donation Procedure

Before an organ is removed from a donor, doctors who are not involved in the procedure must certify that the patient is deceased. The body is then kept on a respirator to keep blood flowing through the organ until it can be removed and given to a waiting recipient. All of this usually takes about 24 hours.

Donation does not disfigure the body and does not interfere with having a funeral, even an open-casket service.

Making Your Wishes Known

Your health care directive is a good place to state your wishes regarding organ donation. WillMaker gives you the following four options.

Indicate that you have already made arrangements or signed a document expressing your donation wishes. If you choose this option, you will be asked to briefly describe the arrangements you have made or the document you have signed, including its location.

Leave specific instructions about organ, tissue, or body donation in your health care document. If you have not made arrangements to donate your organs but you know that you want to be a donor, you can add specific instructions directly to your health care directive. If you choose this option, you can state whether you want to donate any needed organs or body parts, or only specific ones that you name. You will also be able to indicate the purposes for which your donation must be used, including transplant, therapy, research, education, or any necessary purpose that is allowed by law.

Indicate that you do not want to donate your organs. If you choose this option, your health care document will clearly state that you don't want to be a donor.

Leave the decision to your agent. If you named a health care agent, you can let your agent make organ donation decisions. If you choose this option, it will be helpful to discuss your feelings with, and offer some guidance to, your agent.

Other Ways to Make Your Wishes Clear

If you want to be a donor, there are more steps you can take to be sure your wishes are carried out. First, you can put your name on your state's organ registry, where you can sign up to donate any usable organs or tissues at your death. In many states you can also put limits on which organs you want to donate and how they can be used. These state registries, which are run by the state or by a nonprofit organization, provide computerized, confidential lists to authorized medical personnel 24 hours a day. You can find the registry for your state at www.organdonor.gov/sign-up. In most states, you can also register through the DMV, and your driver's license will indicate that you are a donor.

You can also sign up on the national registry at https://donatelife.net. This registry is separate from the state registry, and you can sign up for both. Medical professionals will check both registries at the time of your death. If there is a conflict between your state and national registrations, the most recent registration will be honored.

Finally, and most important, you should discuss your views about organ donation with your health care agent, close relatives, and friends. Even if you've put your wishes in your health care directive and filled out a separate donor card, it's possible that an objection by a close family member could defeat your wishes after death. The best thing you can do is let those close to you know that you feel strongly about donating your organs.

Making It Legal

When you arrive at this section, know that you have finished with the hard parts of making your health care directives. You have overcome the lure of procrastination to assert your right to keep control over your own health care.

However, you still must comply with a few technical requirements before your documents will be legally valid and binding. Very detailed, state-specific instructions will print out with your documents. But here's a brief overview of what you must do.

Signing Your Documents

Every state requires that you sign your documents—or direct another person to sign them for you.

But do not sign them immediately. You must sign your documents in the presence of witnesses or a notary public—sometimes both, depending on state law. That way, there is at least one other person who can attest that you were of sound mind and of legal age when you made the documents.

Your Agent's Signature

In just a few states, including Alabama, Michigan, and Oregon, your health care agent must sign your health care document before acting on your behalf. Sometimes your alternate health care agent must sign, too.

Note for Nevada Readers

In Nevada, there's an extra requirement for residents of hospitals, residential facilities for groups, facilities for skilled nursing, and homes for individual resident care. A medical professional must state in writing that the person signing the document is competent. If this applies in your situation, read the signing instructions that print with your document for directions on what to do. (Nev. Rev. Stat. § 162A.220(2).)

Signing for Someone Else

If you are helping someone else prepare health care documents and that person is too ill or weak to sign them, you or another person can sign the documents at the direction of the person who cannot sign. In most states, the document will print with a special place for you to add the signer's name and signature.

The person making the document and the signer should appear together in front of the witnesses and/or notary public (see below), so that someone can observe the signing and confirm, if it is ever necessary, that it is what the document maker wanted and directed.

If you live in a state that requires your agent to sign your health care document, the document will include a section for the signature, and the instructions that accompany your document will remind you to talk with your agent and get the signatures you need.

Having Your Documents Witnessed and Notarized

In most states, witnesses must sign your documents. In some states, you can have your documents notarized instead of witnessed. In others, you will be required to have both witnesses and a notary sign your document. Each state's rule is listed below. Note that a few states have different requirements for the document directing your health care and the document naming your agent.

Witnessing

Many states require that two witnesses see you sign your health care documents and that they verify in writing that you appeared to be of sound mind and signed the documents without anyone else influencing your decision.

Each state also has rules about who can serve as your witnesses. In many states, for example, a spouse, another close relative, or any person who would inherit property from you is not allowed to act as a witness for the document directing health care. And many states prohibit your attending physician from being a witness. The goal of these laws is to be sure your witnesses do not have a personal or professional interest in your health care and, therefore, a conflict of interest.

If your state has restrictions on who can serve as witnesses to your health care documents, those restrictions are listed below and will also be noted on your documents, just before the witness signature lines.

Notarization

A notary public is an individual who is authorized by the state to verify signatures on documents. It shouldn't be difficult to find a notary. A quick online search should uncover local options, and many hospitals also have a notary on staff.

Depending on your circumstances, you might take your document to the notary, or the notary might come to you. The notary will watch you sign the document and may then sign the notary language on the form or fill in a separate form and attach it to your document.

Be prepared to show the notary some identification and to pay a small fee for the services. If you are a patient in a hospital, the service might be free of charge.

The table below, as well as the instructions accompanying your documents, will tell you if your state requires that your documents be notarized and if there are any restrictions on who can serve as the notary.

Remote Witnessing and Notarization

In some states, you may be able to finalize your health care directive remotely. However, finalizing health care directives remotely is not yet common practice in any state, and most states that allow it are still working out the practical kinks. For those reasons, we recommend finalizing your documents in person.

If you are unable to get to a notary, you might be able to find a mobile notary who will travel to you. All of that said, if you are determined to finalize your documents remotely, get help from a notary or an attorney who is familiar with your state's laws and procedural requirements.

If you cannot find a way to get the witness or notary signatures required by your state, do not let this stop you from expressing your wishes to those who will make decisions for you if you become too sick to make decisions yourself. You could even share your unfinalized document with them—it might not be legally binding, but at least they would have a better understanding of what you want.

State Witnessing and Notarizing Requirements

Alabama

Advance Directive for Health Care

Two witnesses are required. Neither of your witnesses may be:

- under the age of 19
- your health care proxy
- the person who signed your advance directive for you, if you were unable to sign it yourself
- related to you by blood, marriage, or adoption
- legally entitled to any portion of your estate, or
- directly financially responsible for your medical care.

If you grant your proxy the power to direct your burial or cremation, your advance directive must also be notarized.

Alaska

Advance Health Care Directive

If you grant your agent power to direct your burial or cremation, your document must be notarized. If you do not grant this power, you may choose to have your document signed by two witnesses or notarized.

If you choose to have the document witnessed, neither of your witnesses may be:

- your health care agent
- your health care provider
- an employee of your health care provider, or
- an employee of the health care institution or health care facility where you are receiving health care.

In addition, at least one of your witnesses must not be related to you by blood, marriage, or adoption—and must not be legally entitled to any part of your estate.

Arizona

Living Will

Health Care Power of Attorney

Both documents must be signed by at least one witness or notarized.

State Witnessing and Notarizing Requirements (continued)

If you choose to have the document witnessed, you may choose to have one or two witnesses. If you choose to have one witness, your witness may not be:

- any person involved in providing your health care
- related to you by blood, marriage, or adoption, or
- legally entitled to any part of your estate.

If you have two witnesses, your witnesses do not need to meet the last two requirements on the list above.

If you choose to have your document notarized, the notary may not be:

- your health care agent, or
- any person involved in providing your health care.

Arkansas

Living Will

Must be signed by two witnesses or notarized. If you choose to have your document witnessed, your witnesses must be at least 18 years old and may not be your health care agent. In addition, your witnesses may not be related to you by blood, marriage, or adoption, or legally entitled to any part of your estate.

Durable Power of Attorney for Health Care

If you grant your agent power to direct your burial or cremation, your document must be signed by two witnesses. If you do not grant this power, you may choose to have the document signed by two witnesses or notarized. If you choose to have your document witnessed, your witnesses must be at least 18 years old and may not be your health care agent. In addition, one of your witnesses may not be related to you by blood, marriage, or adoption, or legally entitled to any part of your estate.

California

Advance Health Care Directive

Must be either signed by two witnesses or notarized.

If you choose to have the document witnessed, neither of your witnesses may be:

- your health care agent
- your health care provider
- an employee of your health care provider
- the operator of a community care facility

State Witnessing and Notarizing Requirements (continued)

- an employee of a community care facility
- the operator of a residential care facility for the elderly, or
- an employee of a residential care facility for the elderly.

In addition, one of your witnesses must not be related to you by blood, marriage, or adoption—and must not be legally entitled to any part of your estate.

Finally, if you are in a skilled nursing facility, the document must also be witnessed by a patient advocate or an ombudsman. (This requirement applies whether the document is witnessed or notarized.)

Colorado

Declaration as to Medical Treatment

Must be signed by two witnesses or notarized.

If you choose to have the document witnessed, neither of your witnesses may be:

- a physician
- an employee of your attending physician
- an employee of a health care facility where you are a patient
- a person with a claim against your estate, or
- a person legally entitled to any part of your estate.

Medical Durable Power of Attorney

Colorado law does not require that your medical durable power of attorney be witnessed or notarized. However, witnesses or notary is recommended to avoid concerns that the document was forged, that you were forced to sign it, or that it does not represent your wishes. If you choose to have your documents witnessed, your witnesses should be at least 18 years old and your health care agent should not act as a witness.

Connecticut

Health Care Instructions and Appointment of Health Care Representative
(and any health care document produced by WillMaker, including those with additional or different titles)

Must be signed by two witnesses. Witnesses should be at least 18 years old and should not be the person named as your health care representative, if you named one. You and your witnesses may also sign in front of a notary public, but you are not required to do so.

State Witnessing and Notarizing Requirements (continued)

Delaware

Advance Health Care Directive

The document must be signed by one witness. Your witness may not be:

- your agent
- your agent's spouse, domestic partner, or someone who lives with your agent, or
- an owner, operator, employee, or contractor of a nursing home or long-term facility in which you are a resident.

District of Columbia

Declaration

Must be signed by two witnesses. Neither of your witnesses may be:

- under the age of 18
- related to you by blood, marriage, or domestic partnership
- your attending physician
- an employee of your attending physician
- an employee of a health care facility where you are a patient
- the person who signed your declaration for you, if you were unable to sign it yourself
- a person legally entitled to any part of your estate, or
- a person directly financially responsible for your medical care.

If you are a patient in a skilled care facility, one witness must be a patient advocate or an ombudsman.

Durable Power of Attorney for Health Care

Must be signed by two witnesses. Neither of your witnesses may be:

- under the age of 18
- your health care attorney-in-fact
- your health care provider, or
- an employee of your health care provider.

In addition, one of your witnesses must not be related to you by blood, marriage, or adoption and must not be legally entitled to any part of your estate.

State Witnessing and Notarizing Requirements (continued)

Florida

Living Will

Must be signed by two witnesses, one of whom must not be your spouse or related to you by blood.

Designation of Health Care Surrogate

Must be signed by two witnesses, both of whom must be at least 18 years old. Neither witness may be your health care surrogate. In addition, one of your witnesses must not be your spouse or a blood relative.

Georgia

Advance Directive for Health Care

Must be signed by two witnesses. Neither of your witnesses may be:

- under the age of 18
- your health care agent
- a person who is directly involved in your health care, or
- a person who will knowingly inherit anything from you or knowingly gain a financial benefit from your death.

In addition, only one of your witnesses may be an employee, agent, or medical staff member of the hospital, skilled nursing facility, hospice, or other health care facility in which you are receiving health care. (This witness is still prohibited from being directly involved in your health care.)

Hawaii

Advance Health Care Directive

If you grant power to direct your burial or cremation, your document must be notarized. If you do not grant this power, you may choose to have your document signed by two witnesses or notarized. If you choose to have the document witnessed, neither of your witnesses may be:

- your health care agent
- a health care provider, or
- an employee of a health care provider facility.

In addition, at least one of your witnesses must not be related to you by blood, marriage, or adoption—and must not be legally entitled to any part of your estate.

State Witnessing and Notarizing Requirements (continued)

Idaho

Advance Care Planning Document

Idaho law does not require that your documents be witnessed or notarized. However, having your document witnessed or notarized will help avoid concerns that the document was forged, that you were forced to sign it, or that it does not represent your wishes. If you choose to have your documents witnessed, your witnesses should be at least 18 years old and your health care agent should not act as a witness.

Illinois

Declaration

Must be signed by two witnesses. Neither of your witnesses may be:

- under the age of 18
- the person who signed your declaration for you, if you were unable to sign it yourself
- a person legally entitled to any part of your estate, or
- a person directly financially responsible for your medical care.

Durable Power of Attorney for Health Care

Must be signed by one witness. Your witness may not be:

- under the age of 18
- your attending physician, advanced practice registered nurse, physician assistant, dentist, podiatric physician, optometrist, or psychologist
- a relative of any of the health care professionals listed just above
- an owner, an operator, or a relative of an owner or operator of a health care facility in which you are a patient or resident (this includes directors or executive officers of an operator that is a corporate entity, but not other employees of the operator, such as non-owner chaplains, social workers, or nurses)
- a parent, sibling, or descendant, or the spouse of a parent, sibling, or descendant, of either you or your agent or alternate agent, regardless of whether the relationship is by blood, marriage, or adoption, or
- your agent or alternate agent for health care.

State Witnessing and Notarizing Requirements (continued)

Indiana

Advance Directive

Must be signed by two adult witnesses or notarized. If witnessed, at least one of the witnesses must not be your spouse or other relative.

Iowa

Declaration

Durable Power of Attorney for Health Care

Both documents must follow the same requirements:

Must be signed by two witnesses or notarized.

If you choose to have the document witnessed, neither of your witnesses may be:

- under the age of 18
- your health care agent
- your health care provider, or
- an employee of your health care provider.

In addition, one of your witnesses must not be related to you by blood, marriage, or adoption within the third degree of consanguinity (parents, children, siblings, grandchildren, grandparents, uncles, aunts, nephews, nieces, and great-grandchildren).

Kansas

Declaration

Must be signed by two witnesses or notarized. Neither of your witnesses may be:

- under the age of 18
- the person who signed your declaration for you, if you were unable to sign it yourself
- related to you by blood or marriage
- legally entitled to any part of your estate, or
- directly financially responsible for your health care.

Durable Power of Attorney for Health Care Decisions

Must be signed by two witnesses or notarized.

If you choose to have the document witnessed, neither of your witnesses may be:

- under the age of 18

State Witnessing and Notarizing Requirements (continued)

- your agent for health care decisions
- related to you by blood, marriage, or adoption
- legally entitled to any part of your estate, or
- directly financially responsible for your health care.

Kentucky

Advance Directive

Must be signed by two witnesses or notarized. Neither of your witnesses nor the notary may be:

- related to you by blood
- your beneficiary by operation of Kentucky law
- your attending physician
- an employee of a health care facility where you are a patient, unless the employee serves as a notary public, or
- directly financially responsible for your health care.

Maine

Advance Health Care Directive

The document must be signed by two witnesses. Although the law does not restrict who can serve as a witness, your witnesses should be at least 18 years old and your health care agent should not act as a witness.

Maryland

Advance Directive

The document must be signed by two witnesses. The person you name as your health care agent cannot serve as a witness. In addition, at least one of your witnesses must be a person who is not legally entitled to any portion of your estate and who is not entitled to any financial benefit by reason of your death.

Massachusetts

Document Directing Health Care

Health Care Proxy

Both documents must be signed by two witnesses. Neither of your witnesses may be:

- under the age of 18, or
- your health care agent.

State Witnessing and Notarizing Requirements (continued)

Michigan

Document Directing Health Care

Must be signed by two witnesses. Although the law does not restrict who can serve as a witness, your witnesses should be at least 18 years old and your patient advocate should not act as a witness.

Patient Advocate Designation

Must be signed by two witnesses. Neither of your witnesses may be:

- under the age of 18
- your spouse, parent, child, grandchild, or sibling
- your patient advocate
- your physician
- an employee of your life or health insurance provider
- an employee of a health care facility where you are a patient
- an employee of a home for the aged where you live, or
- legally entitled to any portion of your estate.

Minnesota

Health Care Directive

Must be signed by two witnesses or notarized. Neither your witnesses nor the notary may be your health care agent.

If you choose to have the document witnessed, at least one of the witnesses may not be a health care provider or an employee of a provider directly attending to you.

If you choose to have the document notarized, the notary may not be your health care agent.

Mississippi

Advance Health Care Directive

Must be signed by two witnesses or notarized.

If you choose to have the document witnessed, neither of your witnesses may be:

- under the age of 18
- your health care agent
- a health care provider, or
- an employee of a health care provider or facility.

State Witnessing and Notarizing Requirements (continued)

In addition, one witness must not be related to you by blood, marriage, or adoption and must not be legally entitled to any part of your estate.

Missouri

Declaration

Must be signed by two witnesses. Neither of your witnesses may be:

- under the age of 18, or
- the person who signed your declaration for you, if you were unable to sign it yourself.

Durable Power of Attorney for Health Care

If you grant your agent power to direct your burial or cremation, your document must be signed in front of two witnesses and notarized. If you do not grant this power, only the notary is necessary.

Montana

Declaration

Durable Power of Attorney for Health Care

Both documents must be signed by two witnesses. Although the law does not restrict who can serve as a witness, your witnesses should be at least 18 years old and your health care agent should not act as a witness.

Nebraska

Declaration

Must be signed by two witnesses or notarized. If you choose to have the document witnessed, neither of your witnesses may be:

- under the age of 18, or
- an employee of your life or health insurance provider.

In addition, one witness must not be an administrator or an employee of your treating health care provider.

Durable Power of Attorney for Health Care

If you grant your agent power to direct your burial or cremation, your document must be notarized. If you do not grant your agent the power to direct your burial or cremation, you may choose to have your document

State Witnessing and Notarizing Requirements (continued)

signed by two witnesses or notarized. If you choose to have the document witnessed, neither of your witnesses may be:

- your attorney-in-fact for health care decisions
- your attending physician
- a member of your mental health treatment team
- your spouse, parent, child, grandchild, or sibling
- entitled to any part of your estate by operation of law or under your will
- your romantic or dating partner
- an employee of your life or health insurance provider, or
- an administrator or employee of your health care provider.

Nevada

Declaration

Must be signed by two witnesses. Although the law does not restrict who can serve as a witness, your witnesses should be at least 18 years old and your attorney-in-fact for health care decisions should not act as a witness.

Durable Power of Attorney for Health Care Decisions

If you grant your agent power to direct your burial or cremation, your document must be notarized. If you do not grant this power, you may choose to have your document signed by two witnesses or notarized. If you choose to have the document witnessed, neither of your witnesses may be:

- under the age of 18
- your agent or alternate agent, or
- the owner, operator, or employee of a nursing home in which you reside.

New Hampshire

Advance Directive

Must be signed by two witnesses or notarized. If you choose to have the document witnessed, neither of your witnesses may be:

- under the age of 18
- your health care agent

State Witnessing and Notarizing Requirements (continued)

- your attending practitioner or a person acting under the direction or control of the attending practitioner
- your spouse, or
- legally entitled to any part of your estate.

In addition, no more than one witness may be a health or residential care provider or such provider's employee.

New Jersey

Combined Advance Directive for Health Care

Instruction Directive

Proxy Directive

Any document must be signed by two witnesses or notarized.

If you choose to have the document witnessed, neither of your witnesses may be:

- under the age of 18, or
- your health care representative.

New Mexico

Advance Health Care Directive

The law does not require that your advance directive be witnessed. However, witnesses are recommended to avoid concerns that the document might be forged, that you were forced to sign it, or that it does not genuinely represent your wishes. If you choose to have your document witnessed, your witnesses should be at least 18 years old.

New York

Health Care Proxy

Document Directing Health Care

Must be signed by two witnesses. Neither of your witnesses may be:

- under the age of 18
- your health care agent, or
- the person who signed the declaration for you, if you were unable to sign it for yourself.

If you reside in a mental health facility, your witnesses must meet additional requirements. Ask your mental health care provider for more information.

State Witnessing and Notarizing Requirements (continued)

North Carolina

Advance Directive

Must be signed by two witnesses and notarized. Neither of your witnesses may be:

- related to you by blood or marriage
- your attending physician or mental health treatment provider
- a licensed health care provider who is (1) an employee of your attending physician or mental health treatment provider, (2) an employee of the health facility in which you are a patient, or (3) an employee of a nursing home or any adult care home where you reside
- a person legally entitled to any part of your estate, or
- a person with a claim against you or your estate.

Health Care Power of Attorney

Must be signed by two witnesses and notarized. Neither of your witnesses may be:

- under the age of 18
- related to you by blood or marriage
- your attending physician or mental health treatment provider
- a licensed health care provider who is (1) an employee of your attending physician or mental health treatment provider, (2) an employee of the health facility in which you are a patient, or (3) an employee of a nursing home or any adult care home where you reside
- a person legally entitled to any part of your estate, or
- a person with a claim against you or your estate.

North Dakota

Health Care Directive

Must be signed by two witnesses or notarized. Neither the witnesses nor the notary may be:

- under the age of 18
- your spouse or another person related to you by blood, marriage, or adoption
- your health care agent

State Witnessing and Notarizing Requirements (continued)

- a person legally entitled to any part of your estate, or
- a person with a claim against your estate.

In addition, at least one witness must not be a health care or long-term care provider providing you with direct care or an employee of the health care or long-term care provider providing you with direct care. (This restriction does not apply to the notary.)

Ohio

Declaration

Must be signed by two witnesses or notarized. If you choose to have the document witnessed, neither of your witnesses may be:

- under the age of 18
- related to you by blood, marriage, or adoption
- your attending physician
- an administrator of a nursing home where you receive care, or
- the person who signed your declaration, if you were unable to sign it yourself.

Durable Power of Attorney for Health Care

Must be signed by two witnesses or notarized. If you choose to have the document witnessed, neither of your witnesses may be:

- under the age of 18
- related to you by blood, marriage, or adoption
- your attorney-in-fact
- your attending physician, or
- an administrator of a nursing home where you receive care.

Oklahoma

Advance Directive for Health Care

If you grant your agent power to direct your burial or cremation, your document must be signed in front of two witnesses and notarized. If you do not grant this power, your document must be signed by two witnesses. Neither of your witnesses may be:

- under the age of 18
- related to you by blood, marriage, or adoption, or
- a person who might inherit from you.

State Witnessing and Notarizing Requirements (continued)

Oregon

Advance Directive for Health Care

You may choose to have your document signed by two witnesses or notarized. If you choose to have your document witnessed, neither of your witnesses may be:

- your health care representative, or
- your primary health care provider.

If you are a resident in a long-term health care facility, one of the witnesses must be a person "designated" by the facility. Ask an ombudsman at your facility to help you comply with this rule.

If you grant your health care representative power to direct your burial or cremation, in addition to the restrictions above, your witnesses may not be:

- an owner, operator, or relative of an owner or operator of a health care facility in which you reside, or
- a person related to you by blood, marriage, or adoption.

Pennsylvania

Living Will

Durable Health Care Power of Attorney

Both documents must be signed by two witnesses. Neither of your witnesses may be:

- under the age of 18, or
- the person who signed your declaration for you, if you were unable to sign it yourself.

Your documents will print with a notary acknowledgment, but notarizing your document is optional.

Rhode Island

Declaration

Must be signed by two witnesses. Your witnesses may not be related to you by blood or marriage.

Durable Power of Attorney for Health Care

If you grant your agent power to direct your burial or cremation, your document must be notarized. If you do not grant this power, you may choose to have your document signed by two witnesses or notarized.

State Witnessing and Notarizing Requirements (continued)

If your document will be notarized, the notary may not be:

- related to you by blood, marriage, or adoption, or
- legally entitled to any part of your estate.

If you choose to have the document witnessed, neither of your witnesses may be:

- under the age of 18
- your health care agent
- a health care provider
- an employee of a health care provider
- the operator of a community care facility, or
- an employee of an operator of a community care facility.

In addition, one of your witnesses must not be related to you by blood, marriage, or adoption and must not be legally entitled to any part of your estate.

South Carolina

Declaration

Must be signed by two witnesses and notarized. Neither of your witnesses may be:

- related to you by blood, marriage, or adoption
- your attending physician
- an employee of your attending physician
- a person directly financially responsible for your medical care
- a person legally entitled to any part of your estate
- a beneficiary of your life insurance policy, or
- a person who has a claim against your estate.

No more than one of your witnesses may be an employee of a health care facility where you are a patient. If you are in a hospital or nursing care facility when you sign your declaration, at least one of your witnesses must be an ombudsman designated by the state.

Health Care Power of Attorney

Must be signed by two witnesses and notarized. Neither of your witnesses may be:

- your health care agent
- your attending physician
- an employee of your attending physician

State Witnessing and Notarizing Requirements (continued)

- related to you by blood, marriage, or adoption
- directly financially responsible for your medical care
- the beneficiary of an insurance policy on your life
- a person with a claim against your estate at the time you sign your document, or
- a person legally entitled to any portion of your estate.

In addition, only one witness may be an employee of a health care facility in which you are a patient.

South Dakota

Living Will Declaration

Must be notarized or signed by two witnesses who are at least 18 years old.

Durable Power of Attorney for Health Care

Must be notarized or signed by two witnesses who are at least 18 years old. If you grant your agent power to direct your burial or cremation, your document must be notarized.

Tennessee

Advance Health Care Directive

Must be signed by two witnesses or a notary. If you choose to have your document witnessed, both witnesses must be competent adults and neither may be your health care agent. In addition, at least one of your witnesses must not be related to you by blood, marriage, or adoption—and must not be legally entitled to any part of your estate.

Texas

Directive to Physicians and Family or Surrogates

Must be signed by two witnesses or a notary. If you choose to have your document witnessed, your witnesses must be at least 18 years old. In addition, at least one of your witnesses may not be:

- your health care agent
- related to you by blood or marriage
- your attending physician
- an employee of your attending physician

State Witnessing and Notarizing Requirements (continued)

- an employee of a health care facility in which you are a patient if the employee is providing direct care to you or is an officer, a director, a partner, or a business office employee of the health care facility or of any parent organization of the health care facility, or
- a person who is entitled to or has a claim against any part of your estate.

Medical Power of Attorney

If you grant your agent power to direct your burial or cremation, your document must be signed by two witnesses and notarized. Your witnesses must be at least 18 years old. In addition, at least one of your witnesses may not be:

- your health care agent
- related to you by blood or marriage
- your attending physician
- an employee of your attending physician
- an employee of a health care facility in which you are a patient if the employee is providing direct care to you or is an officer, a director, a partner, or a business office employee of the health care facility or of any parent organization of the health care facility, or
- a person who is legally entitled to or has a claim against any part of your estate.

If you do not grant your agent power to direct your burial or cremation, you may choose to have your document signed by two witnesses (subject to the requirements above) *or* notarized.

Utah

Advance Health Care Directive

Must be signed by one witness. Your witness may not be:

- your health care agent or alternate health care agent
- your health care agent's or alternate health care agent's spouse
- a person your health care agent or alternate health care agent lives with as a couple, or
- the owner, operator, employee, or contractor of the nursing home or assisted living facility in which you reside or receive care.

If you grant your agent power to direct your burial or cremation, your document must be signed in front of two witnesses.

State Witnessing and Notarizing Requirements (continued)

Vermont

Advance Directive

Must be signed by two witnesses. Neither witness may be:

- under the age of 18
- your health care agent, or
- your spouse, parent, adult sibling, adult child, or adult grandchild.

In addition, if you are being admitted to or are a resident of a hospital, nursing home, or residential care facility, a designated person must sign the document after explaining it to you. Ask a patient representative for help with this requirement.

Virginia

Advance Medical Directive

If you grant your agent power to direct your burial or cremation, your document must be signed in front of two witnesses and notarized—and your health care agent must sign the part of the document that grants the power.

If you do not grant your agent power to direct your burial or cremation, only the witnesses are necessary.

Your witnesses must be over the age of 18. In addition, your health care agent should not act as a witness.

Washington

Health Care Directive

Must be signed by two witnesses or notarized. If you choose to have your document witnessed, neither of your witnesses may be:

- under the age of 18
- related to you by blood or marriage
- your attending physician
- an employee of your attending physician
- an employee of a health care facility where you are a patient
- a person legally entitled to any part of your estate, or
- a person with a claim against your estate.

State Witnessing and Notarizing Requirements (continued)

Durable Power of Attorney for Health Care

Must be signed by two witnesses or notarized. If you choose to have your document witnessed, neither of your witnesses may be:

- under the age of 18
- related to you by blood, marriage, or state-registered domestic partnership, or
- a care provider for you at your home, at an adult family home, or at a long-term care facility if you live there.

West Virginia

Living Will

Medical Power of Attorney

Both documents must meet the same requirements:

Must be signed by two witnesses and notarized. Neither of your witnesses may be:

- under the age of 18
- your health care representative or successor representative
- the person who signed your document, if you were unable to sign it yourself
- related to you by blood or marriage
- your attending physician
- a person directly financially responsible for your medical care, or
- a person legally entitled to any part of your estate.

Wisconsin

Declaration to Health Care Professionals

Must be signed by two witnesses. Neither of your witnesses may be:

- under the age of 18
- related to you by blood, marriage, or adoption
- your domestic partner
- your health care provider
- an employee of your health care provider, other than a chaplain or a social worker

State Witnessing and Notarizing Requirements (continued)

- an employee of an inpatient health care facility where you are a patient, other than a chaplain or a social worker
- a person directly financially responsible for your medical care
- a person who has a claim against your estate, or
- a person legally entitled to any part of your estate.

Power of Attorney for Health Care

Must be signed by two witnesses. Neither of your witnesses may be:

- under the age of 18
- your health care agent
- related to you by blood, marriage, or adoption
- your domestic partner
- your health care provider
- an employee of your health care provider, other than a chaplain or a social worker
- an employee of an inpatient health care facility where you are a patient, other than a chaplain or a social worker
- a person directly financially responsible for your medical care, or
- a person with a claim against your estate.

Wyoming

Advance Health Care Directive

Must be signed by two witnesses or notarized. If you choose to have the document witnessed, both witnesses must be competent adults who know you personally. In addition, neither of your witnesses may be:

- your health care agent
- a treating health care provider
- an employee of a treating health care provider
- the operator of a community care facility
- an employee of an operator of a community care facility
- the operator of a residential care facility, or
- an employee of an operator of a residential care facility.

Storing and Sharing Your Documents

Ideally, you should make your wishes for your future health care widely known. Give a copy of your health care documents to your agent, if you named one, and store the originals in a safe place where loved ones will be able to find them in an emergency. You might also wish to distribute additional copies or put your health care wishes on record with a state registry.

Making and Distributing Copies

At a minimum, give a copy to the health care providers or medical facility most likely to be treating you. Also consider giving copies to:

- any health care provider with whom you now consult regularly
- the office of the hospital or other care facility in which you are likely to receive treatment
- the patient representative of your HMO or insurance plan
- immediate family members—spouse, children, siblings—and
- trusted friends.

Some people are hesitant to discuss the particulars of their medical care with other people, feeling that it is an intensely private issue. However, in the case of health care directives, you must weigh your desire for privacy against the need for the documents to be effective. Your carefully reasoned medical directive will simply be wasted words unless you make sure it gets into the hands of the people who need to know about it.

Registering Your Documents

In addition to giving copies of your health care documents to your agent, caregivers, friends, and family, you might consider placing information about your documents on file in an official state registry for living wills or advance directives.

In many states, for a small fee you can record information about your document in a state-maintained database that medical professionals can access later. In some states, you must include a copy of your completed advance directive form when you register. In others, you have the option to provide only basic details about your document, such as the name and contact information for your health care agent and the location of the form. After you register, many states provide a wallet card that you can carry with you. You can also copy this card and give it to others, reminding them to contact the registry in the event of a medical emergency.

In practice, doctors and hospitals have been slow to adopt the registry system; many simply do not check them when a patient is admitted. Nevertheless, if your state offers one, you might want to use it on the theory that it is not very expensive to register and it can't hurt you to do so. If medical professionals start to use registries more frequently, your registration might turn out to be helpful.

To find out whether your state has an advance directive registry, do an internet search for the name of your state followed by "advance directive registry" or "living will registry."

Keeping Your Documents Up to Date

Review your health care documents occasionally—at least every few years—to make sure they still accurately reflect your wishes for your medical care. Advances in technology and changes in health prompt many people to change their minds about the kind of health care they want.

In addition, you should consider making new documents if:

- You move to another state.
- You get married. You should prepare new health care documents if you get married, unless your new spouse is already named as your health care agent. You are never required to name your spouse as your health care agent, but if you want to name someone else, be sure you do it in a document created after the

date of your marriage. If you have an old document naming someone other than your spouse as your agent, some states will consider it automatically revoked when you marry.

- You get divorced. If you divorce or separate, revoke your health care documents and make new ones. In most cases, your former spouse's authority as agent terminates automatically if you file for divorce, but you should still create a new document to make your wishes clear.
- You made a health care directive many years ago, because your state's law controlling them has probably changed substantially.
- The agent you named to supervise your wishes becomes unable to do so.

Revoking Your Documents

If you have a change of heart and want to revoke or cancel your health care documents, you can do so at any time.

If you want to revoke the appointment of your health care agent (or an alternate agent), most states require that you either deliver a written notice to your agent and health care providers or personally inform your primary physician that you no longer want your agent to serve. You can revoke other health care choices simply by informing or demonstrating to your health care providers and others who know about your wishes that you want to revoke them.

But the best practice is to revoke any document in writing—if you are well enough to do so. You should also tear up the original document and ask anyone who has a copy to return it to you to be destroyed. WillMaker prints a revocation form that you can keep for later use, if you need it.

As a practical matter, even if you prepare a written revocation, it is important to tell everyone who knows about your document that you have revoked it. And if you registered your documents (discussed earlier) be sure to update or remove your registry.

TIP

If you need a revocation form. If you no longer have the revocation form that WillMaker printed with your health care directive (or if you want to revoke one other than the one you made with WillMaker), you can use WillMaker's generic revocation—you'll find it in the list of WillMaker documents under the heading "Estate Planning."

A New Document Overrides an Old One

If there is more than one health care directive and there is any discrepancy between the two, the statements in the most recent one win. Technically, there is no need to formally revoke an earlier document. However, confusion might arise if an old document still exists—for example, if it covers issues on which the newer document is silent. For this reason, you should do all you can to make sure your old document is clearly revoked and destroyed. And of course you should make sure that your new document is properly finalized, that you give it to your doctor and your health care agent, and that it is placed in your medical records.

CHAPTER

16

Final Arrangements

Most people avoid the subject of death—and are especially uncomfortable thinking about their own mortality. You, too, might be tempted to leave the details of your final arrangements to those who survive you. But there are two good reasons not to do this: care and cost.

Making Final Arrangements in Advance

Anyone who has lost a loved one knows how agonizing it can be to plan an appropriate commemoration. And most people have attended funerals or memorial services that seem uniquely unsuited to the person who has died.

Letting your survivors know whether you'd like to be buried or cremated and what kind of ceremonies you envision saves them the pain of making such decisions at a difficult time. Many family members and friends also find that an open discussion is a great relief—especially if death is likely to occur soon.

Planning some of these details in advance and doing wise comparison shopping can also save money. For many people, after buying a home and car, after-death goods and services are the most expensive things they ever pay for.

Without some direction, your survivors might choose the most expensive goods and services available, to assuage their own feelings of grief or obligation or perhaps due to pressure from funeral industry providers. The best way to prevent this from happening is to write down your preferences. You can use WillMaker to do just that, creating a final arrangements document to point the way for your loved ones.

A Will Is Not the Way

Despite what many people think, a will is a poor place to express your death and burial preferences. It probably won't be located and read until several weeks after you die—too late to help your family. It's better to write up a separate document such as the one you can prepare with WillMaker.

CAUTION

Get organized for your family. Making a final arrangements document won't do any good unless your loved ones can find it when the time comes. Here are two suggestions for making sure your wishes aren't overlooked:

- Use the download version of WillMaker to make an Information for Caregivers and Survivors form. It provides the location of all your important paperwork, including your final arrangements document. This form also lets you document other essential information, such as financial accounts and medical information. To learn more, in the download version of WillMaker, go to the Your Documents screen and select Information for Caregivers and Survivors from the list.
- Turn to *Get It Together: Organize Your Records So Your Family Won't Have To,* by Melanie Cullen (Nolo). This comprehensive workbook walks you step by step through the process of gathering and organizing all your important records and personal information. You can order a customized binder to neatly store your work.

See "Organizing Your Records" in Chapter 1 for other ideas about gathering information for your loved ones.

The Legal Effect of Your Document

Your final arrangements document provides valuable guidance for your family members. It will tell them what kind of body disposition and services you want and direct them to any sources you've set aside for payment. As long as your wishes are reasonable and financially feasible, they should be carried out as you intend.

If relationships among your loved ones are amicable, this should be all you need. You can talk with those who will be most likely to carry out your wishes and give them a copy of your instructions—or be sure they know where to find them when the time comes.

If a dispute arises among your loved ones—for example, between your partner or spouse and other relatives—funeral industry personnel are usually bound to follow any written instructions you left. The greatest sticking points arise when the deceased person has not provided in advance for payment of the arrangements. (See "Paying for Final Arrangements," at the end of this chapter.) Court battles over preferences for body or funeral ceremonies almost never arise, primarily because of the lack of time and the costs of litigation.

Most disputes arise when more than one person is in charge—say you have three children—and they disagree over a fundamental decision, such as whether your body should be buried or cremated. Such disputes can be avoided or minimized if you put your wishes in writing.

If You're Worried About Family Fights

If you are concerned that your family might not agree with your final wishes—or if you expect them to argue with each other after your death—you can add legal force to your document by combining it with a health care directive.

It might not be possible to make your wishes ironclad. (State laws on the subject vary widely, and many are unclear or full of loopholes.) But a health care directive can help, primarily by allowing you to appoint someone to be sure your post-death preferences are carried out.

The primary function of a health care directive is to set out wishes for medical treatment in an emergency or at the end of life. And one of the most important parts of making a health care directive is naming your health care agent—that is, the person who will oversee your medical care and make treatment decisions for you if you are unable to do so yourself. You can also give your health care agent the power to carry out your wishes for the disposition of your body and other final arrangements. (The WillMaker health care directive specifically includes this power.)

To provide guidance for your agent, you can attach your final arrangements document to your health care directive. After your death, if family members object to your wishes or squabble with each other about what's best, your health care agent is legally authorized to step in to ensure that you get what you wanted.

See Chapter 15 for more information on health care directives.

CAUTION

Special rules for Kentucky, New Jersey, and New Mexico. Each of these states requires that you use a document other than a health care directive to name the person who will oversee your final arrangements.

- In Kentucky, you must use a signed, witnessed, and notarized statement called a "funeral planning declaration" in which you appoint someone to have authority over your final arrangements. (Ky. Rev. Stat. §§ 367.93117 and 367.93103.)
- In New Jersey, you must use either your will or the state-authorized form "Appointment of Agent to Control the Funeral and Disposition of Remains." (N.J. Stat. § 45: 27-22.) You might be able to find a PDF of this form on the website of the New Jersey Division of Consumer Affairs at www.njconsumeraffairs.gov.

In Kentucky or New Jersey, (1) use the state's official form to name your representative, and then (2) attach your final arrangements document to that form.

- In New Mexico, to designate someone who is legally authorized to carry out your final arrangements you must use a will. (N.M. Stat. § 45-3-701.)

Unfortunately, as mentioned above, a will is generally not the best place to address these matters. If you live in New Mexico (or any other state) and you're worried that your closest family members will fight over your final arrangements, you might want to see a qualified estate planning lawyer to minimize conflict and ensure that your wishes are respected.

If You Have Already Made Some Final Arrangements

If you have already made arrangements for burial or cremation, you might wonder whether it is necessary to make a final arrangements document. It is probably wise to do so. WillMaker gives you the opportunity to describe any existing arrangements, and it might also direct your attention to issues that you have not yet addressed. The result is a comprehensive document that provides essential directions for your survivors.

Expressing Your Wishes for Organ Donation

There are many ways to express your wishes for organ or body donation. For example, you can indicate your wishes:

- on your driver's license (some states)
- by registering to be a donor with your state's organ donor registry
- by registering to be a donor with Donate Life America at https://donatelife.net, or
- with your health care directive and final arrangements document.

Taken together, your health care directive and final arrangements document will act as a comprehensive guide to your end-of-life wishes. If you indicate your wishes for organ donation in more than one place, be consistent so that you avoid leaving confusing or conflicting instructions.

What Happens If There Is No Document

If you die without leaving written instructions about your preferences, state law determines who has the right to control how your remains will be disposed. In most states, the right—and the responsibility to pay—rests with the following people, in order:

- spouse or registered partner
- child or children
- parent or parents
- next of kin, or
- a court-appointed public administrator.

Getting Started

Before you jump into the details of your final arrangements document, you might want to spend some time thinking about the big picture. It might be easier to answer specific questions once you have a general sense of what you want.

How to approach this is up to you. You might find it helpful to talk with family or friends about end-of-life issues, reflecting on what appeals to you—and what doesn't. Perhaps you have participated in after-death events that you have particularly liked or where you have felt noticeably uncomfortable. All these things can help to point the way.

If you want to do some additional research, you might browse the Funeral Consumers Alliance website at www.funerals.org. This nonprofit organization's consumers section is a good place to begin exploring your options.

When you're ready, WillMaker invites you to put the details in writing. We'll guide you through a number of topics, one at a time:

- burial or cremation
- mortuary or cremation facility
- embalming
- casket or urn
- pallbearers
- transportation to burial site
- headstone, monument, or burial marker
- epitaph
- funeral or memorial ceremonies
- obituary, and
- financial plans.

If You Are an Organ Donor

You should state your preference for burial or cremation even if you have arranged to donate some organs or your entire body. (See Chapter 15 for more about organ donation.) Keep in mind that if one or more of your organs is donated, the rest of your body must be disposed of or buried. And even if you have arranged to have your entire body donated, there is the possibility the donation might not be accepted for some reason. And, finally, after the medical institution has finished using the body for teaching or research in one or two years, it must be disposed of or buried.

You need answer only the questions you want to. While it helps to be as specific as possible, your final arrangements document can be as brief or as extensive as you wish. If there is an issue you don't care to address, simply skip it. If you like, you can always come back to WillMaker later, either to change your answers or to create a more detailed document.

Burial, Cremation, and Nontraditional Options

One of the most important questions WillMaker asks you is whether you want your body to be buried or cremated. WillMaker also offers a third "other" option for those who don't want to be buried or cremated in the traditional ways.

If your body will be buried, you can state your preferences for a burial site. If you choose cremation, you will be asked whether you want your ashes to be scattered, buried or interred, or kept with a loved one. If you pick the third option, you can describe what you'd like instead of burial or cremation.

Body Burial

While cremation is becoming increasingly common, many people still choose to be buried. Depending on your wishes, your body might be buried immediately after death or several days later, after a funeral or other memorial service.

The Burial Process

A body can be buried in the ground, generally in a cemetery plot, or aboveground in the chamber of a mausoleum or family crypt. Typically, burial includes placing the body in a casket. However, if you want your body to be buried immediately, a casket might not be necessary. (Although required by many individual cemeteries, a casket is not a legal requirement for burials in the United States.)

How Much Does Burial Cost?	
Product or Service	**Cost Estimate**
Basic Fee Services	
Funeral director services (nondeclinable)	$2,300 average
General Services	
Transfer of remains	$350 average
Embalming or refrigeration, dressing, and shelter of remains	$1,500 average
Hearse rental and flower transfer from mortuary to gravesite	$700 average
Viewing or visitation, funeral service support, guest register, and funeral booklets	$1,200 average
Opening and closing grave	$3,000 average
Casket or Shroud	
Wood or metal	$3,500 average
Rental (including transport and cleaning fee)	$750 to $2,500
Fiberboard or cardboard	$1,000 average
Burial shroud—fabric with fabric handles for pallbearers	$400 average
Plot, Crypt, or Marker	
In-ground single plot	$350 to $10,000 or more
In-ground plot with vault (required by some cemeteries to maintain level landscape)	$1,500
Aboveground mausoleum crypt	$7,500 average
Aboveground individual or family crypt	$10,000 to $1,000,000 or more
Monument, headstone, or marker	$3,000 average

Burial Costs

Burial can be expensive. The national average cost for a traditional funeral, with burial and headstone or monument, is more than $10,000. Depending upon the products and services purchased, the pricing of individual service providers, and the array of ceremonies included, burial can cost several times as much as cremation.

Leaving Instructions

If you have decided where you wish to be buried, record that information. If you have already purchased a burial site and any other related products or services, describe your arrangements—and attach any related documents (for example, your contract with the cemetery) to your final arrangements document when you print it out.

If you haven't bought a burial site, but you know where you'd like to be buried, you can state your preference. There is no guarantee that it will be available when you die, but your survivors will know what you had in mind.

Cremation

Almost half of the population chooses traditional cremation rather than burial. For some, the relatively low cost makes this choice an easy one. But there are many other reasons why someone might prefer to be cremated—for example, you might want to have your ashes scattered or kept by a loved one at home.

The Traditional Cremation Process

Traditional cremation is the burning of a body at extreme heat, resulting in a fine residue of ash and bone. The cremated remains (sometimes called "cremains," though we'll call them "ashes" here) can be buried, scattered, or kept in an urn. A temporary casket is required to contain the body during cremation. Cremation caskets are generally made of unfinished wood, cardboard, pressboard, or canvas. The cremation facility supplies the temporary casket.

Traditionally, cremation arrangements include local transportation of the body to the cremation facility, visitation with the body prior to cremation, a temporary container for remains, cremation, a memorial service, preparation of an obituary, ordering the death certificate, and the scattering or other disposition of the ashes.

Traditional cremation can have a heavy toll on the environment, and other "greener" forms of cremation have emerged in recent years—for example, potassium hydroxide baths or composting. See "Nontraditional Options," below.

Cremation Costs

As with burial, cost might play a part in your decision. Here are some cost estimates.

How Much Does Cremation Cost?

Product or Service	Cost Estimate
Coordinated by cremation provider	
Transfer of remains, cremation with temporary casket, basic urn, recording and requesting death certificate	$2,500 average
Scattering service	$350 or more
Coordinated by funeral home	
Transfer of remains, cremation with temporary casket, basic urn, recording and requesting death certificate, memorial service	$6,250 average
Urn or niche	
Urn	$50 to $5,000 or more
Niche in columbarium, including opening, closing, and marker	$750 to $20,000

Religious Concerns

Most religions accept cremation. However, if you are thinking of choosing cremation and have religious concerns, speak with your spiritual adviser.

What to Do With Cremated Remains

If you choose to have your body cremated, WillMaker will ask what you'd like your survivors to do with your ashes. You can state that you'd like your ashes to be:

- scattered over land or water
- buried
- stored aboveground, or
- kept with family or friends.

After you make your initial selection, WillMaker will ask you to provide more details about your wishes. If you want to divide your ashes among two or more of these options, select the one that feels most important to you. When you provide details, you can state exactly what you'd like your survivors to do, including how you want your ashes to be divided.

Scattering or Burying Ashes

If you choose to have your ashes scattered or buried, you should be aware of state or local laws that might affect your wishes.

Check state rules about scattering ashes. Some people wish to have their ashes scattered over some area that has special significance for them—such as a garden, a lookout point, or the ocean.

Laws and restrictions on the scattering of ashes vary from state to state. To find out your state's laws, check with a local cremation facility or your state's health department (see "Finding your state's laws," below).

Scattering Services

Most people opt to have family members or friends scatter their ashes in private, in their own time and style. However, there are companies that arrange to transport and scatter cremated remains over land or sea. If you decide to hire one of these services in advance, make sure you understand its pricing structures. Also, attach a copy of any written agreement to your final arrangements document.

Check state and local laws about burying ashes. Ashes can be buried in the ground. Local zoning ordinances might restrict where the burial can take place—such as that ashes must be buried a specified distance from a residence.

If you wish to have a family member or friend bury your ashes, it is a good idea to first check local zoning ordinances to see whether burial is permitted on the site you have chosen. Ashes can also be buried in a cemetery, either in a special urn garden or in a plot. It is not necessary to place the ashes in an urn before burial, although some places might require a plot liner to prevent the earth from sinking over time.

RESOURCE

Learn about your state's burial and cremation laws. Laws about caskets, embalming, scattering ashes, and other end-of-life issues vary by state. Go to www.nolo.com/legal-encyclopedia/burial-cremation-laws to learn the rules and restrictions in your state.

TIP

Cashing in your crowns. If you want your dental work to be extracted prior to burial or cremation, metals can be redeemed for cash. (You can also cash in on replaced dental work during your life.) Garfield Refining Company buys dental metals—gold or semiprecious crowns, bridges, and inlays. For more information, visit Garfield online at www.garfieldrefining.com.

RESOURCE

Finding your state's laws. You can find information about your state's laws and common practices by contacting your state's health department or related agency that governs cemetery and funeral activities. To locate this department online, do a search for the name of your state and "health department."

Nontraditional Options

If you don't want your body to be buried or cremated in the traditional ways, you have an increasing number of nontraditional options. If any of these seem right for you, on WillMaker's Body Disposition screen, choose "I want another form of care," and then leave a description about what you want.

Green Options for Traditional Burial or Cremation

Traditional burial and cremation can be hard on the environment. Embalming chemicals, metal caskets, concrete burial vaults, and cremation emissions take a surprising toll. But you can make earth-friendly arrangements that reduce your environmental impact. Some choices are remarkably simple—and most are significantly less expensive:

- **No embalming.** Embalming fluid contains toxic chemicals—including up to three gallons of formaldehyde. Embalming is rarely required by law or to carry out final wishes.
- **Eco-coffin or biodegradable urn.** You can use a simple wood casket, cardboard box, or fabric shroud for burial. There are many options for biodegradable coffins and urns (for ashes that will be buried), including homemade ones.
- **Home funeral.** While it's more work, your loved ones might find a home funeral to be more satisfying. Most states permit home funerals, but a handful require the involvement of a funeral director. See "Finding your state's laws," above, and "Making Independent Plans," below.

- **No in-ground vault.** Vaults are concrete containers that are placed in the ground to surround a casket. They aren't required by law, but many cemeteries demand them to make landscape maintenance easier. Look for a cemetery that doesn't require a vault or find out whether you can legally refuse one.
- **Green cemeteries.** The Green Burial Council maintains a certification process for cemeteries that want to go green. Learn more and locate green facilities at www.greenburialcouncil.org.
- **Conservation burial.** There are burial areas on protected land managed by organizations that provide sustainable burial services, conservation of the land for future generations, and use of the land by the living. Learn more on the website of the Conservation Burial Alliance (www.conservationburialalliance.org).

It's unlikely that traditional funeral homes will know much about these methods. So if any of these nontraditional options appeals to you, consider doing some research and providing your loved ones with concrete information on where and how to get the services you want.

Innovative Options

Your body doesn't have to be buried or cremated in the traditional ways. New methods of body disposition continue to appear. Here are some interesting options:

- **Aquamation.** This new kind of cremation uses a solution of water and potassium (or sodium) hydroxide to reduce a body to liquid and bone. This process is called "alkaline hydrolysis," and is also known as "flameless cremation."
- **Natural organic reduction (also called human composting)** is a carefully controlled process that allows bodies to decompose naturally. The body is put into a vessel with an ideal amount of microbes, bacteria, carbon, nitrogen, and oxygen. After 6 to 10 weeks the result is about one cubic yard of soil that can be returned to the family or donated.

- **Reef memorials.** Cremated remains are mixed with concrete to create "reefs" specifically designed to support and enhance sea life. The reef is placed on the sea floor in a documented location. Individual memorial reefs can include more than one family member (including pets), and families can take part in the creating and placing of the reef.
- **Tree pod burial.** Cremated or uncremated remains are placed into a biodegradable pod, which is buried underneath a tree sapling. The pod and the remains nourish the soil, supporting growth of the tree. Families can choose the type and location of the tree, which might be planted in a green cemetery, on private land, or in a memorial forest, depending on local laws.
- **Mushroom burial suit.** The body is placed in a suit that contains the spores of mushrooms that facilitate decomposition and neutralize toxins. The body can then be buried in a green cemetery, on private land, or in a memorial forest, depending on local laws.

Legally, the use of these new methods is limited. Some are legal only in some states, while others are legal only in specific geographic locations. If any of these interest you, you'll need to do some additional research so that you can leave clear instructions for your loved ones.

Describing Your Wishes

Because many alternative methods of body care are relatively new, try to be as specific as possible in your description. Your loved ones will need clear guidance to carry out these unconventional wishes.

When describing your choice, consider including:

- **Specific method.** Clearly name the process (for example, "I want my body to undergo natural organic reduction").
- **Provider.** If you have already researched a facility that performs this service, list the company name, location, and contact information.
- **Final destination.** Specify what should happen to the resulting soil or remains, if any. For example, if you chose human composting, should the soil be returned to your family's garden or donated to a conservation forest?

- **Marker.** If you want your final resting place to have a marker—maybe with a plaque or stone—describe what kind of marker you would like, what it should say, and where it should go.
- **Alternative plans.** Because laws regarding these methods are changing rapidly, you may want to include a "Plan B." For instance, you might state that if your first choice is not legally available in your area at the time of your death, you wish to have a green burial or traditional cremation instead.

Mortuaries and Cremation Facilities

From an economic standpoint, choosing the institution to handle your burial or cremation is one of the most important decisions you can make. If you consider this issue now, you'll have to think about your options, shop around if necessary, and then make recommendations to your survivors. That said, you might also want to give your loved ones some leeway. Circumstances might change significantly by the time of your death—for example, you might move or an institution might go out of business. Your survivors might need some flexibility when it comes time to carry out your plans.

A good mortuary is equipped to handle many of the details related to disposing of a person's remains. These include:

- collecting the body from the place of death
- storing it until burial or cremation
- making arrangements for burial or cremation
- conducting funeral ceremonies
- preparing the body for burial or cremation, and
- arranging to have the body transported for burial or cremation.

The mortuary can also help with administrative details, such as preparing an obituary and ordering copies of the death certificate.

If you wish to be cremated, the cremation facility might also be able to provide these services for you.

When you make your final arrangements document, you can suggest the mortuary or cremation facility you'd like your survivors to use. If you want your family to handle the disposition of your remains without involving a mortuary or cremation facility (this is rare, but it can be done), you can say so.

Below, you'll find more information on choosing the right facility—or taking a more independent approach.

Choosing a Facility

It is important that you find the mortuary or cremation facility that best meets your needs in terms of style, proximity, and cost. Comparison shopping for traditional burial and cremation services is fairly easy, because mortuaries and cremation facilities must by law give price lists to consumers who visit their facilities—and must disclose prices and other information to those who ask for it over the phone.

You can compare prices and services at local facilities before you make your choice. You might also consider joining a funeral consumer group, or memorial society, to make the task easier. These nonprofit groups can help you locate a mortuary and make other decisions and plans. For a small membership fee, you will receive information about local service providers, including costs. You can also take advantage of the society's discounted rates for funeral products and services.

To locate a group in your area, contact the Funeral Consumers Alliance (FCA) at www.funerals.org or 802-865-8300. For help locating and evaluating cremation facilities, you might want to contact the Cremation Association of North America at www.cremationassociation.org or 312-245-1077.

Making Independent Plans

There is a trend in America for people to care for their own dead, minimizing or even eliminating the involvement of funeral industry personnel. This could mean everything from preparing the body to burying it or transporting it to the cremation facility.

Most states do allow individuals to act completely on their own. But there are rules about how people may proceed. For example, most states have laws that regulate the depth of a site for a body burial. A few states throw up roadblocks to acting independently, requiring that a funeral director handle the disposition of a deceased person.

If you are considering directing that a family member or friend handle your disposition independently, the following resources can help you make your plans:

- The Funeral Consumers Alliance website, www.funerals.org, offers extensive resources to help you make your own plans.
- *Final Rights: Reclaiming the American Way of Death*, by Joshua Slocum and Lisa Carlson (Upper Access, Inc.), is a guide to funeral planning that helps family and friends choose (and spend) wisely. The authors are leading consumer advocates in the funeral industry and provide a wealth of information, examples, and state-by-state law.
- The Home Funeral Alliance (www.homefuneralalliance.org) provides information, insights, tips, and resources for home funerals.

If you want to research your state's laws and common practices, see "Finding your state's laws," above.

Embalming

When making your final arrangements document, you will be asked whether you want your body to be embalmed. Embalming is a process in which the blood is drained and replacement fluids are pumped into the body to temporarily delay its disintegration. While it has now become a common procedure, embalming is rarely necessary, and refrigeration can serve a similar purpose.

Originally considered a barbaric and pagan ritual, embalming first gained popularity during the Civil War, when bodies of the war dead were transported over long distances. When the war ended, embalming was promoted (mostly by those who performed the service) as a hygienic means of briefly preserving a body.

When Embalming Is Required

Embalming is legally required only in some states and only in a few instances, such as:

- when a body will be transported by plane or train from one country or state to another
- when there is a relatively long time—usually a week or more—between the death and burial or cremation, and
- in some cases, when the death occurred because of a communicable disease.

If Your Body Is Not Embalmed

If you choose not to be embalmed, your body will be refrigerated until the time of burial. If you choose, you can still have a funeral or other service with an open casket.

Embalming Costs

The cost of embalming averages about $1,500, depending on your location and on the individual setting the rate. Refrigeration is usually less costly, involving an average daily charge of $75. Some facilities provide refrigeration free of charge.

Caskets and Urns

Whether you choose to be buried or cremated, you will have the option to state your wishes for a casket or an urn. You might want both—for example, if you'd like a temporary casket for a funeral before your cremation and an urn for your ashes afterward.

Shopping for Caskets and Urns

For more information about buying caskets and urns, you can turn to:

- The Funeral Consumers Alliance (www.funerals.org), which provides information to help you get a fair deal on a casket or an urn. The organization can also help you locate independent casketmakers or artisans if you are interested in a low-cost or specialized container.
- The Green Burial Council (www.greenburialcouncil.org), which provides a list of vendors that sell "certified products" constructed from plant-derived, recycled plant-derived, natural, animal, or unfired earthen materials.

Search online to learn about different products and to compare prices. You'll find lots of options, from niche mom-and-pop suppliers to big retailers like Costco.

Choosing your own casket or urn might seem like more than you want to think about right now, but there's a very practical reason to consider your preferences and make them known: Doing so could save your survivors thousands of dollars.

First, caskets and urns carry the biggest markup of all funeral goods and services. Second, grieving survivors aren't always capable of making sound decisions. This is a setup for overspending. Your loved ones might choose something elaborate and costly, not knowing that you would have been satisfied with simple arrangements.

On the other hand, if you want something ornate and you can afford it, now's your chance to make your wishes known.

Caskets

For immediate burial, a simple container or pine box is all that is necessary. But you might prefer to have a casket—and the cemetery you've chosen might require it. If there will be a service before burial with your body present, the type of container is entirely up to you. You might want something luxurious or something economical, or, if the viewing or service will be at home or in another private place, you might not feel the need for any type of container at all.

If your remains will be cremated but you first want to have a funeral or memorial service with your body present in a casket, your survivors might simply rent one. This is not as odd as it might sound; it is done quite frequently. A rental casket has a disposable liner.

Caskets are usually made from wood, metal, fiberglass, plastic, fiberboard, or cardboard and are available in a wide range of finishes, colors, and styles. The inside of the casket is usually lined with cloth, which is also available in different fabrics and colors. The closure might be simple, or it might be fitted with a gasket or protective sealer—providing short-term protection from the elements—but at significant additional cost.

A wood or metal casket purchased online will run $600–$6,000. The cost at a funeral home will average 35% higher, $900–$10,000. A casket made of cardboard or fiberboard will be about $1,000. As an alternative, a cloth burial shroud with fabric handles for pallbearers will run about $400. Casket rental averages $750 to $2,500 for viewing and funeral services. You might want to shop around and compare prices. Under federal law, a funeral home cannot charge you a fee if you provide your own casket, whether homemade or purchased from an outside source.

Urns

If your remains will be cremated and scattered, the cremation facility will provide a temporary container, and you won't need an urn. If you want your survivors to place your ashes in a columbarium or grave or to keep them at home, they will need a container of some sort.

Cremation urns are available in a wide range of materials and styles, from bronze book replicas to colorful porcelain vases. Attractive biodegradable urns are available for burial on land or at sea. If your remains will be divided, smaller "keepsake" containers are available to hold just a portion of them.

If the cremated remains will be interred or buried, the columbarium or cemetery might impose restrictions on the size, shape, or type of urn that you can use.

Cremation urns start at about $50 for simple wooden boxes and can cost more than $5,000 for premium materials.

Pallbearers

In some funeral ceremonies, the casket is carried to and from the place where the ceremony is held—and sometimes again carried from a vehicle to a burial site. The covering traditionally draped over a casket is called a pall, and the people who carry the casket are called pallbearers.

If you envision a ceremony in which your casket will be carried, you can name the people you would wish to serve as pallbearers. Close friends and relatives are common choices. While women were not historically named as pallbearers, there is no logical reason to exclude them.

Pallbearers need only be physically able to lift and carry. Also consider that some people's psychological makeup might make them better or worse choices for the job.

The number of pallbearers usually ranges from four to eight, but you can name as many or as few as you wish. If you know of no one to nominate—or you know just a couple of people you want to name—a mortuary should be able to provide people to help.

Transportation to Burial Site

You might have a preference about the type of vehicle that will carry your body to the burial site or cremation facility, usually after a funeral ceremony. This might be a horse-drawn carriage, a favorite antique car, or a stretch limousine.

If you have selected a mortuary to handle some of your arrangements, it might have only one type of vehicle available. If the vehicle customarily provided is not what you would want for yourself, check to be sure the mortuary will allow you to provide your own—and be sure that it will not add its transportation charge to your costs. If this is an important issue to you, check with the mortuary you selected earlier and, if its arrangements about transportation are not satisfactory, shop for another mortuary.

Headstones, Monuments, and Burial Markers

Headstones and monuments are upright grave markers (picture the traditional, rounded tombstone) generally used with in-ground burials in a cemetery. In contrast, burial markers are flat and flush to the ground or other surface (picture a plaque) and can be used with an in-ground burial or affixed to a vault above the ground. Burial markers are often used in mausoleums, columbariums, and family crypts. Also, because of space constraints and maintenance considerations, many cemeteries now prefer burial markers for graves in the ground.

Headstones, monuments, and burial markers come in an almost endless array of shapes and sizes, from the common tombstone to elaborate sculptures and designs. For example, a headstone or burial marker might be embossed with flowers, figures, or a photograph. It might bear the logo of a fraternal organization or a military insignia. New "green" cemeteries might use simple stones or just a planting of wildflowers to mark a burial site. Designs are limited only by the constraints of cemetery policy, the craft of the builder, and your budget. (An internet search for "burial monument" or "grave marker" will turn up numerous providers to help you compare styles and prices.)

Traditional headstones and monuments are most often made from marble or granite. Both stones come in a variety of colors and shades. With granite, the darkest shades provide the best long-term resistance to erosion. Burial markers are usually made from stone or from various metals—such as steel, bronze, or copper.

Headstones and burial markers start at about $250 and run into the thousands. An individual mausoleum or crypt costs about $35,000, and a family mausoleum (containing 8 to 10 caskets) can cost several million dollars.

Epitaphs

An epitaph is the words or saying on a grave marker or an urn. Your epitaph can be extremely simple, stating only the years you were born and died. Or it can reflect your personality by including a witty saying, favorite phrase, symbolic engraving, or meaningful poem.

Famous Epitaphs

I am ready to meet my Maker. Whether my Maker is prepared for the great ordeal of meeting me is another matter.

—Winston Churchill

Cast a cold eye
On life, on death
Horseman, pass by!

—W.B. Yeats

3.14159265358979323846264338327950288...

—Ludolph van Ceulen, who computed π (pi) to 35 digits

Here lies one whose name was writ in water.

—John Keats

She did it the hard way.

—Bette Davis

The best is yet to come.

—Francis Albert Sinatra

That's all folks!

—Mel Blanc

Ceremonies

Death often involves at least one ceremony and sometimes more. To sort out the details for yourself and your survivors, you might find it helpful to consider the types of services that can occur at the following times:

- before burial or cremation
- at the time of burial or when ashes are scattered or interred, or
- after burial or cremation.

You might want a ceremony at each of these times—or at none of them. When you make your final arrangements document, you can leave instructions for each type of ceremony. If you don't want any services, WillMaker allows you to say so. Or, if you have no preferences, you can indicate that and leave these decisions to your loved ones.

Ceremonies Before Burial or Cremation

Most people want at least one ceremony or gathering to be held before their remains are buried or cremated, even if it is a simple one. A wake or funeral is a way for your friends and family members to say goodbye to you, to comfort one another, and to grieve.

That said, there might be good reasons why this type of ceremony is not right for you. You might live far from most of your friends and family members, meaning they would have to drop everything and attend the ceremony at great personal cost. In these circumstances, many people opt not to have a large funeral but instead prefer a memorial ceremony—usually held days, weeks, or months after the burial—that more people can attend. (You can of course request a small gathering before your burial or cremation, followed later by a larger memorial ceremony.)

If you do want one or more ceremonies to be held before your body is buried or cremated, it's a good idea to write down your wishes. The more details you arrange while you are alive, the fewer decisions will be left for your survivors at a time when decisions are likely to be hard for them to make.

Here is basic information about common types of services before burial or cremation, to help you make your plans.

Viewing, Visitation, or Wake

A viewing, visitation, or wake is an opportunity for family and friends to view your body or to sit with you after you've died. For many, it is a quiet, meditative time. For others, it will be a time to gather with family and friends for remembering and honoring your life.

A viewing or visitation is commonly held in the viewing room of a funeral home or mortuary. However, you might wish to have it in another place, such as your home, a community hall, or a church. It all depends on your wishes and the options available to you.

Traditionally, a wake is a gathering characterized by both sadness and gaiety—a celebration of the life that has passed and a send-off to whatever comes next. A wake is often held in the home of the deceased person, but many mortuaries now offer their facilities and services for one- or two-day wakes. A wake can be an important part of the grieving process, giving family and friends an opportunity to come together and comfort each other.

If you want a viewing, visitation, or wake, you might wish to consider:

- where and when the gathering should be held
- who should be invited
- whether you will have a casket and, if so, whether it should be open or closed, and
- whether you want music, readings, certain types of food or drink, or other details for the gathering. (For wakes, there is of course no limit to the number of details you could specify. Some people have directed their loved ones to wear bright-colored clothing, bring their favorite pets, or read a favorite poem.)

Funeral

A traditional funeral is a brief ceremony, most often held in a funeral home chapel or a church. The body is usually present, in either an open or a closed casket. Beyond that, there are no absolutes or requirements about what constitutes a funeral. If the deceased person adhered to a particular religion, funerals often include a brief mass, blessing, or prayer service.

In some traditions, only family members attend the funeral, while friends and the general public are invited to attend other scheduled ceremonies. In other locales and traditions, this is reversed, and the funeral is the less private event.

Some concerns you might wish to address when planning a funeral are:

- where the ceremony should be held
- who should be invited
- whether clergy should be invited to lead the ceremony or participate in it and specific names of clergy you would like
- any music you would like played, along with the names of the musicians or singers you would like to perform it
- preferences for a eulogy or other readings, and the name of the person or people you would like to speak
- whether you want your body present at the ceremony or a picture displayed instead, and

- whether you want to suggest that friends donate to a certain organization instead of sending flowers.

If you'd like family and friends to gather at a reception after your funeral, you can specify that as well. Aside from where the reception should be held, you might want to consider the following details:

- who should be invited
- what kind of food and beverages should be served, and
- whether you want to request specific music, activities, or entertainment for the gathering.

Burial, Interment, or Scattering Ceremonies

In addition to or instead of holding a ceremony before burial, it is common to hold a brief ceremony at the burial site at which a religious leader, relative, or close friend says a few prayers or words of farewell. This type of ceremony might also be appropriate after cremation, at the time your ashes are scattered or interred.

If this is something you want and you have an idea of who should be there, who should speak, and what they should say, describe those details.

Ceremonies After Burial or Cremation

Ceremonies after burial or cremation can range from a reception immediately following a burial or the scattering of ashes to a memorial ceremony held days, weeks, or even months after death. Memorial ceremonies can be held anywhere—a mortuary, a religious building, a home, outside, or even a restaurant.

Memorial ceremonies are more often the choice of those who wish to have an economical, simple commemoration. While funeral directors, grief counselors, or clergy members might be involved in memorial ceremonies, they are not the people to consult for objective advice. Many will advocate that traditional funerals—often more costly and less personalized—are most effective in helping survivors through the mourning process. The truth is that most survivors are likely to take the greatest comfort in attending a ceremony that reflects the wishes and personality of the deceased person.

The details you might want to consider for a reception or memorial ceremony after burial or cremation are largely the same as those for wakes or funerals. For lists to jog your thinking, see "Ceremonies Before Burial or Cremation," above.

Your Obituary

An obituary is a notice published after your death. It informs people that you have died and provides some biographical information about you. In addition, the obituary might specify the time and place of your funeral or memorial service and include other details, such as wishes for donations to be made in your name.

Where Will Your Obituary Be Published?

Think about the places where your obituary might be published—newspapers, newsletters, magazines, or online.

You might want to recommend to your survivors that specific publications run your obituary. For example, you might suggest that your obituary be published in newspapers in the various communities where you have lived and worked. If you work for a company or an organization that publishes a newsletter, provide the contact information for the newsletter. If you are well known, you might want to recommend specific magazines or other publications that would be interested in publishing an article about your life.

Many families are also using online obituaries to give word about a loved one's death. Posting an obituary online greatly increases the number of people who are able to view it. And viewers are often able to post comments to the obituary—an effective way for your loved ones to read loving words about you from friends and family across the country or around the globe.

A newspaper usually posts an electronic version of an obituary on its website when you pay to have it printed in the paper, sometimes for an extra fee. Many funeral homes also provide online obituary services to their clients. Or, families can post an obituary on a private memorial website, which usually has both free and paid options.

In the past, newspapers published two types of notices: death notices, which were paid notices supplied by the family, and obituaries, which were statements written by a newspaper's editorial department. Nowadays, the distinction has blurred for many newspapers, and both paid and nonpaid statements are often grouped together. WillMaker refers to both types of notices as "obituaries."

If you are well known in the community or the field in which you work, a newspaper or other publication will likely publish a detailed obituary or even an article about your life, and there won't be a fee associated with that. Otherwise, the length of your printed obituary depends on the local newspaper's printed obituary policy and fees, your budget, and how much you wish to say.

Online obituaries have fewer length restrictions, are usually less expensive, allow you to share photos and videos, and also provide a place for loved ones near and far to post memories or thoughts. Most newspapers also publish their printed obituaries online through a site like Legacy.com, but you can publish an online obituary even if you don't go through a newspaper. Most memorial websites allow you to post simple profiles for free, but charge for additional features like unlimited photos or videos. Try doing an online search for "memorial website" to see some examples.

Making the Choice

When you make your final arrangements document, you can state that:

- you have already written an obituary that you would like your survivors to publish
- you have not written an obituary, but would like to leave some guidelines for your survivors
- you do not want your survivors to publish an obituary, or
- you have no preferences for the publication of your obituary.

If you anticipate that your family will publish only a brief death notice, you might want to indicate that you have no preference and leave the decisions to them. But if you know that any source—be it a newspaper, a website, an organizational newsletter, or a church bulletin—will want to publish information about you after your death, it will help your survivors to know what these sources are and what you do or don't want your obituary to say.

Leaving Instructions

If you prefer to draft your own obituary, WillMaker will ask you to state where it is located, so your survivors can easily find it when they need it.

If you don't want to draft a full obituary, you can provide some guidance about what you'd like your survivors to include in your obituary and where they should publish it.

When deciding what to include, you might want to consider the following topics:

- where and when you were born
- family information, including the names of your spouse or partner, children, grandchildren, parents, and siblings
- where you went to school
- information about your work
- military service
- community or recreational organizations
- awards or achievements
- special interests or hobbies
- whether or not you want people to send flowers in your name
- whether or not you want people to make donations to a particular charity or organization in your name, and
- anything else you'd like others to know or remember about you.

You might also want to select a photograph to include with your obituary. Your instructions can state which photograph you prefer and where your survivors can find it.

Following are a few sample obituaries to help you draft your own obituary or leave instructions for your survivors. For more examples, look at your newspaper or its website. This should give you many ideas for structuring your obituary.

EXAMPLE 1: Paul Ralph Dillon, 67, 12 Sunset Lane, Mill Valley, died Thursday, October 5, in San Francisco. Funeral services will be at 10 a.m. Saturday at Grace Cathedral Episcopal Church in San Francisco.

EXAMPLE 2: Paul Ralph Dillon, 67, 12 Sunset Lane, Mill Valley, died Thursday, October 5, in San Francisco. A native of Springfield, Massachusetts, and a graduate of the Stanford Law School, Mr. Dillon worked as a patent attorney and was a founding partner of Dillon & Winkler, a San Francisco patent law firm. He is survived by his wife, Margaret Evans-Dillon of Mill Valley, and two sons, Mark Dillon of Los Angeles and James Dillon of Sacramento. Services will be at 10 a.m. Saturday at Grace Cathedral Episcopal Church in San Francisco.

EXAMPLE 3: Margaret Evans-Dillon, 71, 12 Sunset Lane, Mill Valley, died Friday, January 11, in Mill Valley. A native of Pleasanton, Ms. Evans-Dillon was an ardent supporter of environmental causes in Marin County and one of the founders of the Marin Environmental Education Program, a series of programs that integrate environmental concerns into local class studies. In 1998, Ms. Evans-Dillon created Mill Valley Waterkeepers to preserve Mill Valley's watershed and plant and animal life. Ms. Evans-Dillon also served on the Board of the Marin Agricultural Land Trust.

Ms. Evans-Dillon was the daughter of Grace and Woodward Evans of Pleasanton. Her father, Woodward Evans, served as city manager and city attorney for Pleasanton. Ms. Evans-Dillon attended San Francisco State University and received paralegal certification from the University of San Francisco. She worked for 12 years as a paralegal in San Francisco, specializing in patent and copyright law, before marrying Paul Dillon in 1973. Paul Dillon passed away in 2019.

She is survived by two sons, Mark Dillon of Los Angeles and James Dillon of Sacramento. Services are at 12 noon Sunday at St. Anselm Church in Ross. In lieu of flowers, memorial contributions can be sent to the Marin Agricultural Land Trust, P.O. Box 809, Point Reyes Station, CA 94956.

Guarding Sensitive Information

Unfortunately, death notices and obituaries can be rich sources of information for identity thieves. Use caution when supplying details for publication. Instead of providing a full birth date, you might give just the month and year—for example, March 1947. For women with a married name, you might choose to omit the maiden name, a common bit of information used to gain access to financial and other critical accounts.

Paying for Final Arrangements

Whatever arrangements you make, you have two main options for covering costs. You can:

- pay everything up front (in a lump sum or installments), or
- decide what you want and leave enough money for your survivors to pay the bills.

If you don't do any of these things and your estate doesn't have enough money to cover the costs, your survivors will have to pay for any final expenses.

Paying in Advance

If you want to pay in advance, either all at once or under a payment plan, be sure you're dealing with a reputable provider of goods and services, and document your arrangements very clearly.

There are reasons to be cautious about paying up front. Though there are a number of legal controls on how the funeral industry can handle and invest funds earmarked for future services, there have been many reported instances of mismanaged and stolen funds. A great many other abuses go unreported by family members too embarrassed or grief-stricken to complain.

In addition, when mortuaries go out of business, customers who have prepaid might be left without a refund and without recourse. Also, many individuals who move during their lifetimes discover that their prepayment funds are nonrefundable—or that there is a substantial financial penalty for withdrawing or transferring them. In addition, money paid now might not cover inflated costs of the future, meaning that survivors will be left to cover what's left.

Setting Aside Funds

A safe, simple, and flexible option is to set aside funds that your survivors can use to cover the costs of your final plans.

After making your plans and estimating the cost, you can tuck away that sum (perhaps adding a bit to cover inflation or unexpected expenses) in a money market or other accessible fund. Tell the bank or financial institution that you want to set up a pay-on-death account. You can designate a beneficiary a good choice might be the executor of your will or successor trustee of your living trust—who can claim the money immediately upon your death. The beneficiary will have no legal obligation to use these funds for your final arrangements, so make sure that person understands what the funds are for and that you trust the beneficiary to do as you ask.

Leaving Instructions

WillMaker asks you to write out your financial plans in a few sentences. You'll also want to make sure your survivors have immediate access to any of the documents they'll need to carry out your arrangements, such as a prepayment contract or bank account information.

What to Do With Your Finished Document

After you have printed, dated, and signed your final arrangements document, you might need to take a few more steps to ensure it works as you intend.

If you have paperwork to keep with your document, such as receipts or contracts, gather everything together. Attach the papers to your final arrangements document or create a binder or folder where you can store everything in the same place.

If you'll use your final arrangements document in conjunction with a health care directive (as discussed at the beginning of this chapter), you should attach your final arrangements document to the directive.

Store your documents where your loved ones can readily find them. You might want to make photocopies for people who should be aware of your wishes, and tell them where to find the originals, if necessary. It's a good idea to keep a list of folks to whom you've given copies, in case you need to retrieve them later.

Changing or Revoking Your Document

You can change or cancel your document at any time. There is no formal way to do this, so simply tear up the original. If you've given copies to others, be sure to get those copies back so you can destroy them, too. Then make a new document that reflects your current wishes.

CHAPTER

17

If You Need More Help

You probably won't need a lawyer's help to make a will or any of the other WillMaker documents. But you might come up with questions about your particular situation that should be answered by an expert. This is especially likely if you have a very large estate, must plan for an incapacitated minor, or have to deal with the assets of a good-sized small business. Throughout the program, WillMaker highlights these and other indications that you might need legal advice.

Learning More

If you've read most of this manual and started making your own will or other document, you might know more about wills than a fair number of lawyers do. If you have questions that these materials don't address, you might want to consult some other self-help books or websites before you consult a pricey expert. It's often worth the money to pay a good lawyer for advice about your specific situation; it's rarely worth it to pay by the hour for education. Reading some background information before hiring a lawyer is usually the best approach.

Here are some Nolo books that provide more in-depth information about estate planning:

- ***Nolo's Guide to Estate Planning,*** by Liza Hanks. This book explains how to draw up a complete estate plan making use of a will, a living trust, and other devices. It introduces more complex estate planning strategies, including various types of tax-saving trusts for the very wealthy.
- ***8 Ways to Avoid Probate,*** by Mary Randolph. If you're interested in learning more about some of the probate-avoidance techniques discussed in this manual, check out this book.
- ***Prenuptial Agreements: How to Write a Fair & Lasting Contract,*** by Katherine E. Stoner. Estate planning is often an important

component of writing a prenuptial agreement. If you're planning to be married and considering a written agreement, this book will walk you through the process, including lots of guidance to help you communicate and negotiate a plan that will please both of you.

- ***Special Needs Trusts: Protect Your Child's Financial Future,*** by Kevin Urbatsch and Jessica Farinas Jones. This book will help you understand and draft a trust for a loved one with a disability. Even if you decide to have a lawyer draw up or finalize the trust, you will be armed with the information you need to get the best possible help.
- ***The Executor's Guide: Settling a Loved One's Estate or Trust,*** by Mary Randolph and Jennie Lin. This is an invaluable handbook for anyone asked to serve as an executor. It can also help you prepare your estate for your own executor, to make the job as easy as possible.
- ***The Trustee's Legal Companion,*** by Liza Hanks, Shalla Buckley, and Carol Elias Zolla. This book is a detailed guide for people who find themselves serving as the trustee of a loved one's living trust. It clarifies the trustee's duties and explains when and how to get help from professionals.

You can find Nolo books at Nolo.com or through your favorite bookseller.

Free Legal Information on Nolo.com

Go to Nolo.com for clear and dependable information about estate planning and almost every other legal topic. It's Nolo's mission to provide accurate legal information written by legal professionals and vetted by Nolo's expert editorial staff. Whether you have a specific question or just want to browse by topic, you can count on Nolo to give you unbiased, straightforward, plain-English legal information.

What Kind of Expert Do You Need?

If you have questions, the first thing to decide is what type of expert you should seek. Questions about taxes might be better (and less expensively) answered by an experienced accountant rather than a lawyer. Or if you're wondering what type of life insurance to buy, you might be better off talking to a financial planner.

Consult a lawyer if you have specific questions about a provision of your will. Also see a lawyer if you want to get into more sophisticated estate planning—for instance, if you want to establish a charitable trust or a detailed plan to address property distribution in a complicated family situation.

Different Ways to Get Advice From a Lawyer

Although many consumers (and some lawyers) don't know it yet, the way lawyers and their customers structure their relationships is changing fast. Lawyers used to insist on taking responsibility (and fees) for creating an entire estate plan. But, in what has become a very competitive market, many lawyers now offer piecemeal services, tailored to just what a customer wants.

This means you no longer have to walk into a lawyer's office, turn over your legal problems, and wait for an answer—and a bill. Instead, you can often buy what you need, whether it's a bit of advice, a single estate planning document, a review of a document you've prepared with WillMaker, or regular coaching as you handle a probate court proceeding on your own.

If you adopt this approach, you and the lawyer should sign an agreement that clearly sets out your roles and states that the lawyer is not acting in a traditional role, but instead giving you limited services or representation. Without this type of agreement, lawyers fear that dissatisfied clients might later hold them responsible for more than they actually agreed to take on. The agreement should make things clear to you too, so you know what to expect from the lawyer. (For more, see "Working With a Lawyer," below.)

Finding a Lawyer

Finding a competent lawyer who charges a reasonable fee and respects your efforts to prepare your own estate planning documents might not be easy. It's important to find a lawyer who specializes in estate planning. Most general practice lawyers are simply not sufficiently educated in this field to competently address complicated problems. Here are some ways to look for the help you need.

Personal Recommendations

The best way to find a lawyer is to get a recommendation from someone you trust. So ask your relatives and friends—especially those you know who have substantial assets and have likely made an estate plan. You might also want to ask those who run their own businesses. They are likely to have a relationship with a lawyer who either practices estate planning or knows someone who does.

Finally, you might check with people you know in any social or other organization in which you are involved. Senior citizens' centers and other groups that advise and assist older people might have a list of local lawyers who specialize in wills and estate planning and are well regarded.

Group Legal Plans

Some unions, employers, and consumer action organizations offer group legal plans to their members or employees, who can obtain legal assistance free or for low rates. If you are a member of such a plan, check to find out whether your issue might be covered free of charge. If it is and you are satisfied that the lawyer you are referred to is knowledgeable in estate planning, this route is probably a good choice.

Some plans, however, give you only a slight reduction in a lawyer's fee. In that case, you might be referred to a lawyer whose main virtue is the willingness to reduce fees in exchange for a high volume of referrals. Chances are you can find a better lawyer outside the plan and negotiate a similar fee.

Attorney Directories

A lawyer directory will give you the names of attorneys who practice in your area. You will probably find several who specialize in estate planning and will give you an initial consultation for a low fee.

Lawyers.com and Avvo.com are part of the Nolo family and provide excellent and free lawyer directories. These directories allow you to search by location and area of law, and list detailed information about and reviews of lawyers.

Attorney Referral Services

Your local county bar might have an attorney referral service, which differs from a directory in that a referral service will gather some information about your legal needs and match you with attorneys who might be a good fit for you. Usually you'll get only a few names of attorneys to consider, chosen for you by the knowledgeable people running the referral service, rather than having an entire directory to choose from on your own.

Working With a Lawyer

Before you talk to a lawyer, decide what kind of help you really need. Do you want someone to advise you on a complete estate plan or just to review the documents you prepare to make sure they look all right? If you don't clearly tell the lawyer what you want, you might find yourself agreeing to turn over all your estate planning work.

One good strategy is to do some background research and write down your questions as specifically as you can. If the lawyer doesn't give you clear, concise answers, try someone else. If the lawyer acts wise but says little except to ask that the problem be placed in the lawyer's hands—with a substantial fee, of course—watch out. You're dealing with either someone who doesn't know the answer and won't admit it (common) or someone who finds it impossible to let go of the "me expert, you plebeian" philosophy (even more common).

Lawyer fees usually range from $100 to $400 or more per hour. But price is not always related to quality. It depends on the area of the country you live in, but, generally, fees of $250 to $400 per hour are reasonable in urban areas. In rural areas and smaller cities, $150 to $250 is more like it. The fee of an experienced specialist might be 10% to 30% higher than that of a general practitioner, but the specialist will probably produce results more efficiently and save you money in the long run.

Be sure you settle your fee arrangement—preferably in writing—at the start of your relationship. In addition to the hourly fee, you should get a clear, written commitment from the lawyer about how many hours your problem should take to handle.

RESOURCE

For more information about working with lawyers and paying a fair rate, visit www.nolo.com/legal-encyclopedia/lawyer.

Doing Your Own Legal Research

There is often a viable alternative to hiring a lawyer to resolve legal questions that affect your estate planning documents: You can do your own legal research. Doing your own legal research can provide some real benefits if you are willing to learn how to do it. Not only will you save some money, you will gain a sense of mastery over an area of law, generating confidence that will stand you in good stead should you have other legal problems.

Fortunately, researching wills and related estate planning issues is an area generally well suited to doing your own legal research. Most problems do not involve massive research or abstruse legal questions. Often, you need only check the statutes of your state to find one particular provision.

RESOURCE

Start with Nolo. Go to Nolo.com for lots of free, dependable legal information in plain English. If you would like an in-depth resource, try *Legal Research: How to Find & Understand the Law,* by Cara O'Neill and Jessica Gillespie, which gives detailed instructions and examples explaining how to conduct legal research.

Every state provides its current, pending, and recently enacted statutes on its legislative website. You can usually browse current statutes by section, but pending and recently enacted statutes most often require a search of the state's bill tracker. Some states' websites are better than others, so prepare to do a little investigative work to find what you need. Similarly, because some states are slow to update their current statutes, it's always a good idea to check for recently enacted modifications. For general information about state legislatures—like how they work or how to find their websites—look to the National Conference of State Legislatures at www.ncsl.org.

Another possible resource for legal research is law school libraries, which often have robust online resources, including free databases and legal guides. State schools (compared to private schools) might be more likely to offer open-to-the-public resources.

Or, if you prefer to do your research the old-fashioned way, you can look up your state laws at a local law library or, sometimes, at the main branch of a public library. Once there, ask a librarian to help you. Plan on spending most of your time researching in the library itself because you won't usually be able to check out the most useful resources.

Index

C

E

G

H

I

M

N

O

Q

R

S

T

V

W